My Double Life

My Double Life
Memoirs of a Naturalist

Frances Hamerstrom

Illustrations by
Elva Hamerstrom Paulson

The University of Wisconsin Press

A North Coast Book

The University of Wisconsin Press
114 North Murray Street
Madison, Wisconsin 53715

3 Henrietta Street
London WC2E 8LU, England

Printed in the United States of America

Library of Congress Cataloging-in-Publication Data
Hamerstrom, Frances, 1907–
My double life : memoirs of a naturalist / Frances Hamerstrom:
illustrations by Elva Hamerstrom Paulson.
328 pp. cm.
"A North Coast book."
Includes her Strictly for the chickens, originally published in
1980.
ISBN 0-299-14200-0 (cloth)   ISBN 0-299-14204-3 (paper)
1. Hamerstrom, Frances, 1907–   . 2. Ornithologists—United
States—Biography.   3. Greater prairie chicken—Wisconsin.
I. Hamerstrom, Frances, 1907–   Strictly for the chickens.
II. Title.
QH31.H32A3   1994
598'.092—dc20
[B]   94-17999

To our gabboons—a politer term would be "apprentices"—
who have struggled beyond the call of duty on hawk and owl research
on the Buena Vista Marsh

Dan Berger
Gary Hampton
Glen Fox
Ray Anderson
Ross Lein
Gary Anweiler
Paul Drake
Chuck Sindelar
Gary Page
Bill Scharf
Tom Ahlers
Joe Platt
Larry Crowley
Ron Sauey
Skip Walker
John Hart
Frank Renn
Dale Griffy
Eric Bienvenu
Brother Edwin Mattingly
Max Albrecht
Karl Lang
John Champion
Alan Beske
Deann De La Ronde
Keith Janick
Danny Thompson
Joe Schmutz
Sheila Schmutz
Tina Smith
Keith Bildstein

Curt Griffen
Mark Ashby
Randy Acker
Rodd Friday
Bruce Phillips
Charley Burke
Mark Kopeny
Monica Herzig
Mac Ehrhardt
Betsy Haug
Dale Gawlik
Dan Groebner
Bill Gilbert
Charlie Munn
Greg Sulik
Jeff Pope
Rebecca Paulson
Mark Manske
Kevin Turner
Dan Goltz
Scott Anderson
Michael Tlusty
Jennifer Leak
Kiki Strecker
Juan Esteban Martínez-Gómez
Annie Wendt
Félix Manuel Guererro-González
David Sikorski
Carlos Armenta Contreras
Nora Delia López-Rivera

When I was a small child I longed one day to become so famous that I did not have to hide how odd I was—how unlike other people. Few people really held my attention. It was birds and mammals, reptiles and insects that filled my dreams and eternally whetted my curiosity.

Other, more normal loves intruded, often to my delight, and so it was that I have led a double life from childhood, when grownups forbade wild pets and tried to squelch my companionship with creepy crawly creatures, to the present, when I still cannot explain my passion for the wild and the free. This book describes my development on the long, rewarding road to discovery and toward becoming a defender of our natural world.

Contents

x

My Double Life

Anna's muff

There comes a time in early childhood when it becomes clear that grownups are less than perfect. I was six when I made several discoveries.

My earliest memories were not of the United States and the huge brick house near Boston where I was born, but of Europe—various cities in Europe, for the family lived abroad for four years. The first place I considered home was a large apartment on the second floor of 14 Heubner Street in Dresden. Anna is the first nursemaid I remember. Bertram and I were repeatedly told that no nursemaid would stay more than a week or two because we were naughty children. My father's vehement and unreasonable temper, and my mother's dramatic and far from silent spells of sobbing, may really have had more to do with the repeated departure of yet another nursemaid.

At any rate, Anna stayed. Anna had a muff. Anna started walking out with a soldier and she put two lengths of rope into her muff—where nobody could see them—every time she took us for our afternoon walk in the park. Anna headed straight for a little bay in the bushes where there was a long park bench. It took her just a few minutes to pull the ropes out of her muff, fashion a harness for each child, and tie us to separate ends of the bench. "Remember," she said, "if you make a noise I shall pinch you again."

We were both black and blue from Anna's pinches. Our buttocks and the soft areas between our ribs and our hips showed signs of Anna's pinching. "Quiet, or I'll pinch again," were her parting words. Then Anna went walking with her soldier. Each day she came back to take us home after what seemed an eternity.

Bertram and I remembered to be quiet. Anna had been forbidden to spank us, so she pinched—giving each pinch of her strong fingers a sharp little twist. It never entered my head to dislike Anna for her unusual punishments. It was another episode with the muff that troubled me deeply.

3

Anna, who pinched us.

The president of a good school, Herr Director Thümer, and his two maiden daughters were coming to tea—and there was no cream in the house. It was Sunday, and it was illegal to buy cream or groceries on Sunday. My father, who was a criminologist, had already given me numerous lectures on having a sense of moral perspective, moral turpitude, and knowing right from wrong. My father called Anna to the rescue.

"Anna," he roared, "there is no cream in the house. Herr Director Thümer is coming for tea and there is no cream."

Anna said, "Yes, Mr. Flint, I know a little shop."

My father waited for her to say more.

Anna smiled, and announced, "I shall take the children for a walk and—I have a large muff."

My father handed Anna some money. They understood each other perfectly.

Anna put on our galoshes, our coats, our hats, and our mittens. We

4

walked rather a long way and then we moved into an alley. Anna knocked on a back door. It was opened and there was some whispering. Anna handed an unprepossessing man some money and he handed her a bottle of thick, heavy cream. Bertram was probably too young to realize, but I knew: it was illegal.

On the way home we saw a policeman. Anna walked quite close to him and said, "Good afternoon."

He could arrest us! But my terror of getting arrested didn't compare with the terrible discovery of that afternoon. My father, of whom I was afraid, but whom I had looked up to, had deliberately condoned breaking the law.

What is true?

Anna controlled us not only by pinching. She told us bogeyman stories of naughty children driven into culverts where they got stuck forever, and other tales of improbable horror.

My mother felt that all children should be exposed to the classics. She loved reading aloud and Helen Bannerman was an author she approved of; so we begged her to read *Little Black Sambo* over and over again. This story of a little black boy, and eating ever so many pancakes, and tigers running around in a circle until they turned into butter was obviously such nonsense that no stock was to be taken in any of it. Anna's bogeyman stories struck me as improbable, but some of them just might be true.

With Christmas coming Anna had a new method of disciplining us. In Germany Knecht Ruprecht comes at Christmas. He carries a whip. Only good children get presents from the bag he carries over his shoulder. "All naughty children," Anna said, "are beaten unmercifully on Christmas morning. You can hear them screaming."

Was it true? Or were Knecht Ruprecht and Santa Claus just fairy stories like *Little Black Sambo?* The only way to find out was to ask. Mother was unhappily evasive. Cook said, "Don't let Anna's stories scare you." Grandmother gave me the best answer, "No dear, there is no Santa Claus, but let's pretend there is."

Bertram was old enough to be frightened by the stories, but too young to understand. I tried to tell him, "There isn't any Santa Claus and there isn't any Knecht Ruprecht, so don't be afraid."

Bertram and I spent many happy hours playing in the fenced-in garden in front of the house.

People walked past on the way to the corner store and returned the same way. But we were more interested in watching ants, and playing in the sandbox.

Not long after we learned about Santa Claus an absolutely amazing thing happened. A black man walked past our garden. I shouted and Anna came running outdoors. She grabbed my arm and jerked me aside. "Don't yell, and don't point. The poor man can't help being black."

6

Anna gave me a good shaking and went back into the house. Neither Bertram nor I had ever seen a black man before. Maybe *Little Black Sambo* was true? At any rate it was time to take action. The poor black man would undoubtedly come past our garden again after he had been to the store. How lonely he must be!

I pulled Bertram over to the pile of coal by the back door and got to work. We would show him that he was *not* alone. I blackened my face and neck and hands with coal dust. I blackened Bertram's face and hands and neck with coal dust. And I was very careful to get plenty of coal dust inside our ears because I had noticed that the black man's ears were black all the way in.

Anna found us just as I was adding a little more coal dust behind Bertram's ears. She screamed, "You naughty, naughty child." Then she lowered her voice. "Wicked, it was wicked of you to make fun of him. He cannot help being black."

Sobbing, I tried to explain. "Can't you see? He was lonely. It must be awful to be the only black person in the world."

"*You* will go to bed right now. And without supper."

"But, he was . . ."

"Not another word."

Anna drew the shades, undressed me, and put me to bed. I lay there alone. Perhaps there *was* a Little Black Sambo? And Knecht Ruprecht? Was he coming with his whip?

Apartment house in Dresden, 14 Heubnerstrasse. We lived there on the first floor.

7

An actress comes to dinner

My parents entertained a variety of notables. Carl Zeiss and my father shared the same passionate enthusiasm for telephotography. "Look," Zeiss would explain, "that castle was eleven miles away and here it is, photographed as though it were just across the river!"

My father muttered, "Fabelhaft," appreciatively.

Then Zeiss opened a large black bag and pulled out a round piece of glass. "Look, such a lens—and not a bubble in it!"

My father held the lens carefully up to the light, shaking his head in admiration.

"Frances!" My father's voice was always loud. "Come here. Look at this lens—not a bubble in it!"

"Yes Father."

My interest in pieces of glass, especially those without bubbles, was minimal. But I knew what to say: "Fabelhaft."

Then someone really *fabelhaft* came to dinner. It was an actress. She wore make-up. Bright reddish lipstick, and her nose was powdered. It was quite a contrast to my mother's rather large and very shiny nose. My father disapproved of make-up. The actress smelled of tobacco, so I knew that she must have come by train. Trains always smelled of tobacco. And ladies don't smoke.

After dinner the grownups withdrew into the drawing room, and the children were called in to say goodnight. The actress lowered herself into a chair, crossed her *knees*—not her ankles—and pulled a pink enamel cigarette case out of her evening bag. She leaned a little farther back and put a cigarette between her lips.

Father jumped to his feet. He dashed to a small table and seized a box of matches, and then with a flourish, he lit the lady's cigarette!

The actress had a lovely, low, lilting voice. She smiled up at my father, gave a little sigh and murmured, "I so *adore* my after-dinner cigarette."

Christmas that year was the first time I ever remember doing anything naughty. I did two wrong things, but only one was found out. The first was launched because Bertram was taken to the barber to get his hair cut for the first time in his life. Anna brought him home afterwards. His hair was very short indeed and his cheeks were smudged with tears. I could hardly wait to find out what happened.

Bertram said, "The barber tied a towel around my neck so tight I could hardly breathe. Then he pushed my head and pushed my head and cut my hair. After that he rubbed my whole head and he got a brush and brushed all around my neck."

For Christmas, among my many toys was a large doll with a porcelain face, eyes that would open and shut, and curly hair. Bertram and I played barber. Bertram tied a handkerchief around the doll's neck as tightly as he could. I got some scissors from the sewing table, and pushing with considerable violence and cutting with dispatch—the doll got a haircut.

Anna appeared, and Anna was in a hurry. "Come children" (she didn't notice the bald doll), "come right now. The Warteiners have invited you to come to see their Christmas presents."

Anna hurried us next door to the Warteiners and left us there, saying she'd be back in about an hour.

"Let's play barber! I will let *you* put the towels on."

The older girl hesitated.

"Find some scissors and a brush. If you are good, I will let you brush up the hair at the end."

It was the happiest day I had playing with dolls in my whole life.

Alex and Gerhardt, the big boys, came into the Warteiner nursery and shouted their approval. Alex was smoking a cigarette!

"Alex, I very much need a cigarette."

"What for?"

I half-closed my eyes, as I had seen that lovely lady do, and said, "I *adore* my after-dinner cigarette."

Gerhardt gave a little snort. Both boys stared at me. Finally Alex asked, "Do you know how to smoke?"

"No, but you could teach me."

He did. And then I begged a cigarette from him to take home with me.

At teatime Anna discovered my beautiful doll with her hair lying all around her on the floor. And Herr Warteiner came over to report the damage done to the Christmas dolls at their house.

I was punished and put to bed.

I sneaked out into the hall and got some matches. Then I climbed out of my window and sat on the roof. I smoked all by myself, and I murmured, "I so *adore* my after-dinner cigarette."

Before the haircut.

My first pet

Vienna, Berlin, Budapest, Basel, Paris, Amsterdam, and then too, Garmisch-Partenkirchen, the Alps, and Munich. My father's occupation—international criminologist—caused him to travel a great deal. We—my mother, my father, Bertram, and I—traveled in an Oldsmobile roadster. My father drove, skillfully and at high speed, my mother next to him in a bucket seat. Bertram sat on a folding camp chair in front of my mother's knees and just behind the dash. I, buffeted by wind, sat in a rumble seat built for one, and I had a strap to hang onto so I wouldn't bounce out.

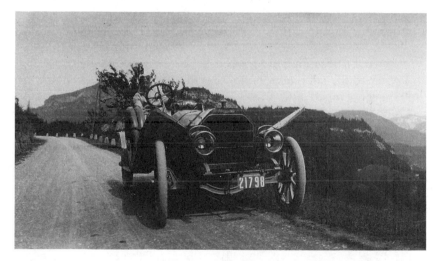

"Merry Wheels," the Oldsmobile we traveled in.

The nursemaid, and sometimes one of the maids, went on ahead by train with the wardrobe trunks, hatboxes, books, and the many pounds of paraphernalia deemed necessary for travel in those days. It was their duty to have everything ready for us when we arrived. To the best of my knowledge, my father never, not even once, found their preparations suitable. Somebody always cried when we got to the hotel.

This was all before my seventh birthday. I remember the places we stayed because of what happened in them. In Leipzig, a lion got loose from the zoological garden and everybody was told to look out for a lion. In Paris, I discovered that Mother spoke French even worse than she spoke German. Of course I spoke Bavarian, Saxon, High German, French, and English—and was expected to speak them all correctly. It was to come as a great surprise to me later when I got back to the United States to find that most American children spoke only one language!

In Munich, my grandmother took me to see Fasching, the big annual carnival, and a masked man in a black-and-white costume jumped into the cab and frightened us badly. The cab driver cracked his whip, the horse almost broke into a gallop, and the masked man took off just as the whip cracked. In Berlin, Fräulein Lehman, a nursery governess, took me for a walk. Suddenly she said, "Look! There is the king! See, he is under those trees." I had never touched a king. I broke away from Fräulein Lehman and ran full speed to touch that king. I ran so fast that I bumped into him! He turned around, and looked at me and said, "Excuse me." So the only king I ever touched apologized to me.

In winter Bertram and I looked out of the windows every evening and watched the lamplighters light up the gas street lights. They were little boys, not much older than I, and they carried long poles. At the top was a hook that made it possible for them to raise the glass shade, and then they could touch a small flame to each light, which burst forth in all its glory. What exciting lives those boys had—and what freedom! I was punished for saying, "I would rather be a lamplighter than who I am."

I picked my first edelweiss in the Alps and I saw my first golden eagles there. I never got to be a lamplighter but long later eagles were to become part of my life.

In Garmisch-Partenkirchen, a sleepy little village, we stayed in a pension. It was stylish, but in those days private bathrooms were essentially unknown. The toilets were rather like those in an expensive club— a long row of stalls. So I learned how wicked the French are. Two little French boys locked every single door from the inside and then crawled out under the doors. Then they watched the guests wait, and wait, for their turn to go to the toilet. And the French boys watched and giggled. And I watched these remarkable boys with profound admiration.

It was in Dresden that the most *real* episode occurred. My nurse and Bertram and I walked past a fenced-in garden. The garden gate was partly open, and a hare was trying to get out.

I conducted my first drive. "Fräulein, you will take Bertram across the garden. Then you walk along the fence on one side. And make Bertram walk along the other side. Then the hare will come to me."

I stood by the gate watching and when the hare got near, I crouched. It dashed for the gate and I plunged. I caught it, and I didn't let go.

"It's a pet." I held on tightly. "We will take my pet home."

On the way home, Fräulein found a spinach leaf lying on the sidewalk. "Hares eat spinach," she said.

Bertram carried the spinach leaf.

My parents were out when we got back. I carried the struggling hare upstairs to my bedroom, put the spinach leaf in a little dish and— very gently—let the hare go near the spinach leaf. Then I tiptoed downstairs. But I had left the window open. The hare was gone.

It was my first wild pet. Hundreds of wild animals were to become part of my life. This was the first.

Sometimes we stayed in country inns, and sometimes in big cities. Wherever we stayed, the children ate supper at five o'clock, were read to after supper, and then went to bed at seven o'clock. We were called at seven o'clock in the morning. Twelve hours' sleep was not considered enough for growing children, so we had to take a nap after lunch every day. Of course it was impossible to sleep thirteen hours a day, but the shades were drawn and we had to lie in bed with our eyes closed . . . at least as long as somebody was watching.

When my father was out of the house, I always got out of bed, because I wasn't afraid of anybody else. One naptime I got ahold of a pair of scissors and cut the tiny hairs off Bertram's legs. But that was entertainment for only one nap. The next way of passing the time was far more satisfactory. I wrote notes and we threw the notes out of the window and watched to see who would pick them up. The notes always carried the same message:

> *Help! We cannot escape!*
> *We are poor kidnapped children!*
> *Help us!*

Day after day we watched the notes flutter down to the street. We never saw anyone pick one up.

The American child

There was nothing placid about our existence, but in the autumn of 1914 it was plain that all the grownups were unusually upset and nervy. Nobody told the children why. We were told, "We are going home. Isn't that lovely? We are going *home.*"

"Home" was dozens of hotels, kind cooks who gave me a mug of beer when I was sent below-stairs to get my morning glass of milk, and merry bellboys who delighted in pranks.

World War I had started. My father, who always seemed to know influential people, was pulling strings to get us aboard an ocean liner sailing for America. We sailed on the *Kaiserin Auguste Victoria,* the last German ocean liner to cross the Atlantic during wartime.

My grandmother felt that my mother was not capable of bringing up children—no discipline, no method—so she engaged Fräulein Taggesell to see to my upbringing. Fräulein Taggesell, soon known as Fräuta, stayed for almost twelve years, and had a profound influence on my life.

Fräuta took me for daily walks around the deck. We were high up, traveling First Class, and way below in steerage I could see the immigrants: colorful people, the women danced with swirling skirts, men danced with their hats on and some had bobbing feathers in their hats. And there were baskets of poultry—and geese right among the people. I was forbidden to even consider going below to talk with those strange folk, but I did long to see them up close.

On our daily walks Fräuta liked to pause in a sunny nook near some lifeboats. Before long an officer liked to pause there too and talk with Fräuta, and one day he was joined by another officer, who, after receiving a brief nod from Fräuta, pulled out a packet of cigarettes, struck a match, and was about to light a cigarette when his eye caught mine. He thought he had noticed something. . . .

"Fräulein," he said firmly, "the First Mate would be delighted to show you the view from the bridge—and in the meantime, I shall show this young lady the engine room, which *she* will find of interest."

15

Then he called over his shoulder, "Let's meet on the fore deck in about half an hour." I was whisked away—down into the depths of the ship and then down a little ladder into the engine room.

He looked at me, this exquisitely dressed six-year-old child, and he shook his head. Again, he pulled out the packet of cigarettes, gave it a little tap so one or two cigarettes stuck out and were easy to reach, and he held the package out to me. I took one and waited politely for a light. We stood by a small railing and smoked together. Men going about their business stared as they passed. That remarkably perceptive ship's officer had realized that Fräulein—under no circumstances— would have accepted a cigarette. And that a certain little American girl was just longing to have a smoke with him.

News spreads quickly aboard ship. Very soon, the sailors, too, found ways of separating me from Fräuta and my parents and managing a smoke with this small, regal child.

A few days after we left Europe, we encountered what was said to be "the biggest storm in forty-five years." Huge waves washed over the steerage deck, so the immigrants came up to First Class. They brought their livestock up with them and I could walk right up to some geese that had been tied to a chair. They ate rolls right out of my hand. I had never had goose friends before.

When the storm abated, the ship and its passengers were much as before. Passengers spent long hours lying in deck chairs, covered with steamer blankets. And one little passenger was sneaked off from time to time so that still another incredulous member of the crew could watch the little girl puff contentedly and gracefully on a cigarette. "This," they would say, "is the American child."

Some time after we got back into the United States, my mother said, "You know something puzzled me aboard the *Kaiserin Auguste Victoria*. They called you 'the American child.' There were dozens of American children aboard that ship." Mother sighed and beamed at her small daughter. " 'The American child'—I suppose because you were so beautiful."

My seventh birthday was on board ship. When I got back to the United States of America all my living memories were of another world.

We docked, I believe in New York. Within the first hour, while going through customs and watching my father see to the luggage, I saw at least twenty black men. Mind you, I had only seen one before in my whole life. And I saw several black women, and I actually saw black children too. I had a lot of thinking to do.

And lots of the people in the United States of America were chewing—they kept chewing and it didn't seem that they had anything to eat.

I asked Fräuta, "What are all those people chewing?"

"*Kaugummi*. It's chew rubber." And then she added, "No beautiful woman ever chews gum."

I still agree with her.

Americans were no great surprise to me. By the time I was seven years old, I had lived in seven countries, I spoke five dialects or languages, and the United States was "just another new country—known as 'home'."

It did come as a surprise to me that not all American children spoke several languages—and were supposed to speak them correctly. Most American children did not even speak English—they spoke American—a fact that was to bring me much trouble later.

Aboard the steamship. I had been smoking about a month at this time.

Just a bowl of goldfish

I had not expected to find that I had *two* grandmothers. The unexpected one, Grandmother Chase, lived alone, with one son, and then besides: there was her companion, Miss Patchell; Waliser the coachman, Timothy the gardener, Maggy the cook, a seamstress, a waitress, an upstairs maid, a scullery maid, and various accommodators. The maid servants slept up in the third storey—where a stuffed moosehead was mounted near the top of the stairs. The men servants either slept in the village with their families, or above the stables.

Grandmother Chase, known as "Granny," invited us, poor Helen (so plucky) and dear Laurence (her husband) and the two dear children (Bertram and me), and my governess Fräuta to stay at Chesham, the family house in Brookline just outside of Boston. Chesham was a great house—not just big, *great*. There were plenty of rooms left over for guests after we all moved in. We stayed a year.

Granny's son, Uncle Billy, lived in a suite, more or less shut off from the rest of the house. I don't know where his valet Dimitri stayed. I was sometimes allowed to wade in Uncle Billy's bathtub. It was made of tile; steps led down into it; and it surely could have accommodated two Roman emperors simultaneously.

Uncle Billy's grand piano was in the library and so were most of the books in the house. The library was so-to-speak neutral ground. It was Uncle Billy's domain, but the rest of the household were welcomed there from time to time. Uncle Billy had some low tastes. He preferred operettas to classical music and he liked to read the funny papers. Bertram and I were supposed to prefer classical music, and we were never allowed to even look at the comics. One Sunday afternoon Bertram and I noticed that one of the cushions of a window seat had slipped aside, and that just a small corner of the Sunday funny section of the newspaper peeped forth. Bertram and I pulled this treasure out and slipped into Uncle Billy's bathroom where we could read in peace.

After glorying in this naughtiness, we returned the funnies—trying to push them under the seat cushion. But something was in the way. The something was a bar of Baker's chocolate, *and* a packet of cigarettes. Dear Uncle Billy.

Bertram and I were absolutely forbidden to go below-stairs, where the servants seemed to conduct a never-ending party in the kitchen–living room. It was not very hard to get down there because I was encouraged to take an interest in flower arrangement. Dear little Frances busy in the flower room, snipping stems and arranging garden flowers in vases, was smiled upon. The flower room was just one step from the staircase down to the kitchen. Maggy let me cut cookies with a cookie cutter. And she let me eat all the little pointy fragments left over after cutting round cookies. I still consider uncooked cookie dough one of the world's great delicacies.

There was a lot of laughter below-stairs. Sailors, policemen, gardeners, and others came to court Granny's maids. Norah, the waitress, was walking out with a sailor.

Bertram and I lived in a household with about twelve grownups—plus visiting aunts, uncles, and Grandmother Flint—most of whom kept telling us what to do and, most particularly, what *not* to do. It was Norah's sailor who taught me skills that have never left me—and may, upon occasion, have saved my life. He taught me to tie knots—good knots to be trusted. And I have dangled from cliffs trusting the knots he taught me. (Upstairs, I was learning lace-making.) He taught me how to climb ropes; and I have been at home on a rope ever since. And he taught me how to fall. Over and over again he threw me onto the kitchen floor. First he made it easy for me to roll with the tumble so as not to get hurt, and then he tossed me with vigor, making it progressively more difficult to roll.

Granny kept complaining that every time she got a new maid (fresh from the Old Country) properly trained, the girl got married and left her service. I was prepared to have the young maids leave. I was not prepared to find Maggy, the old cook, crying and leaving with her suitcase packed. She had told me such wonderful animal stories.

Hilda, the new cook, welcomed me below-stairs, but she was afraid that uncooked cookie dough might be bad for me.

I missed Maggy—she had such a wonderful smell, and she never worried about uncooked dough, and the animals she had known as a child were part of my longings.

"Chesham," my Grandmother Chase's house. I preferred below-stairs to the big porch above.

I slipped through this hallway to find my way to the kitchen stairs.

20

I suppose Maggy had been fired. Nobody told children about things like that. Some months later, I happened to be near the door when the bell rang. Dimitri opened the door and there stood Maggy, wrapped up in a shawl and smiling. She held out a bowl of goldfish. The goldfish were swimming, and breathing and blowing bubbles. They were alive! I held the magic bowl in my hands, hardly able to breathe with delight.

Then one of the grownups spoke. "Tell Cook you cannot accept this present." I held more tightly onto the bowl.

Two of the goldfish alive, real, swam behind some waterplants and reappeared.

"Say 'Thank you' to Cook."

My whole world was in my hands.

"Thank you."

"Now, hand Cook the bowl."

The bluejay's funeral

Chesham murmured mysterious events of the past. Auntie May died of scarlet fever and my mother cut her own hair off too, so Auntie May would feel better before she died. This gave me a lot to think about. I saw no practical use for this information.

My mother, who had an excellent sense for the dramatic, pointed to the telephone one day. "Children, look at the telephone! When I was a little girl my father had a telephone installed. Our number was EIGHT. It was the eighth telephone installed in Boston."

"Why?"

"He wanted to be able to call his office, but we children wanted to make sure it worked. We used to ring EIGHT and say "Bring six apples.""

And, sure enough, six apples were brought in from Boston.

I liked to hear these stories of the olden days, but the big woods on the Chesham property had an even stronger appeal for me.

There were chestnut trees, and we could eat the nuts. And there were hollow trees in which one could hide valuable possessions. One morning I found a whole package of razor blades. I had never owned a knife, and these sharp, but slightly rusty tools were quickly hidden in a hollow tree. When I came into the house to have my face, hands, and

The rich are not always happy. At Chesham.

22

knees scrubbed for lunchtime, Miss Patchell was in conference with my father.

"It isn't the first time I've told you, Mr. Flint: Mrs. Chase's liver trouble is a serious matter . . ." Then Miss Patchell caught sight of me. "Run along now, we were just discussing your Granny's health."

But I had heard what they were talking about: *liver,* Granny's liver.

As soon as my father was out of sight I asked Miss Patchell, "What does a liver look like?"

Miss Patchell was not only Granny's companion, she was also a trained nurse, and loved to explain things. She took paper and pencil, and made quick sketches. "See, the liver is shaped like this, and it is shiny, then the heart lies here, and higher up are the lungs—two of them."

"You mean," I asked incredulously, "my grandmother is like that inside?"

Miss Patchell was not pleased at the question. "I forgot how young you are." She suddenly looked very severe. "Frances, go prepare for luncheon."

I don't know how many acres Granny owned. The lawn swept down to the stable and was kept up by Timothy. Flower beds and ornamental shrubs peeked forth here and there, and the big woods lay on a steep hillside. The driveways were well graveled, and the entire property was surrounded by a stone wall next to the streets and by a fence along the back line. So Bertram and I were given a good deal of freedom to roam at will as long as we didn't leave the property. Sparrows roosted in the English ivy that covered part of the house, orioles nested in the tall elms, robins feasted in the cherry trees, and sometimes bats flew out of the stable. I longed to get closer to these creatures . . . to see what they were really like.

And then, I found a bluejay. A dead bluejay. I stood holding it in my hand. It was so close—so real—and it was mine.

Just then Eddie Fraser, the only neighborhood boy we were allowed to play with, appeared and said, "Let's see what you've got."

I didn't let go. I showed it to him.

"It's dead! We'll have a funeral!"

Eddie was at least two years older than I, and at least four years older than Bertram, so he could boss us around any time he pleased. "Frances," he ordered, "you pick the flowers, and Bertram, go get your express wagon."

Eddie helped pick flowers and piled them on the express wagon. "Now put the bluejay on the flowers."

I still held the bird tightly in my hand. "I don't want to."

Eddie said, "This is a *funeral*."

I put the bird carefully on the flowers in the bed of the express wagon.

"What hymns do you know?" he demanded.

Fräuta's favorite was *Eternal Father, Strong to Save,* so we sang that one. Eddie pulled the express wagon. Singing, we trudged up the long driveway,

> "Eternal Father, strong to save,
> Whose arm does guide the restless wave.
> Oh, Father, now we pray to thee,
> For those in peril, on the sea."

Singing as loud as we could, we passed the house and then, with some difficulty we pulled and pushed the wagon into the woods. At last we paused. Eddie said, "This is the place."

He dug quite a deep hole with his hands, took the bird from me and buried it. Then he covered the closed grave with flowers and made a cross of sticks. "This marks the spot," he said.

I thought of that bird all through lunch, all the time I was supposed to be taking a nap after lunch, and then, when it was almost dark—after supper—I went alone to the grave and dug the bluejay up. I took it to the tree where I kept my razor blades; selecting one of the least rusty blades, I opened the bluejay. It had a heart. It had lungs. And yes, a very shiny liver.

Saint Frances

When I was eight years old, my parents bought a house in Milton near Boston. The drawing-room walls were of dull gold-textured paper. Little gold chairs sat here and there. The armchairs and sofa featured a rich, dark red, like American Beauty roses.

A bearskin rug lay under the grand piano. I often marveled at the bear's lifelike head and the way his teeth were set in, and then again I used to lie on the bear's thick dark fur and cry softly when people had been unfair.

There were little shelves under the piano easily reached by a child. No maid would ever think to crawl under the piano to dust those little shelves, so they were among my safe places for matches, cigarettes, lump sugar, and other small valuables.

Afternoon tea was served in the drawing room. Ladies came—and my Grandmother Flint was often among them. They sipped tea out of Dresden china cups, and ate little cakes.

Fräulein laid down the silver-backed hairbrush and gave my head a little pat. "The ladies are here. It is time to go down." My face, hands (including fingernails), and hair were perfect.

Then she gasped, "Frances! your knees!"

She steered me into the children's bathroom and gave both knees a good scrubbing.

"Remember your head."

It was easy to remember my head. Day after day I walked up and down the big graceful staircase with a book on my head, so I would have good posture when I grew up.

I went downstairs slowly and evenly as though the book were still on my head. Then I entered the drawing room and walked past the piano without giving it a glance.

I went straight to the oldest lady, curtsied, and was prepared to shake hands with her if that was what she expected—some did and some didn't. Then came the questions.

"Are you in school yet?"

"No my governess is teaching me."

"Your governess does it all?"

"Oh no, I have music lessons, and dancing lessons, and riding lessons, and skiing..."

It seemed that my mother did not want me to tell about the walking lessons, the lace-making lessons, and the variety of tutors that spent so much time teaching me to do things correctly.

The next lady asked, "Do you like poetry, my dear?"

"Oh *yes!*"

"Do you know *Hiawatha?*"

I nodded.

"Please recite it for me."

"Am See der Gitchigummi. Am funklenden..."

The ladies started laughing.

The lady persisted. "Could you recite it in English, please?"

"I only know it in German. Nobody told me that there is an English translation."

My grandmother explained to the ladies, "Sometimes Frances remains and has a little cake with us." And then, turning to me she said, "You may go to your room."

I walked upstairs as though I had a book on my head. Somehow I had done the wrong thing today... it happened so often. The ladies were still laughing when I got to the top of the stairs. I learned not to volunteer too often. "Frances is such a quiet child." Grandmother never failed to add, "She has such a spiritual quality. It is rare in one so young."

Afternoon teas went well for several months: until the day I caught a swallowtail butterfly and brought it in to show to the ladies. It was going into my insect collection, but it was so lovely I wanted to show it first.

I took it straight to Grandmother. "Look!" she exclaimed, "all the little animals trust her."

The butterfly waved its wings slowly.

"Grandmother, the butterfly doesn't..."

"Don't interrupt, dear. Frances has a way with all living creatures. She..."

I held the butterfly right up to her face so she could see that I was holding it by the legs.

Grandmother continued, "This is a rare quality. See how the butterfly sits trustingly on her..."

"*Grandmother,* can't you see I'm holding..."

26

"You must learn not to interrupt."

"One hardly knows how to speak of something so precious." The ladies nodded. Grandmother lowered her voice, which took on a dreamy quality. "Saint Francis—it brings to mind . . ."

"*I am holding* . . ."

"Under no circumstances are you to use that tone. You may be excused."

"May I explain?"

"You are to leave the room."

My next action followed swiftly. I went out our big front door and closed it firmly behind me. Then I put the butterfly down on the cement floor of the porch and squashed it with my foot. I squashed it until there was nothing left.

At supper that evening Grandmother soon started the conversation. "Laurence, a most interesting thing happened this afternoon. Frances brought a beautiful butterfly to show us at tea. It *trusted* her. It sat quietly on her finger and . . ."

"Its legs. I was holding . . ."

My father gave me a withering look. "You have been taught not to interrupt."

"I *have* to!"

"Leave the room!" he roared.

"Saint Frances . . ." My grandmother's voice carried well.

I want a toothache

It was early on that I discovered that books and magazines let you know things that grownups either did not know, or preferred not to discuss. Learning to read had been no problem for me—probably because of Fräulein's skillful tutoring. The day I discovered that I could read a book all by myself still sparkles in my memory. The book was *The Sunbonnet Babies.* I hid halfway up the stairway to the third storey and read it from cover to cover.

I had long ago learned not to volunteer too often, so I kept my new skill secret. I read books in French and German. Nobody had told me, "Now that you can read in English, you must learn to do this in other languages too." I read in treetops, and I read by candlelight in my clothes closet, and I carried books back of the stable, where I could also read in peace. I read Ernest Thompson Seton, and Frances Hodgson Burnett, and Mark Twain. I read a book called *The Little Buffalo Robe,* which I have never been able to find again.

When I got a little older—about eleven—I read Charles Darwin. Then my mother pointed out a shelf of paperbacks in French that "were too old for me to read" so I devoted some months to reading Balzac, Guy de Maupassant, and Victor Hugo. It was good to feel so wicked, but after a while I switched back to Darwin.

Another discovery was that grownups outside of our household knew a lot of things I wanted to know. I had learned how to stuff birds from my friend the hunchbacked taxidermist, and now I was to learn something more, this time about insects. Fräulein took me to the Boston Museum of Natural History. It had been on our way home from my dentist appointment. My insect collection took up about six shoeboxes by now, and it troubled me that I could only label the butterflies and moths that happened to be in my very small insect book. I can imagine what happened that day—the first of many—at that museum. Fräulein, who loved walking, may have wished to see all the animals, but I found some cases of insects, high on slender pins, and every insect was labeled!

A curator, Mr. Charles Johnson, drifted by and watched me peek under each insect to read its Latin name. I suppose Fräulein and Mr. Johnson talked for a while, and then we were invited into the range where the big insect collection was housed in stacks of handsome wooden boxes. That day opened a new world for me, but how to get back into it?

"Fräulein, do you remember taking me to the Boston Museum of Natural History after I went to the dentist?"

"Yes."

"If I had to go to the dentist again, would you take me there?"

"But your teeth are perfectly all right, Frances."

"What if they weren't?"

"It is a silly question, but of course I would take you to the dentist, and perhaps to the museum."

First I tried hitting my teeth with a heavy screw driver . . . harder . . . and harder . . . and *harder!*

But I couldn't seem to hit hard enough.

That night I dreamed about the museum and all those labeled insects on special pins.

It was during my geography lesson that an idea came to me. I had my pencil in my mouth, which I was not supposed to do.

"Excuse me." Fräulein nodded absently as I headed for the bathroom. My idea had to be tried out immediately.

I stood in front of the mirror and pushed the pencil between two teeth—up close to the gum. Then, still pushing hard, I rolled the pencil. Blood came! I kept rotating the pencil between my fingers and looked again. More blood—and a slight swelling.

Fräulein looked up as I returned. "We now come to the agricultural crops of Spain." Fräulein looked at my face more closely. "Frances, I have seldom seen you looking so happy. Has something nice happened?"

"In Spain there are grapes. There is Spanish wine. And olives, and wheat."

It seemed so ridiculous to be reciting the crops of Spain when I had just found a way to get back to Mr. Johnson and the museum.

"What day is it?" Fräulein was puzzled by the interruption.

"Yes, what day of the week?"

Fräulein shrugged. "It is Friday. Now we will proceed with the lesson."

I selected Monday. Monday for my toothache.

Fräulein kissed me good morning, and closed the windows. I got up quickly, plunged into my cold bath and waited patiently for Fräulein to dry me off. Then I brushed my teeth. I dressed quickly with Fräulein's help, and then I locked myself in the bathroom with a nice pointy pencil.

First I tried applying proper pressure to my Friday experiment. It hurt.

So I picked two teeth on the other side of my mouth and worked the pencil for all I was worth. This hurt too, but it was much easier to start in a new place.

I was late for breakfast. I put the fingertips of my left hand gently on the side of my mouth and mumbled, "I'm sorry to be late."

My father snorted over his newspaper and said, "Promptness is something you *must* learn."

I toyed with my food.

At last my father noticed. "*Frances,* you are not eating your breakfast."

I put my little hand up against my cheek and spoke very softly. "I think I have a toothache."

"Let me see your mouth."

I got up and went over to Father's chair. And then I lifted up my lip so he could see the right place. "Helen! how long has this been going on?" Mother looked distraught.

Fräulein spoke up. "Frances was at the dentist last week. He said her teeth were in excellent condition."

"Make an appointment for this morning, or early this afternoon. I don't like that swelling."

A few hours later Fräulein was watching the dentist anxiously. "The lesions are odd—not exactly cankers. Let's treat them with alum." And yes, just a dab of alum was followed by a trip to the Boston Museum of Natural History.

Death of a kitten

The dining room was ablaze with forsythia—hundreds of yellow blossoms. Each year my mother picked numerous unpromising stems, kept them well watered, in sunlight in the conservatory; and then, one day, the vases of forsythia in the dining room glowed against the paneled woodwork.

After lunch, Fräulein and I went up to her room. I lay flat on the floor without a pillow for half an hour while Fräulein read aloud to me. Then she lay down on her bed and I read aloud to her. The books we read alternated: first a French book, and then a German book. Fräulein made sure that I maintained the correct position whilst reading: upright, with a straight back, in a straight-backed chair; book held exactly fourteen inches from my eyes. (This after-luncheon routine was maintained rigorously for almost twelve years.)

The readings were followed by a walk. I put on my jacket and started to button it up. Fräulein said, "It is spring. You need no jacket today." And she let me wear my sandals instead of the boots or galoshes I had been wearing for months. I wore a pale pink dress and white socks.

"We are going to Hyde Park to post a letter for your father."

Usually we walked along country lanes, or across meadows or woodlands on nearby estates. The road to Hyde Park went down a steep hill. It was lined with houses and took us straight into town.

We sang rounds along the way—songs about merry-making and springtime. When we got to the top of the steep hill, we noticed a group of men standing in the middle of the road.

Fräulein said, "Your father will need the letter posted." And I realized that if it hadn't been for the letter, she would have changed the direction of our walk. We would have gone home another way.

When we got quite close to the group of men I could see exactly what they were looking at. A small kitten had been run over by a car. Its hindquarters were squashed flat into the pavement, and it was trying to get up with its front feet. Those little forefeet scratched and twisted helplessly in the air. It meowed softly.

Fräulein took my hand and veered toward the sidewalk. "Come, child."

And then I broke away from her. I looked all around. There was a snow shovel up on the porch of the nearest house. I seized the shovel and ran back to the kitten. I pushed my way between the spectators— and then I bashed the kitten to death. I hit it and hit it till its suffering was over and it would never move again.

Then I put the shovel back on the porch.

My dress that day was of the palest pink cotton. It was spattered with bright red flecks on the way home: and my short white socks had flecks of red running in small streaks.

Fräulein made no comment whatsoever on the way home. We never spoke of the incident.

After supper I overheard Fräulein talking with my father. "All those men just stood there. . . .

"That little one has courage."

She said it in German, "Die Kleine hat Mut."

The Floss on the Mill

Sunday dinner at Chesham came at least once a month, but always caught us unprepared. Father had been warming up the Locomobile, and snapping in the scratched isinglass curtains that served as windows. He did not complain of cold fingers, but snorted and swore under his breath, as the top corners—one by one—buckled out and slapped his face; or—worse still—buckled *in*. He had to retrieve each curtain that buckled *in* by walking around the car, climbing in the door on the other side—and over the little seats to the window.

Mother watched from her dressing room. Her heart must have gone out to him as he flexed his stiff, red fingers, for she forgot to dress: an undertaking that she accomplished with haste and abandon, but never with speed.

Fräulein was always ready and so were we. Our bright red coats and little mink caps lay on chairs, with the mittens and mufflers tucked in the left sleeve of each coat. The klaxon sounded. Each child rushed to his chair and put on his clothes. Fräulein helped Bertram with his, and hurried us out to the car. "Your poor father is waiting."

Mother had, alas! mislaid her blouse. Father opened the front door and shouted upstairs, "Helen, is the house locked?"

Mother's agitated soprano reached us as we sat shivering in the car. "Well, there's the cellar door."

We had no trouble hearing Father's, "*Helen,* we shall be late."

It seems that Mother started to struggle into another blouse. She called ". . . and the greenhouse door . . . and the back door . . .

"I've found my blouse!"

Father was shaking the greenhouse door. "Damn!" he shouted. We all knew the key to the greenhouse door was broken. Nobody had dared to tell him. Mother ran down the staircase to Father's aid. "Let's put a chair against it."

Father shook his head pityingly. "A chair does not lock a door."

While Father went to the stables for hammer and nails, Mother found her hat, gloves, purse, and overcoat, and climbed into the car.

It was cold in the car. I begged to be allowed to wait indoors. Fräulein gasped at the suggestion. But no, we must *not* keep your father waiting.

We could hear Father nailing the door shut and the splintering of the woodwork. Then he came out. I wondered whether Mother knew the pantry window was unlocked? We said nothing. As Father turned to lock the big front door, Fräulein suddenly stiffened.

"Oh!" she exclaimed. She rushed out of the car clutching at her muff and gloves.

"Oh! One moment please. Oh! Mr. Flint, I left a book indoors—it's right there by the door."

We all looked at her in amazement; Fräulein was *never* late. Father shook his head and locked the door after her in silence. He climbed into the driver's seat and we jerked out of the drive in low gear; with a rasping shudder the car plunged into second—a pause—then a nasty clash of metal and third was attained. As we started down the hill the car snapped into high. My father looked at his watch.

My father, who kept his cars in repair in a machine shop that he had built for that purpose, had to be very angry before he shifted gears clumsily. We left Granny's house long after mid-afternoon. Snow had started falling, the wind was picking up, night was not far off, we had miles to go, and still one after another had to run back into Chesham for one reason or another. Of course, my father had hoped to reach Milton before darkness fell.

Near Jamaica Plain it became clear that we would never make it back to Milton without the headlights. Father climbed out of the car, opened the little door in front of a headlight, made some sort of an adjustment, and struck a match—which went out in the wind. He tried again and again. And when one headlight was burning satisfactorily, he put his hands in his pockets for a while to warm them up. Then he struggled with the second headlight—by which time it was night.

We got back late for supper, but Fräulein soon had us eating our cereal and toast. Bertram played with his food, but Fräulein didn't notice. She was very quiet. At last she asked our advice quite as though we were grownups.

"I've left a book at your grandmother's house. It's one of your father's books, *The Mill on the Floss*. Should I telephone about it?" Bertram, who had entirely recovered from the long, cold expedition, asked in a most innocent tone, "You mean *The Floss on the Mill?*"

34

I was about to correct him, for it's a famous book about the mill on the Floss River—when I saw he was mixing Fräuta up on purpose!

Fräulein spoke softly. "I had forgotten. Of course, *The Floss on the Mill.*"

This wonderful fib of Bertram's caused me to choke over a piece of toast but I managed to say, "I should telephone right away. It might get lost."

We giggled as Fräulein went to the telephone. Then we listened. We heard Fräulein speaking very distinctly. "*The Floss on the Mill . . .*"

We could also hear Father pulling nails by the greenhouse door; then louder, "*The Floss on the Mill*—a little blue *book.*"

She hung up muttering about not hearing very well.

Then she went to Father. We had not anticipated this. Bertram and I looked at each other in consternation.

Father was on his knees, examining the nail holes in the floor near the door. We held our breath.

"Mr. Flint, I'm sorry to say that I left one of your books at Chesham today."

The floor creaked as my father straightened his back and turned. "We'll get it later," he said shortly.

Father was getting up with a little grunt. "What book was it?"

"*The Mill on the Floss.*"

Fräulein had forgotten again.

The Milton house, with my mother standing at the front door.

35

Go comfort your poor father

I found the grownups either weak or not to be trusted.

My brother Vasmer was born when I was seven. Having a baby in the house didn't necessarily make things run more smoothly. Then, when I was nine, Mother announced that there was to be another dear little baby. "Why," I asked, "when you can't look after the children you have properly, do you want more?"

Mother liked fairy stories. She liked museums, and art galleries. She liked flower gardens and knew precisely how to direct a gardener. She loved to read aloud to her children. She had exquisite taste. She enjoyed merriment, and she liked to giggle. She adored my father and in her eyes he could do no wrong. As long as he lived she put up her hair in the Gibson Girl manner, wore old-fashioned clothes and button boots. My father knew how he wanted his wife to look.

Mother cried very often, but afterwards she wore a smile. What was true and real had much less interest for her than "seeing things in a happy light."

If my father was wrong, and he often was, she glossed this over. I never knew her to confront him with a mistake. The mistake I remember best still burns in my memory. He accused me of lying. I knew that I had not lied. Mother knew that I had not lied. I have no idea now what it was all about. I just remember that I was punished and placed in disgrace for telling a lie and thereafter my father made it plain to all that, "Frances has no sense of moral perspective."

His punishments became more severe and unexpected.

World War I was well underway and our household harbored an enemy alien—Fräulein.

If Fräulein ever cried, she did it in secret. But one day I found her close to tears. "What is wrong?" I asked.

"Frances, I must go to the police station and get fingerprinted."

"Well?"

"I must walk there and get fingerprinted."

"Are you *afraid?*"

Fräulein didn't answer. Perhaps she gave her head a slight nod.

"Never mind, Fräuta, I will come with you and get fingerprinted too. I think it would be fun."

So, instead of our usual walk, we went to the police station. The police brought out their ink pad and paper and seemed to enjoy showing a little girl how it all worked. Then Fräulein's turn came. Plainly, she was badly frightened.

I didn't bring the matter up again on my way home.

So Fräulein was another fallible grownup.

I wore dresses imported from Liberty's in London, my governess and tutors were the very best available, but I had no spending money. Uncle Trot (whose real name was Theophilus Parsons Chandler II) *slipped* me a little money. Nobody knew that I was accumulating cash— real spending money. More than anything else I wanted a hockey stick so I could play ice hockey with the neighborhood boys. At last I bought my hockey stick and hid it in a stall in the stable. When the ice was thick enough and Neddy Trafford and Winkie Wadsworth and the rest had started up practice, I went to the stable to get my stick. It was gone! The paper it had been wrapped in lay on the floor, but my brand new hockey stick was gone.

There was a smell of fresh paint in the stable. I moved cautiously toward my father's workshop. The ceiling was newly painted—a light cream color. There was a straight stick, to which a wide paintbrush had been attached with two screws, on his workbench. And on the floor beside it, lay the sawed-off bottom of my new hockey stick.

"*Frances,*" my father demanded, "what are you doing in here?"

"I was looking . . ."

"Fräulein simply lets you run wild. Go to your room," he roared, "and you may not come down for luncheon. *Stay* in your room until you are told to come out."

"But . . ."

"Go!"

Again I was in the wrong. And for some mysterious reason, Bertram was in the wrong, too. I heard my father boxing his ears and calling Bertram an old woman. Little Bertram's ears so often ached— and later it turned out he had been somewhat deafened. Bertram came upstairs crying softly and went to his room.

Late in the afternoon, Fräulein came into my room. She put her hand on my forehead to make sure that I didn't have a fever. Then she told me what to do next. "Your father is alone in his study, sitting in his chair. He is sorry that he was so strict. Please go comfort him."

Fräulein brushed my hair and then I went downstairs. I went into his study and sat on the arm of his Morris chair.

"Keezums." It was his pet name for me. Apparently I had pronounced Frances *Frankees* as a toddler.

He put his arm around me. Then he said "Keezums" again. He added, "You know I have your best interests at heart."

I didn't say, "Daddy, all I want is to run away."

I did some stock-taking. My mother is weak. She didn't stand up for me when I was accused of telling a lie.

Fräulein is afraid. She is afraid of silly things like the dark—and she was afraid of getting fingerprinted.

My father is to be feared and avoided forevermore.

I have tried prayer and found out it does not work.

I am alone in this world.

As I look back on it, ten or eleven was startlingly young to reach such a conclusion. I planned never to marry. I stood alone for the next twelve years—distrustful, determined, and leading my first double life.

The secret garden

Most of my hide-aways were in treetops, clumps of rhododendron, or in the wild open fields and woods between our house and the Neponset River.

One winter Bertram and I built the best hide-away I ever saw. It was an igloo. We cut blocks of snow and built up the walls, then we plastered up a ceiling with softer, less crumbly snow. At first, we made the doorway small, so no grownup could get in—and then we improved on this splendid design by adding a curved tunnel no grownup could crawl through to *look* inside. We iced this magnificent secret retreat so it was essentially indestructible.

Bertram and I crouched happily within. He ate chocolate. I smoked. It was peaceful.

Back of the stables was a wild, almost entirely enclosed area—a wasteland of burdock, trees, bushes, weeds, and ferns.

My mother encouraged my interest in gardening and had given me a flowerbed that was to be all my own. First I did some weeding around the peonies and fleurs-de-lis. Then I worked up an area that was so choked with weeds that it had to be spaded. Irmentrude, our waitress at the time, was a German. She saw what I was doing and came rushing out of the house. "Miss Frances! Miss Frances! Stop! Stop now! Remember your *Wappen!*"

"My *Wappen?*"

"Yes. How you say it in English? *Wappen.*"

I put down the spade, and answered, "Coat-of-arms."

Irmentrude gasped, "I will find someone to do this work for you."

Each shovelful of digging had produced new wonders: beetles, fat, white grubs, millipedes, and two kinds of earthworms.

So the family coat-of-arms ruled out manual labor—in front of people. I gave "Frances's very own flowerbed" perfunctory attention after that, but soon found it a useful seedbed from which nicely started plants could be moved to my secret garden.

I converted a huge pile of bricks into a Dutch-pattern walk. I

going to be dressed as boys
and all the boys as girls.
We were all very excited
about it but Vasmer got
sicker and so I did not go
latter he had phemonia
but he got quite well.

Chapter

I sadly repent all my
nauty-nesses to Fräuta
but perhaps it is too
late she talks every day
about going and I am
very unhappy. I have
resolved to be good and I
have tried very hard but
it is a resolve that is very
hard to keep there are
so many temptations.

planted grape hyacinth and snow drops. And made a decision: only white or blue flowers shall grow in this garden.

I took Fräulein to see how beautiful my garden was and asked her to keep it a secret. The very moment I asked her to keep it a secret, I realized I had made a mistake. Poor Fräulein spent a lot of time looking for me, as I was forever escaping. And now she would go behind the stables to look for me.

After a reasonable interval I said, "Fräuta, there is poison ivy growing all over, on the way to behind the stables."

Fräulein simply answered, "Then, of course, no one will go there."

Silence.

I did not tell her that the lush growth of poison ivy on the way to the secret garden had all been planted by me.

My mother and I shared a number of attributes: a love of books, a delight in flowers, an appreciation of fine textures—and—I believe, a life-long immunity to poison ivy.

I grafted seckel pear twigs onto a young, seedling pear tree in my secret garden the way Moynihan, the gardener from across the street, had taught me. I cut the twigs, and then I trimmed them short. I cut off the whole top of the pear tree and made two little notches to receive my twigs. The base of each twig was cut on a slant, so the strong juices running that spring day would push the sap right up into my twigs. Then I sealed all the exposed areas with beeswax, and wrapped the whole with bicycle tape. Both grafts took. I invited Moynihan to come to see how well they were growing, and he was pleased with my aptitude.

The parent seckel pear tree grew about a mile from our house. Fräulein sometimes let me pick one pear when we went by it on our walks.

When Fräulein had her day off, one of the maids looked after me, but they never wanted to walk to the pear tree. They just wanted to watch me while I stayed at home. And then the day came when Fräulein was away, and the maids were too busy to look after the children, for there was to be a big dinner party. The whole household was in an uproar. Somebody said, "Why don't you take your little brother Vasmer for a walk?" I took Vasmer by the hand and we disappeared before anyone could change his mind.

At first we started out at random, and then I took Vasmer to the pear tree. I ate one and gave Vasmer one. The pears were not quite ripe, but they tasted good. We each ate another. They *did* taste good. Then we settled down to a major feast of under-ripe pears. We sat in the grass under the tree and ate pears. Finally Vasmer said, "Frances, I feel sick."

After three months of being dangerously ill, little Vasmer, with me.

"Time to go home." I hurried him along.

"You're going too fast!"

"But I'd better get you home if you're going to be sick."

"Can you carry me?"

"You know I can't carry you home. I'll just help you walk."

At last we got to the front door. Mother was arranging the flowers, the maids were setting the table, and my father was giving orders.

"Vasmer is sick!" I shouted.

My father ordered no one in particular, "Take his temperature!"

Mother called, "Where is Fräulein?"

"In Boston."

Cook found a thermometer. Vasmer's temperature was over 103°!

"Get the child to bed. Get Dr. Withington." Father stomped into his study and telephoned Dr. Withington himself.

The next few weeks were terrible indeed. Two trained nurses were engaged. Vasmer hung between life and death. Every now and then, one of the grownups would say, "Would you like to look at your little brother again?" And each time I realized it might be for the last time.

I knew that I shouldn't have let Vasmer eat all those pears. Here my brother was dying, and it was all my fault. Guilt caused me constant agony.

Vasmer was suffering from double pneumonia. At last he got better. It wasn't until years later that I learned that double pneumonia is not caused by over-indulgence in unripe seckel pears.

The cocker and the fish hook

Every summer I spent two weeks at West Chop on Martha's Vine-yard island visiting the Gierash family. Mr. and Mrs. Gierash had five lively children, but the parents were "separated." Mr. Gierash spent two weeks with his family every summer and I was always invited to spend the same two weeks to help ease the tensions. There were four boys, and Dorothea, who was about my age. The tensions were not like those at Milton. Mr. G. never shouted. He loved to hear his wife play the piano and sing. Every evening she dressed in floating paisley dresses and sang. But, instantly, if her husband walked into the room, she stopped.

In some ways it was like my family. There was a constant undercur-rent of trepidation and unhappiness, which seemed entirely natural to me. The children went their own way, sailing, swimming, playing ten-nis, and fishing, but appeared promptly at meal time. It was fishing that got me into trouble. Dorothea and I took bamboo poles, fishline, hooks, and bait and went down to the end of the wharf to catch cunners, chocksies, and tautaugs. The family's cocker spaniel had romped out onto the wharf too, and had to be shooed away from the bait.

"Go home," we'd yell, but the spaniel just got out of our way and returned to sniff our tin can of electric worms, snails, and clam parts. It made daring little dashes to upset the can and actually get at some of the fishy tidbits, but our bait was far too valuable to let this noisy little dog have even a morsel. Dorothea and I fished in relative peace and proudly brought our catch in at lunchtime. The rest of the day was uneventful, but the night was not. Just after I'd gone to bed, there was an uproar. People ran up and down the upstairs hall and up and down the long staircase. It didn't take me long to put on my bathrobe and slippers and join the excitement. The family was assembled on the verandah near the living room. The cocker spaniel was yipping and wailing, and one of the big boys stood holding a bamboo fishpole.

"Frances," asked Mrs. Gierash, "did you leave this fishpole here?"

"Yes."

Mr. Gierash explained, "You see, the baited hook was near the floor and you caught the dog."

The dog continued yipping and wailing and various people tried to coax it into their arms to be cuddled. "The hook is right in his lip. See what happens if you leave baited hooks around."

I dove for the dog and caught him on the first try. The hook— rather a large one—was almost through the upper lip. One of the boys had cut the dog free from the pole, and about six inches of fishline hung from the cocker's mouth.

"Somebody get me some wire cutters. It's easy. I can get that hook out in a moment."

Nobody moved.

Bobby, one of the boys, came closer and crouched.

"*How* are you going to get it out?"

"Bobby, I'll hold the dog. You cut off the top of the hook. Then I push the hook the rest of the way through."

The dog settled more comfortably in my arms and Bobby rose to get the wire cutters. The yipping had stopped.

But the voices of the people mounted to a crescendo.

"Let that dog go!"

"Call the veterinarian. Phone the mainland, now!"

"This is a high-strung animal!"

"Put those wire cutters back where they belong!"

"Give me that poor dog."

I let go my gentle hold on the cocker. He jumped and rushed anew among the legs of the people— yipping and wailing in full throat.

I suppose it was ten o'clock by now. Mrs. Gierash called the mainland several times before she could find a veterinarian who was willing to give up more than a full day to come to the island by the Vineyard steamer, arriving early in the afternoon and leaving on the same steamer the following day.

I went back to bed. Now and again I could hear yips and wails, and the excited voices of people. Nothing to be done. I went to sleep. At breakfast I learned how heartless this had been of me. I had slept while the poor, high-strung dog suffered—simply gone to bed and slept. At lunch, I heard more about this insensitivity of mine.

And then the veterinarian came. He took in the situation at a glance. "I'm just going to pull this through and clip it off. Will someone bring me some wire cutters . . ."

A night in the woods

One night after I had been put to bed, I heard strange animal sounds coming from the big spruce tree near the house. It sounded like young animals, and maybe I could catch them. Anyway I wondered what the sound was. I got dressed very quietly. Then I tiptoed out onto the sleeping porch, and climbed down onto the verandah. The climb consisted of various minuscule handholds, and lastly a jump down onto the verandah floor. No grownup, I'm sure, had any idea that anyone—particularly a child—could climb from the sleeping porch window down to the ground floor—much less get back up again.

The light was still on in my parents' bedroom and in my mother's dressing room, so I moved very softly to the spruce tree. I could hear crickets, but if there were any animals in the spruce they were now silent.

So I crawled under the spruce to wait. It was like a tent under the branches . . . and well-hidden as well as comfortable. At last I dozed.

The Milton house, where I climbed out the window from my sleeping porch.

When I got wide-awake again, there was still no animal sound and I got to thinking of something my father once said. "Some people need alarm clocks, and others can wake up when they want to—at will."

I started murmuring, "I *will* wake up at six. I *will* wake up at six." So it was that I spent my first night out, sleeping under the spruce tree quite near the house.

Waking up early enough in the morning was no problem. Long before it was time for Fräulein to tell me my bath was ready, I was securely back in my nightdress, tucked into bed, and ready to be kissed good morning.

This was the first of many, many happy nights sleeping under the stars. Soon I slept in my secret garden. I wandered about in the woods of our neighbors and found more "bedrooms."

There was an old horse blanket in the stables. I made it mine, and it made some of the chillier nights seem warmer. It helped to keep mosquitoes off. With that blanket over me and my hair brushed over my face, mosquitoes didn't bother me a bit.

Night sounds are different. Sometimes a dog would come and sniff, and sometimes I thought I might have heard a deer, but the night time was mostly full of sounds of smaller animals: the liquid descending trill of the screech owl came from the Traffords' apple trees, and a frightened robin sometimes shifted its night perch at the edge of the Hollingsworths' woods down by the Neponset River bottoms. The Millikens had a small marsh below their formal gardens. That was my *frog bedroom*. In the spring, the frog music pushed away all other sounds so I could just hear frogs.

Sometimes I had to run home because rain or dew was wetting my hair and this would have been hard to explain to Fräulein. To make up for having to go home, there were other nights when I kept waking up and each time the world was different. I remember moonrise and how the moon moved all the way across the sky. Every time I woke up, it had moved again until moondown. No grownup had ever told me how huge and reddish the setting moon glows just above the horizon—I found out alone.

There is a magic to lying alone under the sky, listening to the sounds of small creatures, and finally drifting off to sleep.

It was not long before I learned that this magic does not come naturally to everyone.

One summer while I was visiting Dorothea, she unexpectedly said, "Let's sleep outdoors tonight."

"Sure."

Dorothea had not expected such an offhand reply to this exciting suggestion.

"I mean in the *woods!*"

"All right."

"We will need a tent, and matches and candles, and sheets and blankets and pillows. What else?"

"How about something nice to eat?" I suggested timidly.

"To *eat?*"

"Yes." I spoke with more authority. "Brownies and sardines."

Dorothea did not welcome bringing food for this great adventure, so I slipped into the pantry and quickly ate some brownies.

Walter, the oldest son, gave me the first hint that the night in the woods might indeed be a great adventure. He helped us find a spot to pitch his pup tent under some gray pines. "Better have it pretty close to the house so you can yell if you need to." I thought he was just teasing us, but I couldn't be quite sure.

This was my first night in a tent—a real tent—not just sliding under a spruce tree to sleep. I tried to stay awake to savor this new experience, but my eyes fell shut and I seemed to be begging, "Pass me the wire cutters. *Please* pass me the wire cutters." Perhaps if the lacework of the leaf patterns fringing the starry sky had not been cut off by the tent I would have fallen asleep with delight in the night.

Suddenly Dorothea whispered, "Did you hear that?"

"I heard crickets."

"No, the *big* noise." Dorothea pressed close to me. A car door slammed in the far distance. At last I slept—until Dorothea sucked in her breath and lay trembling.

Suddenly she lurched to a sitting position, threw off the covers, and shouted, "Run!"

I watched her rush for the house. The moon was up. Nothing else moved. There was no sound. Bewildered, I picked up our sheets, blankets, and pillows and walked toward the house. The last part of the way I ran as fast as I could. I will never know what, if anything, frightened us. I do know that this bizarre and scary experience had no connection with my many outdoor bedrooms where I slept wrapped in my horse blanket, while my parents—quite unsuspecting—slept peacefully in their beds.

Six trout

Somewhere, under a flat rock, slippery with mossy overgrowth, the bones of six trout started to disintegrate over sixty years ago.

"Bertram," my father had announced, "it's time to take you fishing," and as an afterthought he added, "and Frances may come too." He bought us fishing rods and every evening, after supper, we were taught how to hold our rods and we practiced casting exquisite little artificial flies at croquet wickets on the lawn. Long after the mosquitoes had driven my mother into the house, Father kept us practicing. Mosquito welts rose on Bertram's skin until Fräulein protested, but a governess didn't have much say in our household. Father scowled if we conspicuously slapped at a mosquito even when it wasn't our turn at supervised casting at croquet wickets. "There is no point in doing anything unless you can do it properly."

My father, an excellent amateur mechanic, tinkered with the car for a couple of days, for we were to travel from Boston clear up into Vermont—almost 100 miles!

The expedition was delayed a day. I no longer remember whose fault it was. Perhaps Bertram had one of his frequent earaches, or Mother had forgotten to arrange for the right food or perhaps it was my fault.

Instead of starting out on a crisp, clear day with the northwest wind to cheer us, we pulled out of the driveway in a drizzly rain after Father had snapped all the isinglass curtains of the long touring car into position. He muttered that the turnbuckles had been badly designed and Mother replied, "Yes dear." Mother had no idea what a turnbuckle was, nor could she tell one trout fly from another. Father also mumbled about the roiling of the waters. Neither Bertram nor I dared ask how roiling would affect the trout fishing. I peered through a scratched, discolored isinglass curtain, daydreaming about the feel of a trout pulling down the tip of my rod, jumping in the sunlight and ending up in my little creel. Then the creak of the windshield wiper and the splash of the puddles would bring me back to present reality; had it been my fault that we started a day late? And I worried about the roiling of the waters.

Somewhere near the Massachusetts-Vermont state line we drove into sunlight. My father consulted a map and thereafter we wended our way along dusty, winding back roads. At last he eased the car into an old sawmill opening near an ancient wooden bridge. Bertram and I rushed to the bridge to look for swimming trout, Mother spread a linen table cloth on the grass and unloaded hampers of diagonally cut, crustless sandwiches filled with deviled ham. And there were stuffed eggs!

Father was pulling one tip off his Thomas rod to try out the other when we children came back from the bridge.

"Picnic's ready," my mother called in her high clear voice.

Father looked at the display of dainties on the tablecloth as though he were about to be bitten by a rattlesnake.

"Helen!" He shouted, "When were those eggs stuffed?"

"Yesterday," my mother answered nervously. Then she gave a little gasp. "Oh! It was day *before* yesterday. I forgot we started late."

Father spoke without hesitation. "You know perfectly well that stuffed eggs are particularly subject to spoilage. We cannot afford to have the children sick out here in the wilderness."

Mother hastily picked up the plate of eggs and dumped them behind a heap of sawdust. For a moment I wondered if squirrels would eat them and get sick and spit up like children.

After lunch Bertram and I followed Father to the bridge.

I looked at Father, drew a deep breath and asked, "How about the roiling of the waters?"

"Frances, you can see perfectly well for yourself that it has not rained here for a long time."

I believe now, that it was at that moment that my father made a decision. "Be careful not to roil that water wading in muddy places. I will fish upstream and you children may fish down to the next bridge and back."

Bertram and I longed to whoop with joy. We were to fish alone in the wilderness! But we both had a fair amount of sense and managed to look dutiful.

Father looked a little troubled. "You're not afraid, are you? Perhaps it would be better if you came with me?"

We shook our heads and I added, "We can stay together and help each other."

My father smiled. "Now, Frances, that's a very fine sentiment. Be sure to stay together."

Bertram and I, about to fish trout alone in the wilderness.

Bertram and I moseyed along the bank floating flies on top of the water. Then we stopped to whisper at a pool where the current carried our flies way, way out, farther than we could cast them.

It was so quiet in the wilderness. Our flies moved alluringly way beyond our reach. Suddenly we heard Father's voice upstream. He said only one word. It was *"Damn."* For a moment I could picture Mother laying down the book she was reading and then sighing as she always did when she heard a swear word. Bertram and I moved on downstream soundlessly.

We hooked six trout: three apiece. And we did help each other. Bertram, being much younger, was pretty clumsy so we devised a system. He kept the tip of the rod up and the line taut as well as he could while I stalked the fish with the landing net and brought it ashore.

It seemed as though we had fished miles of wilderness and on the way back I even wondered if we might have gotten lost. I was very glad to see the bridge near that first pool where the flies had floated so far out. I wanted to cast there again but Bertram whispered, "What if Father hasn't caught *any* fish?"

We considered this possibility fearfully and then pried up a flat rock, slippery with mossy overgrowth, and buried our fish wrapped in ferns.

We saw Mother asleep with her book on her lap when we got to the car so we looked to see if squirrels had eaten the stuffed eggs. But only ants were feasting on them. And there were ants all over the linen tablecloth on the grass.

When Father got back, he grumbled, "This stream isn't as good as it used to be." Then he noticed that Mother was asleep. "Helen! Why isn't the food put away?"

Mother hastily jumped out of the car and packed away the remains of the picnic. Bertram sneaked behind the car and peeked inside Father's creel. He gave me the ZERO sign with his thumb and forefinger.

Somewhere in Vermont, under a flat rock, slippery with mossy overgrowth, the bones of six trout started to disintegrate over sixty years ago.

Bertram and I learned very long ago that it isn't only the fish you bring home that matter.

How beautifully she holds her head

It was when I was about ten that school was added to my other lessons. Having spent about four years in Europe, and besides seldom being allowed to play with other American children, I had a pronounced foreign accent, was painfully shy, and blushed when spoken to by a stranger.

Milton Academy was one of the oldest private schools in New England, and perhaps the best and most aristocratic in the nation. Children, with well-modulated voices, spoke respectfully to teachers. Good taste predominated. The school was drenched in beauty and riddled with the hysteria of World War I. My foreign accent was primarily a mixture of British and German. The British component was acceptable, but not the German. I rolled my *rr*'s when I said "rroses." Teachers soon bombarded me with questions.

"I understand you've lived in Europe? Germany perhaps?"

"Yes."

"Do you have German friends?"

"Yes."

"What does your father do?"

"I don't know."

"Is there a German living in your house?"

"Fräulein Taggesell; she's my governess."

The children were more direct. I found a note slipped into my coat pocket with a perfectly horrid drawing of a girl with two braids— me—kissing the Kaiser. And Dickie belched in my ear every time he passed my desk. I ate alone, and at recess I sat alone and watched the others play. After a while Myra LeSourd, Esther Osgood, and Mary Field asked me to play jackstones with them. We sat in the sun on the big steps into the sunken lawn of our beautiful brick building and played. We tossed the little ball up into the air and swiftly swept up those odd little objects known as "jacks."

One day a girl stopped to watch. Then she jeered, "Teachers' children *have* to play with her."

It was true. Myra, Esther, and Mary were all children of teachers. Their acute embarrassment showed. I went straight back into the school leaving the game unfinished. Never again did I put them to the public discomfort of being seen playing jacks with me. I have always admired their courage.

War stories kept coming from unexpected sources. A man stopped to talk with me while I was playing by the rhododendrons near the house.

"Is there a radio on your roof?"

"I don't know."

"Well, you do know that your father is a German spy?"

I ran away from the man. Years later I learned that my father, an international criminologist, had acted as an undercover agent for the United States during the war.

Every day my mother read the newspaper—especially the long, long list of young men killed in the war. Sometimes she cried, and sometimes she sat at her elegant little writing desk in the drawing room, and wrote a letter of condolence to a friend who had lost a son.

It was soon after the stranger had asked me about the radio on our roof that I was invited to play a game at school. It was called "Friends."

The leader announced, "Everybody who has no German friends go to the east side of the field."

"Now," he announced in clear patriotic tones, "everybody who has a German friend go to the other side of the field."

"Here we go. Run at each other."

I stood my ground. The mass of children came rushing toward me. They knocked me down and piled on me. When it was over I got up slowly and limped into the schoolhouse to wash up. I was a different person. "Friends" had changed my attitude. The next time Dickie belched in my ear I said, "See you in the coatroom." He came to the coatroom with a few other boys. Dickie was bigger than I and heavier. I beat him up. I sat on his stomach and banged his head on the floor, and then I got the scissors hold on him till he cried, "Uncle."

Just a few more fights and I had won a sort of security. Nobody in the whole school was going to mess with me. They might slide notes into my pockets, and the secret pressure never ceased. And trouble kept coming so unexpectedly.

Miss Thacher, headmistress of the Lower School, taught us reading. The book was *Heidi*. Miss Thacher read aloud to us and then we took turns reading aloud. We got to the Fräulein Rottenmeier. I pronounced this name correctly starting with "Rotten" like "rotten apples." Miss Thacher corrected me. "It is Rotenmeier—'Rote'—like 'Boat.' It is Rotenmeier."

"There are two *t*'s," I argued, "so it's got to be Rottenmeier."

Miss Thacher said, "Rotenmeier sounds better."

"But it's *wrong*."

Miss Thacher said, "We do not use the German pronunciation."

Miss Thacher would undoubtedly have had more sympathy than I for Mother's friend who destroyed everything she owned that had been made in Germany. When Mother took me there to call, all the Meissen china with its exquisite hand-painted flowers had disappeared, and the delicate porcelain shepherds and shepherdesses had been removed from the china cabinet. "Smashed," she said. "I broke them."

But reminders of the war were few at home. At school they were daily and insidiously persistent.

One day Miss Vose called me into her warm, sunny classroom after school. I noticed that she shut the door. "Frances, I've been wanting to tell you something." She rearranged a few papers on her desk.

"It is not a disgrace to speak German. I can speak German too."

Startled, I looked at this amazing teacher. She had dared to be kind to me. . . . To be sure, she had shut the door so no one could overhear us, but she had trusted me.

The sudden kindness unnerved me, far more than trouble. I walked down the school steps, head up, fighting back tears. It was then that I heard one mother say to another, "Did you notice how beautifully that little girl holds her head?"

Wall-flower

Dancing school was different. At school, other girls sometimes sat alone and read during recess, or lay under a tree and did nothing because they wanted to. I could always pretend that if nobody wanted to be seen playing with me, it was really just because I happened to prefer being alone. Not so at dancing school. If nobody wanted to dance with me, *everybody* knew that once more I was a wall-flower.

It was Mr. Foster, I believe, who ran the dancing classes at the Milton Club. All the girls sat on one side of the room and all the boys on the other. We sat in stiff little gilt chairs and waited for Mr. Foster's signal. He had a little "clicker"—something like a castanet—with which he directed his classes. At the start of each dance Mr. Foster clicked and the boys got up, glided across the room, and selected a partner. (The boys preferred to rush across the ballroom floor to try to get the most popular girls, but the clicker slowed them down. . . .) When each boy stood in front of his partner, he bowed, his partner rose gracefully from her chair and curtsied. An elegant and pretty sight it must have been.

My mother sat with other mothers and chaperones and saw this sight every Saturday afternoon in autumn, winter, and spring for *nine years.*

There was little variation. The boys crossed the room and bowed; the girls rose gracefully and curtsied; the couples proceeded to dance around the room clockwise across the highly polished hardwood floor; and three to five girls were left over—sitting by the wall. They were the ones nobody wanted to dance with. I was, over and over again, a wall-flower, left sitting in plain sight for everyone to see that nobody wanted to dance with me.

"Remember, no running! Speed is unseemly.

"When you hear me click, you will go to select your partners.

"Bow slowly, give your partner time to curtsy. And remember, *no* running."

Mr. Foster clicked.

The little boys moved across the room in one giant wave. They

56

Nobody wanted to dance with me.

bowed to their partners. One almost looked as though he was about to bow to me—but he moved away quickly when he saw who it was. I was the tallest girl in the room—taller by far than most of the boys. Nobody danced with the tall girls.

There were always more girls than boys in dancing school. This afternoon there were four extra. We sat on little gold chairs—where everyone could see us . . . where everyone could see our disgrace.

Between dances the girls and boys formed separate lines and practiced steps: how to point the left toe—how to point the right toe— left toe, right toe. "Now," Mr. Foster announced, "you will take your seats and we will try it with the music and partners." It was the announcement that I always dreaded.

Remember, I reminded myself, smile and maybe somebody will dance with me. Smile.

Mr. Foster clicked. The boys crossed the room gliding—all except one. Horace Fuller ran; and Mr. Foster noticed. "Fuller!" Mr. Foster clicked for silence. "You ran. Your punishment will be sitting out this next dance. You will sit against the wall—where everyone can see your disgrace."

So while the couples danced everybody could look at Horace and behold his disgrace. It might have occurred to some grownup that throughout almost every one of the five dances every Saturday afternoon everyone could see *my* disgrace.

I looked to see how Horace was taking *his* disgrace. He was more or less crouched on his chair. He was leaning forward and closely watching the feet of the dancers as they went by. Suddenly a foot shot out. A boy dancing right near him stumbled and almost fell down. My admiration for Horace rose. He was trying to trip any couple that came near enough.

A good example makes for a change in attitude. I decided to do something to make boys dance with me.

The next week, I was told that Mrs. Swan, who was sitting next to my mother, remarked, "I wonder what is wrong with Frances's stomach."

I was wearing my dark blue velvet dancing-school dress. A wide silk Roman scarf was tied around my waist with a big bow in the middle of my back. The front of the scarf bulged. It was the repository for raisins, figs, and lump sugar. Anybody who asked me to dance could be sure of something absolutely delicious to eat.

The difficulty I had assembling my bait, and the stickiness inside my scarf, and on the Liberty velvet imported from London, amounted to nothing compared to the hope that I had found a way to attract partners.

A popular girl can get the word out quickly, but, not having anyone to confide in, how could I let the boys know about the treasure trove just over my stomach?

After a few weeks I gave up carrying food. Instead I brought five marbles to dancing school. Every time Mr. Foster clicked his clicker, I dropped a marble—but only when the class was assembled together in the middle of the room. The marble made a nice loud plop on the ballroom floor—sometimes bounced once, and always rolled.

"Who made that sound?" Mr. Foster lined us all up and looked us over . . . especially the boys.

Then he clicked. Another marble fell. "Silence!" He raised his voice. "This is not to occur again."

Just then, I dropped a marble by mistake.

"Silence!" Mr. Foster's voice cracked. But this time the clicker was the signal for the music to start: the beginning of two-step practice. Mr. Foster could not shout above the two-step.

I had one marble left. Once I had heard one of my cousins come out with a shocking expression. He said, "Oh, what the Hell!"

When the music stopped, Mr. Foster assembled the class. "If this happens again, the boys will have to empty their pockets."

It was at this moment that I whispered, to myself, "Oh, what the Hell!" and dropped my last marble.

Dropping marbles was for *vengeance*—it certainly had never occurred to me that it might get me an invitation to dance!

After Mr. Foster had given us a long lecture on deportment and courtesy he declared, "You will now select partners for the two-step." For just a moment he lifted his left hand and looked doubtfully at his clicker. Then he clicked. This time no marbles fell and the boys rushed as fast as they dared to select partners. Horace was coming straight for me! He bowed. I curtsied.

Horace got a good hold on my waist and we launched into a lively two-step. "I saw you drop marbles."

"*Did* you?"

"I won't tell."

Horace danced with force—the way I liked to dance. Then he put his mouth right next to my ear. "Let's see how many couples we can knock down."

"Yes."

It was glorious—but we were forbidden to dance together again.

Frances dear, you look flushed

Just about the time that the lilacs were in full bloom, summer vacation would start. No more school until September—and no more dancing school. I watched the lilac buds swell each spring and looked forward to the glorious time when two of my troubles would be over. Of course there were troubles at home too, but they didn't involve public disgrace.

The long summer lay before me, with time to look for birds' nests, collect insects, and hide in treetops. It was when the blueberries were ripe that I knew that the last good eating berries of summer were gone. And then, when the goldenrod buzzed with bees, and masses of butterflies gathered by the Michaelmas daisies, dancing school would be coming again.

We had a big meadow next to our property. It was starting to turn into woods. There were endless places to hide—ever so many wildflowers to add to my collection; and quantities of animals lived in my meadow: animals to watch, and animals to eat. Sometimes I cooked various wild vegetables or birds after building a *very small* fire; I cooked these in tin cans or pushed them onto green, pointed sticks and held them over the flame.

Most of the berries that grew in my meadow were good to eat: strawberries, raspberries, blackberries, "brambles," chokecherries, blueberries, and shadbush berries. There was one berry that was *not* good to eat. It gave me a fever. It also gave me an idea.

"Frances, do come try on your new dresses. The box has just arrived from London and your Grandmother Flint is here."

There was a mourning dove nest that was just about to hatch. I wanted to watch a chick get born but this was far too hard to explain.

"Frances! and look, dear," Grandmother continued, "there is another surprise. A cape for you to wear to dancing school." She took it out of its tissue-paper wrappings gently and held it up. "Look, Helen, at the workmanship. Look at those tiny stitches and the lining is just a shade lighter pink than the cape itself."

"Do try it on right now."

It was a command. It was the same every year. My dresses were always babyish and wholly unlike those that other girls wore.

I put the cape over my shoulders. Mother slipped the hood over my head murmuring, "My Posey-girl."

"Why can't I wear . . ."

"You look like a little princess."

I tried on the dresses, one by one. Of course they all fitted. Dainty smocking in heavy silk held the yoke of each dress in position, and from the bottom of the yoke, the dresses bulged shapeless and babyish to the hem.

It was the same every time a box came from London. There was absolutely no point in arguing.

Grandmother murmured, "Not every little girl is so fortunate."

And dancing school was just the same. This year I was still half a head taller than most of the boys; never the less I could hope that *somebody* would want to ask me to dance. It was when I was sitting by myself on one of those little gilt chairs that an idea came to me. The solution was in my meadow!

Next week, a few hours before it was time to leave for the Milton Club, I sneaked away to my meadow and ate quite a few of the berries that gave me a fever.

Just before I went into the dining room for lunch, I pinched my cheeks hard. I thought the fever was coming all right, but I wanted it to show. I needed to *look* sick.

My father noticed first. "Frances, you are toying with your food." Toying with food was not allowed.

I put down my fork and knife and tried to smile bravely. Mother noticed. "Frances dear, you look flushed. Are you all right?"

It was Fräulein who came out with the perfect suggestion. "If you don't mind, I'd like to take Frances's temperature."

She led me up to the children's bathroom, shook down a thermometer and put it under my tongue. "Almost 101°!" She nodded. "And now you will go into bed."

I lay in bed, huddled under the blankets. The wind was rising and now and then I heard a small unidentified sound near my windowsill. It reminded me of Mr. Foster's clicker. I snuggled under the bed clothes and smiled.

It is strange that nobody seemed to notice that it was on dancing-school days that Frances came down with a fever.

Then winter set in. Snow covered the ground; and nowhere in my meadow could I find another berry. Perhaps, I thought, I can find some if I push my way through the blackberry cane. The canes were strong and stout with large, slightly recurved triangular thorns. It was almost time to get dressed for dancing school and I hadn't found a single berry.

I looked again at the canes. I took two in my mittened hands and held them a long time.

"If you're going to do it, do it now." I closed my eyes and, holding both canes firmly, I raked them down across my face—hard.

Then there was blood on the snow. When I got home and looked in the mirror, I sobbed with pain and fright. Great bloody streaks ran diagonally across my face—but I was safe.

Mother asked, "Whatever happened? And on a dancing-school day. What a terrible pity that you will have to miss it."

Cold cream

The poison ivy that I had planted to keep the grownups out of my secret garden served more than one purpose. It gave me a place where I could be alone; it gave me a place where I could have my wild animal hospital and my wild pets: snakes, squirrels, turtles, birds of many sorts, fish, and mice. And it gave me a fine secret place to keep my guns and ammunition.

Fräulein sometimes found it her duty to mention various little unpleasantnesses to my father. I'm sure that she sometimes tried to tell my mother about these things but Mother had a way of foiling anybody who tried to bring up any unpleasantness. It went something like this:

"Mrs. Flint, I feel I should tell you something."

"Yes Fräulein?"

"It's about Frances . . . she . . ."

"Fräulein, did I ever tell you about the time that Cousin Susie Creasy visited the zoo in Dresden and the elephant trumpeted the very moment that he saw Cousin Susie Creasy . . . and . . ."

"Mrs. Flint . . ."

"Cousin Susie Creasy was wearing an enormous hat and it was decorated with large tropical flowers and fruits . . ."

Fräulein must have persisted. "Mrs. Flint, Frances has been eating . . ."

"Little children were feeding Lily—the elephant in the Dresden Zoo—peanuts—peanuts. It has always interested me that peanuts are called Erdnüsse—earth nuts—in the German language. Don't you find that interesting?"

"Yes, Mrs. Flint."

"At any rate, when Cousin Susan Creasy got close to the elephant pen, Lily trumpeted again. And then she reached through the bars and took Cousin Susie Creasy's hat right off her head!"

"Yes, Mrs. Flint. How extraordinary."

"Dear me," Mother would sigh after one of these feats, "It's almost lunchtime. Perhaps the children should start washing up."

Well, Fräulein had *tried* to tell my mother. . . .

Fräulein waited until after luncheon, when my father was in a good mood, before approaching him (in fact, one of the valuable lessons I learned from Fräuta was: if you want to ask a man for something important: always ask him after a meal, not before it). Fräulein lingered just outside the doorway to my father's den. She listened, and when she was sure from his breathing that he wasn't asleep, she said, "Mr. Flint? May I have a word with you?"

"Come in, Fräulein. Come *in!*" Father didn't say, "What is it now?" but he always made it perfectly plain that he had been interrupted.

"Mr. Flint, I thought I should tell, cold cream is disappearing from the children's bathroom."

"*Cold cream?*"

"Yes."

"Why do you tell me this?"

"Children sometimes develop abnormal appetites."

My father heaved himself out of his Morris chair.

"What on earth are you talking about?"

"It is disappearing . . ."

"You said that."

To the best of my knowledge, Fräulein never once cried in the presence of any member of our household. She must have been close to tears now. "It's Frances, Mr. Flint; I fear she is eating it."

"Harrumph!" My father roared like a wounded bull whenever he was displeased.

"Come to the children's bathroom right away." My father stormed up the exquisite staircase to the upper hall and into our bathroom. "Show me."

"Mr. Flint, this jar was almost full yesterday."

Father snatched it from her. "It's half-empty!"

"*Frances,*" he roared, "Frances!"

Fräulein murmured, "The children are having their naps!"

I opened my door and peeked out of my room.

"Fräulein says you've been eating cold cream."

"I heard her."

"What have you to say for yourself?"

"Nothing."

"*Have* you been eating cold cream?"

Silence.

I hung my head, looking as guilty as possible.

"*Answer!*" My father bellowed. "Answer, or you will take your punishment."

64

Father turned to Fräulein. "Frances is to practice on the piano—especially exercises—for two hours a day for two weeks."

Two weeks! Why that meant for two whole weeks I would not be allowed outdoors to walk with Fräuta—or to play.

Then I tried not to smile my quiet secret smile. The nights were mine—and the early mornings: I could climb out of my window and feed my pets, and oil my guns, and sleep in the woods. All was not lost.

Father had not found out that I was the proud owner of two guns: a BB gun and a twenty-two. It so happened that Father took good care of his guns. He kept them well oiled and often told Bertram, "Never neglect a gun. Keep it well oiled against rust." After these little lectures Father locked his gun oil in an ornate cabinet in his den.

Under the stables by my secret garden was where I hid my guns. It was damp and tiny rust spots appeared on the barrel of my twenty-two. For some weeks now I had been oiling my guns carefully, and trouble with rust was over. A remarkably effective gun oil is cold cream.

My treetop world

My childhood held a nebulous mosaic of worlds that belonged to me because no grownup could interfere with them as long as I kept them secret. They were varied and precious: my animal hospital, my guns, my meadow, my nights under the sky, and my treetop world, which I perhaps considered the safest of all.

Treetops were part of my life. When the leaves were on the trees no grownup could spot me. I felt as safe as though I were in a deep hole way underground. Sometimes I climbed high into the treetops with my mother's pearl-handled opera glasses to watch the warblers. Sometimes I climbed to a small pool right in a treetop, where birds came to drink, and sometimes I just hid in the treetops when I wanted to cry.

No one had told me about tree surgeons.

One day when I came home from school a great silvery branch, rich with a succession of flicker nesting holes, lay broken on the lawn. I crouched and listened at each hole to see whether anything alive was trapped deep within. Nothing stirred. Then I looked up at the route I had shinnied and climbed to listen to the calls of young flickers buzzing like eggbeaters. My path just led to a hole in the sky—nowhere. The whole limb had been sawed off.

A truck, heaped high with wood, mostly dead, stood at the far end of the driveway. The open-ended maple branch—home of the flying squirrels—had been smoothly sawed off too and was nowhere to be seen, probably just thrown onto that truck. The phoebe's hunting perch hung broken, twisting and twisting and untwisting slowly in the late afternoon.

Numb with pain, I looked to see what was left. Lord knows I had no heart to climb. But I was relieved to see that my great maple was still standing. A raccoon sometimes spent a day down in a big hole left by a branch lost long ago. In winter frost rimmed the hole—frost from his body heat when he was in residence—and in summer, spiders spun their webs across the entrance. Old cobby webs suggested that nobody was at home, but fresh, neat webs could have been spun while the raccoon slept down in his hole.

Protest would have been impossible even if I had not been in school. My father was in power; he would not have listened.

After a few days I felt like climbing again—my fingers and toes found each familiar hold as I swung up into the old maple and disappeared from view. I could hide there; perhaps that's why the coon liked it too. As I climbed higher, I paused to check the coon hole on my way up. It had been stuffed with cement and painted a bilious green. The delicate, torn cobweb at its lower edge had no story to tell.

My first falcon

Snow blew in big puffs around the corner of the house, and twirled behind the hydrangea bushes. Moynihan walked up the driveway much more slowly than he usually walked. He was slightly bent over to shelter something.

I ran to meet him. Ever so gently he pulled a bird out from under his coat. "Something else for your hospital—look out for her feet."

And then the something else was in my hands.

"It's a hawk. You'll have to feed it meat—just meat."

I opened my jacket and held the bird under the thick cloth—as much to hide it as to protect it from wind and snow.

"Oh, Moynihan! She's beautiful. How did you get her?"

"She was just a-hanging and couldn't seem to get away . . ."

"Where?"

"Up against that poultry wire that the sweet peas got trained up on last summer."

The bird had huge eyes—dark, like pools in a swamp. She was brown and black, with a light, streaked breast. Then I looked more closely. She had a *notched beak*. "Moynihan," I almost whispered, "she's a falcon!"

If kings and queens could train falcons in ancient times, so could I.

"Fräuta, how did the kings and queens train falcons in ancient times?

"I don't suppose anyone really knows. I have a feeling that they had someone to train their falcons for them. Perhaps we could find a book . . . ?"

My family had hundreds of books, but I was quite sure that none would deal with the matter at hand. The early autumn flurry of snow had melted entirely, so after lunch I got on my bicycle and pedaled two miles to the Milton Public Library. (I was not allowed to enter the public library. One might pick up diseases from the people there. They probably had germs.)

The librarian was a nice person, dressed in gray, and a lady. She found me books. "These are rare volumes. You may read them here, but you may not take them out."

I opened the biggest book first. The print was strange.

"It's printed in Old English. I doubt that you can read it. It belongs in the rare book section. Shall I take it back?"

"No!"

The librarian sighed, and went back behind her desk.

The print was rather like my German books. I could read Old German printed; I could write Old German script; and besides I could read and write modern English. The trick to reading Old English was simple. Just find a few words that you can recognize and in a few minutes you can decode the rest. There'll always be a few words you don't know, but frequent guessing often brings words closer than a dictionary ever can.

I was just puzzling over a long word when the librarian interrupted me. "Are you pretending to read that book?"

I ignored the question. "What does *austringer* mean?"

"Austringer? Who taught you to read Old English?"

"Nobody."

"Well!"

She took my hand. "Now let's go to the dictionary."

It was the biggest dictionary I'd ever seen. It was fastened to a special stand. And there was what I wanted.

Austringer: one that keeps goshawks.

I also looked up *Jess:* a short strap fastened around a falcon's leg, to which a leash can be attached.

Creance: a fine line for a hawk during training.

Rangle: gravel fed to hawks.

Musket: male of sparrow hawk.

Then I looked up the falconer's knot. It was a new knot—one that the sailor had never taught me. There was a picture, so I tried the knot out with my shoelace.

Then the lady in gray was at my side again. "The library is about to close. . . ."

"Oh!" I jumped up. "I'll be punished."

Going to the library was naughty, but not really wrong.

Will she die without rangle?

I knew perfectly well that what I was going to do next was wrong. My falcon needed jesses—and I was going to steal the leather. Sometimes, when my mother was going out in the evening, I was allowed into her dressing room while she added the final touches. She put some sort of powder onto the suede surfaces of her ivory-handled nail buffer, and polished her short, rounded fingernails; she poured a small amount of Eau de Cologne onto her fingers and dabbed a little at the base of her throat. Then she went into the bedroom and pulled out the second drawer of her massive bureau and selected a pair of opera gloves.

The opera gloves were of white kid. They were long, reaching almost to the elbow. Each pair was wrapped in dark blue tissue paper to keep the leather from yellowing.

I needed one glove, but I reached down toward the bottom of the pile of tissue-wrapped gloves and I took two so I wouldn't be found out; one glove would surely be missed, but a whole package might not be. It was stealing—different from filching lump sugar and figs. I knew I was doing wrong and I thought about it quite a lot.

Cutting up the glove didn't trouble me at all. It was beautiful leather, strong and soft.

I can't remember what I did about supplying my falcon with a leash, swivel, or perch. She liked to sit on my hand and I liked carrying her about behind the stables and in my meadow.

My kestrel was the most secret friend and possession I've ever had. I dreamed of someday hawking on horseback. Knowing perfectly well that the reins are always correctly carried in the left hand, I made a point of carrying my bird on my *right* hand—a habit that has persisted more than seventy years.

My falcon learned to come to my glove when I whistled; she sometimes preferred to ride on my head, and she ate uncooked meat that I easily helped myself to from the kitchen and pantries. Rangle was my major problem—*rangle:* gravel fed to hawks.

71

The driveway was frozen solid. Sleet and snow molded the gravel into one impenetrable chunk. Perhaps among the gravel I could find some suitable rounded stones. The rest of my outdoor world was not only frozen solid, but covered with snow too. I broke two kitchen knives trying to dig rangle out of our gracefully curved driveway. Then I gave up.

As soon as I found out that I couldn't give my bird rangle I started worrying. Maybe she's sick? Perhaps she won't live until spring?

But she did. She lived and I took her hunting. At dusk, English sparrows flocked in to roost in the ivy that covered the stone walls of the church. It seemed my falcon could see even better than I as deep dusk turned into street-light night. She fairly pounced into the ivy to make her kills. I rewarded her with tiny scraps of butcher meat, and stuffed sparrows into my pocket.

The year was 1919. I was twelve years old. I had learned from the old, old books. There were no modern falconry books in the library. I was alone. And I thought I was the only living falconer in the world.

My relationship with my falcon was intensely personal and intensely secret. I never talked with anyone about her. I never gave her a name.

For part of my life, she was my whole world.

I lose a friend

Moynihan taught me so much: how to graft fruit trees, how to find bee trees, when to plant bulbs, and names of flowers and insects and birds.

But one day we were lying under a rhododendron bush together watching ants—a long procession of ants. Then, suddenly Moynihan's voice sounded different. He unbuttoned his trousers and touched me in unexpected places.

"Moynihan," I said haughtily, "you forget yourself."

I got up very slowly. Head held high, I walked away from him with dignity.

The next day Moynihan rang the front-door bell. He had made a present for Miss Frances. It was an exquisite partridge-tail fan with a beautifully fashioned leather handle.

I never saw Moynihan again. I never told the grownups . . .

I had lost a friend.

I learn to order the meals

My Grandmother Flint, who visited us frequently, pointed out on numerous occasions that I was not being brought up properly.

Among her complaints was, Frances is not being taught how to handle servants. She must learn to direct them, maintain discipline, and how to order the meals.

Mother, somewhat aghast at all the things she was supposed to teach me, settled for having me learn how to order the meals.

At about ten o'clock in the morning, Cook lumbered up the back stairs, crossed the upstairs hall and knocked on the door of my parents' room. Mother, in her high girlish voice, called, "Come in."

Cook at that time was Elisabeth—a large woman with a large bosom and a large behind, and untidy hair. Mother sat at her small upstairs desk and I sat in a straight-backed chair beside her.

"Elisabeth, Miss Frances is going to order the meals this week."

Elisabeth, who of course remained standing, pursed her lips and looked down at me with raised eyebrows.

"For lunch today," I announced, "we will have cream puffs and ice cream." (Elisabeth made wonderful cream puffs and ice cream was my other favorite dessert.)

"Will that be all, Miss Frances?"

"No. Let's have a leg of lamb. *Not* overdone," I added severely. "Be sure it is a little pink in the middle. And roast potatoes . . . and green peas—*fresh* green peas."

Elisabeth looked at my mother inquiringly. Mother had nothing to volunteer, so Cook pointed out, "There's no fresh green peas to be had in December. How about Hubbard squash?"

"No!" I shouted, "I *hate* it."

This brought Mother's attention back to the matter at hand. "*Frances* dear!"

Elisabeth suggested Brussels sprouts. Then, quite guilelessly she asked me, "How many will there be for luncheon today, Miss Frances?"

I hadn't given this a thought! "Well, my father will be in Boston,

74

Fräulein will be taking Bertram to the dentist. There will be *two* of us today Elisabeth, my mother and I."

"Perhaps the two of ye would be a-finding the leg of lamb a bit big?"

"But I like lamb."

Elisabeth turned to my mother. "There's enough meat left over for cold cuts: beef, ham, and tongue. Yesterday's boiled potatoes didn't all get eaten, so you could have potato salad, and start over again for dinner this evening."

"Yes Elisabeth." Mother kept looking out of the window. I suspect she was planning the spring planting of perennials. She was good at gardening. The thought of food bored her.

"If you ordered a leg of lamb for dinner this evening, there'd be enough left over for minced lamb when all your ladies come tomorrow."

Mother had obviously forgotten that Sewing Circle was coming. She said, "Oh *yes,* and let's have peas. They go so well with lamb."

"Peas are not yet in season."

Mother murmured, "Oh! I forgot. Well, let's make it *canned* peas."

At dinner, Father carved the lamb. He seldom praised Mother but this time he exclaimed, "This is one of the best meals I've had in this house."

Mother smiled. "Little Frances planned this meal."

We had extra big cream puffs for dessert. I ate mine slowly, savoring every moment of its delicious taste and texture. I never got to eat one of Elisabeth's cream puffs again, for the next morning there were angry voices in the kitchen. Father had found three empty whiskey bottles buried in the flour barrel. "Drinking!" And Elisabeth's hairpins and comb were in a drawer right in with the kitchen silver!

We children listened from upstairs.

"Drinking!" my father shouted again.

Then we seemed to hear Elisabeth yell back.

"You like your little nip too, Mr. Flint. I'm giving you a week's notice."

"Pack your bags and go!"

Mother, who handled all money matters with marked ability, sat down at her pretty little downstairs desk and wrote a check for one week's salary. Elisabeth left.

My father got into our Marmon touring car and headed for Boston and Miss Eldridge's Employment Agency to hire another cook.

A day or two after Bessie, the new cook, came, the parlor maid gave notice. She had only been with us four days.

Bessie had arrived in time for one of my parent's formal dinner parties. All the leaves were put in to extend the big dining-room table. This always caused complications because Mother could no longer reach the little button under the rug to push it with her foot to call the waitress. *Just* when we needed things to go smoothly!

Father hired an "accommodator." These were usually trained waitresses who took short-term jobs with catering services or in private houses when more help was needed. This accommodator was small and frightened.

After the guests were seated, my father—much to my mother's annoyance—made his perennial jovial statement. "Today, it's just camp life. I hope you can all put up with it." The guests disclaimed this idiotic witticism with polite murmurs.

Meanwhile Mother had been feeling under the rug with her pretty little foot. By now she was holding onto the edge of the table with both hands and sliding farther and farther down in her chair to reach that bell. It was time to call Bessie to have her fill the guests' glasses with ice water. Bertram and I had a secret, and could hardly wait for the next development.

At last Mother took matters into her own hands. "Bertram, would you please call Bessie."

Bertram looked up startled. Twice, he tried to raise his voice so Bessie could hear him through the closed pantry door. "Bessie!" Bertram tried to overcome his shyness and tried again—just a little louder. "*Bessie!*"

This time my father heard him. "Stupid!" he said, "go into the kitchen and *get* Bessie."

Bertram laid his napkin on the table, pushed his chair back, and disappeared. A moment or two later, Bessie appeared, bearing the huge silver pitcher my father had won for being a crack pistol shot.

Normally we were not punished in front of guests, but this party was not starting out smoothly. Bertram and I looked at each other. We thought we knew what was in that pitcher: water, and ice—and about three dozen small black pollywogs. Bessie poured into each glass, taking care not to have too much crushed ice go into any one glass. No pollywogs came! Perhaps a maid had found the pollywogs and dumped them. When she got to Mr. Martin one pollywog swam into his glass—small and black.

Bessie didn't notice.

By the time she was halfway around the table more and more pollywogs slid swimming into the glasses along with the ice water.

76

My godmother, Mrs. Duffett, gasped when she saw what was going into her glass. Bessie saw too—at the very same moment. Bessie screamed.

This rattled the little accommodator. She tried to put the soup tureen in front of my father, but she came in from the wrong side. "Has no one," my father roared, "ever taught you from which side to serve?"

The accommodator pushed the heavy tureen just far enough onto the table so it wouldn't fall off. She headed for the kitchen, but got to the fireplace instead . . . where she reached up and seized the mantle-piece and hung there sobbing. Bessie tried to get her into the kitchen, but that small person refused to let go of the mantle-piece. She cried as though her heart would break, and she wouldn't go.

Finally my father got up from his chair at the head of the table and pried her fingers loose, and led her gently into the kitchen.

Then he said, "Bedtime for the children." Bertram and I gladly got up to leave. Fräulein excused herself, too, and we were put to bed. Before I went to sleep I made sure that my secret aquarium with its small black pollywogs was safe.

I hire a cook

Rhododendrons have long shiny dark leaves. These cast an almost black shadow. Deep in the shadow, beneath the shiny dark leaves Bertram and I had a place where we could hide together and watch the world go by.

We watched the maids who had been told to "pack up their things and go" walk down the driveway lugging packages, string bags, and baskets. It was a mile to the railway station in Hyde Park and some of them had rather a lot to carry. This struck us as sheer comedy—rather like watching robins trying to pull up worms that wouldn't come.

Bertram and I called one wizened old woman—who did not like children—"the Monkey," but to her face we always politely called her "Cook"—at least until the day she stumbled down the driveway laden with her worldly possessions. When she got quite close to our rhododendron clump Bertram jeered, "Good-bye Monkey! The Monkey is going!"

Cook struggled on down the hill and out of sight. Then, about ten minutes later, we saw somebody striding purposefully up the hill. It was Cook! She had left her possessions somewhere and was walking much faster. She went right past our hiding place. When she was almost out of earshot, Bertram called, "Here comes the Monkey! The Monkey is back!"

She went straight to the front door (which clearly showed that she no longer worked for us) and rang the bell. Somebody let her in. After a long wait, Father stepped out on the front porch and bellowed, *"Bertram!"*

Bertram gave me an agonized look. Then he crept out of our rhododendron hide-away and walked slowly up to the house.

It was plain that Cook had told my father about "the Monkey." The house was far enough away so I couldn't hear what was being said, but I could hear Bertram crying. Father had boxed his ears again.

I don't know why I hadn't called Cook "Monkey." Perhaps I was just a little bit sorry for her—like that robin having trouble pulling up worms. It certainly wasn't because I had come to realize that servants are "people."

Every time Bertram was punished and I was not, it put me on some sort of pedestal. I was used for comparison, and sometimes given special treats or responsibilities. This time the repercussions of the Monkey episode were unexpected.

"Frances," my father announced, "it is time you learned to run a household. I want you to hire a cook."

"Me?" I gasped.

"Fräulein will take you to the employment agency, but *you* will conduct the interview, and select a cook."

"Yes, Daddy."

Fräulein was quite flustered after lunch, and exclaimed, "We must hurry and get to the employment agency. I will leave you there and have tea with one of my friends while you are interviewing cooks."

The agency was up a long flight of stairs. There was a faint smell of overcooked cabbage, cheap perfume, and mould. Miss Eldridge sat at her desk in a rather bare office. Fräulein introduced me. "This is Miss Frances." Fräulein started over, because Miss Eldridge would need to know my last name if I was going to do anything so grownup as hire a servant.

"This is Miss *Flint*—Miss Frances Flint. She will hire a cook."

Miss Eldridge nodded pleasantly and beamed at dear little Miss Flint. Fräulein said, "I'll be back in about an hour to take Miss Frances home."

Miss Eldridge took me by the hand and led me to a room that was far larger than her office. There was a bench along the wall and everybody sitting on that bench looked at me.

"Miss Flint is here to engage a cook. The Flints have a small staff. There are four children. Their estate is one mile from the railway station and the train trip to Boston is about fifteen minutes. Wages are standard." Miss Eldridge patted my shoulder and left the room.

The people sitting along the bench continued to stare.

"Who can make cream puffs?"

About three of the women raised their hands. One smiled.

I had been taught not to point, but I pointed. "I'll take you."

Miss Eldridge was just settled into her chair again, when I trotted back into her office. She looked anxious.

"Is anything wrong?"

"No."

"But you were going to hire a cook?"

"I did."

"You *did!* Which one did you hire?"

"The one with the blue hat."

The look of tolerant amusement faded from Miss Eldridge's face to be replaced by something like respect. "Why, that's Mrs. O'Brian. She is one of the best and most experienced cooks we have listed!"

I sat down in an armchair near a newspaper from which peeked a comic section . . . to wait for Fräuta, but more needed to be done. Miss Eldridge left the room and came back followed by Mrs. O'Brian. "When would you like Cook to start?"

"Mrs. O'Brian, we don't have dinner until eight o'clock and there is nobody in our house who can cook. Could you start today?"

She did.

Mrs. O'Brian stayed far longer than most of our cooks. After she left I was often sent to hire replacements. They came and went. I got to feeling quite at home in the employment agency. Miss Eldridge always welcomed me cordially. And each time I went again into that big room I saw all those people in their shabby clothes, sitting on the bench like sparrows sitting on a wire.

The lie

The Hull House was high on a hill overlooking Boston Harbor. It was four storeys high and almost entirely surrounded by verandahs connected by outside stairs. Each morning, when the fog lifted, the spider webs on the lawn lost their little beads of moisture and disappeared—leaving only a memory of exquisite patterns all over the grass.

When the sun beat down, butterflies set the salt marsh between the hill and the sea alive—and there were flies with iridescent wings, and shiny-backed beetles. After breakfast, I took my butterfly net and my cyanide jar and collected insects painstakingly. My efforts became more and more professional. Each insect was mounted on a pin and carefully labeled. I fastened corrugated cardboard to the bottom of shoe boxes, so I could push pins into the cardboard and mount my collection.

The Hull House had been designed by my Grandmother Flint. It was full of places where a child could hide things. I kept my insect collection in my room, but Bertram and I hid our aquarium under the verandah—and very secret things we hid behind the enormous water tank that took up most of a dark corner near the trunk room in the top storey.

In some ways Grandmother Flint allowed us more freedom than we ever had at home, and in other ways she was stricter. Bertram and I could roam as we pleased as long as we arrived promptly with clean faces, hands, and knees at meal time. On the other hand, we were expected to account, each evening, for worthwhile time spent during the day. "Remember, Frances, *fun* is not important: work is." I listened.

Often we sat high on the verandah above the mezzanine after supper. We watched ocean liners, and the Nantasket steamer, the cargo boats, the fishing boats, and the yachts. And when it got dark, we watched Bug Light blink its message to passing ships. It was the smallest lighthouse I'd ever seen.

Sometimes, too, thunderstorms rolled and roared across the har-

bor. One summer, both maids ran upstairs to hide from the vivid lightning. They cowered in terror under their beds. Grandmother, having investigated, said, "That was no way to behave.

"Frances and Bertram, we will now continue reading Kipling."

Bertram and I dutifully took the chairs we always sat in when she read aloud, and Grandmother sat in a wicker armchair by the lamp. From time to time bright lightning flooded the room; and now and again the lamp light flickered. Grandmother had a beautiful voice for reading, and she never put on any false accents or over-dramatized the stories. We leaned forward to listen, but thunder—crash upon crash of thunder—drowned out her words.

Just as I looked out of the window, I saw lightning strike the house! It hit the pedestal globe on the railing of the long verandah's corner. The great wooden globe flared and dropped from sight.

Grandmother kept reading. "What the Bandar-log think now the Jungle will think later."

"Grandmother, I saw . . ."

"Don't interrupt."

She continued ". . . and that comforted . . ."

"Grandmother! Lightning just struck the house!"

"Be quiet. You must not let your imagination run away with you."

"But Grandmother, I saw . . ."

"Frances! Insisting that something that you have imagined is true is an untruth. It is a *lie!*"

"But, Grandmother . . ."

"You will go to your bed immediately. There will be no further discussion."

I cried in bed. I cried until I fell asleep. And I was not looking forward to breakfast and further admonitions. In the morning I went slowly down to the dining room.

Grandmother was already at breakfast. "Good morning Frances."

"Good morning Grandmother."

"Frances, I have something important to say to you."

I put down my spoon and waited for the worst.

"I owe you an apology."

"*What?*" Not being allowed to say "What?" I quickly added, "What did you say?"

"I made a mistake. The house *was* struck by lightning last evening. The corner of the house is charred, and the maids found the balustrade globe lying scorched on the lawn.

"I apologize." Grandmother was smiling. "You did *not* tell a lie."

It was the first time one of the grownups ever apologized to me.

The scars of childhood

I am proud of my scars. Ours was a neighborhood of boys. We liked to be brave like Indians and suffer horrible wounds silently. We were playing Indians when Neddy Trafford gave me my first good scar. We carried slingshots, bows and arrows, BB guns, and painted our faces. We spoke to each other gruffly in the tone we thought the Indians must use.

One day, when we were playing far from the house under a big oak tree, Neddy, who started many of the games, ordered, "Dance!"

"I won't."

"Dance, or I'll shoot."

I wasn't going to do that silly, jumping-up-and-down dance again for him or for anybody else.

Neddy reached for his BB gun.

"Dance, or I'll shoot."

"No!"

Neddy shot my leg at point-blank range. The BB was out of sight under the skin. Everybody crowded around to see where it went in. Then Neddy pulled out his jack knife and sat on my stomach. Others sat on my hands and feet for "the operation"; Neddy dug out the BB and put it in his pocket.

I didn't cry.

I didn't tell.

It was a good, honorable scar and it lasted many, many years.

My next scar was not quite so honorable. The Newton family lived next door to us. Connie Newton was about my age, but we had little in common. I found it hard to understand anybody who *liked* being a girl. Fig Newton, the oldest of the three boys, was fun to play with. (The others were too young.)

Fig sneaked up on me one day when I was whittling a slingshot with my new jack knife. He pounced on my back, covered my eyes, and growled, "Guess who this is."

84

My knife—which I kept very sharp—slipped and made a half-moon-shaped cut near the base of my left thumb.

Lots of blood! I borrowed Fig's handkerchief, wrapped my hand so the blood wouldn't show, and sneaked into the children's bathroom where I made myself such a neat-looking bandage that it looked like the work of a grownup.

A day or two later I decided to look at my wound. The bandage was stuck and I had quite a bit of trouble pulling it off in little jerks. A nice wound, over an inch long and now bleeding again almost all the way. There was a little place at the upper end of the cut that already seemed to have healed. I scratched it with my fingernail till it bled almost as well as the rest. Then, as I couldn't find anymore bandages in the medicine cabinet, I put the old bandage back on.

At lunch, my father said, "Frances, I think I'll take a look at your hand after lunch."

"It's just a little cut."

After lunch I ran up to the children's bathroom, ripped off the bandage and firmly replaced it with about an inch and a half of adhesive tape. This gave me a splendid idea

After lunch my father usually took a nap in his Morris chair. And after his nap he didn't seem to notice my little bandage. Normally he took quite an interest in our cuts, bandaged them skillfully, and admonished us, "Untreated wounds are apt to leave scars." As the days passed, he never seemed to notice that the moderately small strip of adhesive tape *still* seemed to be on my cut. Little did he suspect that my cut was being treated every day—for the opposite reason.

Every day, after breakfast, I jerked off the adhesive tape. Next I pulled the cut open as wide as I possibly could and put on a new strip of tape to *hold* it open. This tended to encourage bleeding.*

---

*I am now 86 years old. The handsome moon-shaped scar near the base of my left thumb is still easy to find.

Under the sofa

The boys in our neighborhood were divided into two groups. There were the little boys—too young for me to play with. These included two little Newtons, Levy Millikin, Clippy (Cleveland) Amory, Amor Hollingsworth, and my own little brothers: Vasmer and Putnam. The big boys were Neddy Trafford, his brother Harry, Winkie Wadsworth (sometimes), Fig (Frank) Newton, and my own brother Bertram.

We had several ways of getting rid of the little boys so we could play without them. Our favorite was to run slowly so the little boys thought they could keep up with us. Then faster and faster, but letting them keep us in sight, so they knew we were heading for the big barn on the hillside. The huge door stood invitingly wide open and we made sure that the little boys were going to follow us into the barn. Then we grabbed a rope just outside a window, slid to the ground and ran away. This left all the little boys spending the rest of the afternoon looking for us *inside* the barn.

Then we played. Sometimes the clarion call would ring, "Let's have a milk fight!"

The Traffords kept a cow. Fights were staged when the cow was in her stanchion ready to be milked. Then we got on both sides of the cow and tried to see how much milk we could squirt on each other. The result was a glorious mess. But the cow did not like this game. Furthermore, she could kick—and her eyes stuck out so far from the sides of her face that she could probably see just where she was going to kick. We figured that we were safe; as long as we were on both sides she wouldn't know which foot to kick with.

The Traffords lived in an enormous colonial house set high on a hill. It was empty every Saturday evening. All the maids were gone, and Mr. and Mrs. Trafford got all dressed up and went away till late at night. I believe it was Winkie who suggested a promising new pastime: "Let's get drunk."

Of course the Trafford boys knew where the key to the wine cellar was. The wine cellar had one weak light bulb hanging from the ceiling—enough to gleam on bottles and bottles and bottles.

"Let's just take a little from each bottle," Neddy suggested. "Then it will never be missed."

We poured a little, from each bottle that we could get open, into water glasses and took sips now and then to see what effect the liquor was having. Finally, when we had filled about four water glasses, Neddy announced, "Time to go upstairs and drink."

We sat in the living room and drank as we presumed the grown-ups did, smiling and holding our glasses up to toast each other. Once we got into the spirit of the thing we got up and staggered around the room, clutching at door frames and chair backs to keep from falling. We tottered and we hiccoughed.

Our idea of how drunks behaved was vague, mostly picked up from cartoons and things the grownups had let slip. Drunks sometimes got rough. We started bumping into each other and apologized—most formally—by saying, "Oh! excuse me, I thought you were a lamp-post."

Suddenly Harry yelled, "They're coming!" And sure enough there were car lights coming up the long driveway.

Somebody turned out the lights. There was a scuffling sound, and then I stood all alone in the dark.

"Neddy?" I called softly.

No answer.

I could hear the front door opening, so I crawled under the sofa. It was the only place to hide.

Mr. Trafford switched on the lights, saying something uninteresting like, "That was a pleasant evening, and you looked perfectly beautiful."

Mrs. Trafford gave a little low laugh.

Mr. and Mrs. Trafford sat on the sofa. Mr. Trafford's ankles were just inches from my face. They made love.

Mr. and Mrs. Trafford started saying very tender things to each other—things that were not intended for my ears.

I didn't dare let them know I was under the sofa, and the longer I put it off, the more impossible it was for me to announce my presence. At last they went upstairs to bed.

I sneaked out the front door, and ran all the way home. I had a new idea of what grownups were like.

Think lemonade

My father frequently let his children know that the family had moved to Milton so we could go to Milton Academy—perhaps the finest private preparatory school in the whole country. There were about 100 in the Girls' School, and about 300 in the Boys' School—just across the street.

Some people referred to the Girls' School as *Miss Goodwin's*. Miss Goodwin, the principal, was slender, gray-haired, exuded charm, and was magnificently qualified to deal with parents and other people who might assist the school in its worthy endeavors.

Miss Weeks was dumpy—not instantly impressive, but she was fair. I respected Miss Weeks.

Opening exercises took about twenty minutes each morning. Sometimes I managed to do yesterday's homework during exercises. A poem was considered equal to a two-page theme; and I could dash off a whole poem in fifteen minutes.

Miss Goodwin was in charge of opening exercises. She commanded attention. She smiled. She read from the Bible. Then a hymn was sung, and lastly, came messages for the day.

Mother was a social Episcopalian, and—in my opinion—far from devout. But maybe she was worrying about Jesus way out in the desert. One evening she said, "Frances, have you noticed how often WATER is mentioned in the Bible?"

"But," I exclaimed, "lemonade isn't mentioned at all!"

I glanced through my mother's Bible and did notice numerous mentions of water. And then I started giggling. Each time I read "water" I substituted "lemonade" in the sentence. I could hardly wait for school to start the next morning!

Just before opening exercises, I passed the word in the coatroom. "Every time Miss Goodwin says the word 'water': *think* 'lemonade'."

"Tell everybody." I added, "Opening exercises will be a lot more fun."

As soon as we were all assembled, I quickly started writing the poem that was to save me from not having written a theme.

The tender leaves
Of poplars tall
Cast quivering shadows
on the wall—
A wall of ancient stone.

The leaflets whisper in the breeze
And softly then the wind does moan
I sit beside the ancient wall
And I am all alone.

The mosses on the ancient wall
Are masked . . .

"Hoo-ha-ha-ho!" Elsie de Normandie shrieked. She was having hysterics. Louise Hunt had buried her head in her arms to suppress her laughter. About eight girls were suppressing laughter with very little success, but it was Elsie's shrieks that held everybody's startled attention. We could *see* Miss Goodwin ringing her little bell for silence. After a nod from Miss Goodwin, Miss Weeks went over to Elsie, patted her shoulder and led her—helpless with laughter—from the schoolroom.

As I had been making up my poem, I hadn't heard Miss Goodwin mention *water* so I didn't have anything to laugh at. My enjoyment of the situation was inconspicuous and quiet. No one would ever have suspected that Elsie's hysterics and various other spontaneous bursts of laughter *well scattered* around the schoolroom had anything to do with *me*. And after recess there was no way anybody could ever find out who had started "Think lemonade."

Recess must have gone rather like this:

"Elsie, what was so funny about opening exercises?"

"When Miss Goodwin reads, THINK 'LEMONADE' every time she says 'water.' Remember, *tomorrow.*"

"Think 'LEMONADE' when Miss Goodwin says 'water'."

"Think 'LEMONADE' . . ."

The message traveled fast.

Miss Goodwin wore a gray knit dress often graced with a single string of real pearls around her neck. She commanded attention just from the way she stood behind her desk. She smiled. She opened the Bible.

Milton Academy is one of the oldest schools in the United States. I am willing to wager, that never before—in the history of this very fine institution—did so many pupils lean forward in their chairs to catch every single word of a biblical reading.

Miss Goodwin's well-modulated voice always gave her readings a somewhat gloomy dignity. It went something like this: They came to the Mount. And behold, Mary knelt before Jesus and washed His feet with lem . . .

The room rocked with laughter. There was no way that Miss Weeks could lead all the hysterical girls into another room.

Some of the littlest girls in the first two rows cried. They didn't know what had happened.

Miss Goodwin didn't look quite so sure of herself during the morning reading on the third day.

She looked a trifle worried. Her worries were well founded. "Thou shalt smite the rock, and there shall come water out of it, that the people may drink. And Moses did so."

I don't remember what happened, but perhaps, when I was doing my homework each evening I liked to think of Miss Goodwin doing hers. The careful avoidance of the word WATER when selecting biblical passages for morning exercises must have required an odd type of concentration.

The last of the Mick fights

The main tree-house was on our property—about thirty feet up in a straight-boled, towering oak. It took us months to build it and when it was done five—or even six—of us could sit in it. And besides, it had storage space for food, cigarettes, and a Sears Roebuck catalogue. Of these, the Sears catalogue was the most wicked. Neddy, Winkie, Fig, and I studied the underwear pictures day after day, and from these we deduced what grownups must look like naked.

We also collected magazines about fighting: wrestling, jujitsu, and boxing. We practiced half nelsons and camel bites, and tested pressure points. We touched the spots that might knock your opponent out, or even kill him.

Gradually we decorated the tree-house with pictures, a carpet, and plenty of ashtrays, and we felt wonderfully secure: no grownup could reach us.

It wasn't long before this sense of security evaporated: the Micks discovered our tree-house. The Micks, in our opinion, were from down in the slums. We were not allowed to play with such boys, but every now and then they came up onto Brush Hill in small, belligerent groups. We welcomed them by shouting, "Mick fight! Mick fight!" and throwing stones at them.

After the Micks found our tree-house, we were very careful to pull up our rope ladder so nobody could reach us. We stored stones, and other heavy objects to hurl at the Micks if they ever came back—and they did. It was unsettling.

There was only one solution. Neddy said, "Go down to Hyde Park and beat them up."

Winkie added, "No girls. You stay home."

I gave him a camel bite until he yowled, "Quit it. You can come."

Slowly removing my fingers from his kneecap, I muttered, "Don't worry, I'll wear Bertram's clothes and hide my hair." We waited until dark and then walked the long, long mile down into Hyde Park—and there were the Micks. One of them yelled "Fight!"

92

Then there were more Micks—too many Micks—and they didn't fight fair. Three of them had Neddy down, and just as I ran to help him, a good-sized Mick with blond curly hair, punched me. I kept my thumb outside my fist the way boys do, and punched him. I picked the knockout spot on his temple and down he went in the street. He didn't move. I hit another Mick and we fought for quite a long time. The blond Mick still lay still. He hadn't moved yet!

Our magazines said that you can kill somebody by punching just right near the temple. Was he breathing?

Just then a Mick yelled, "Cheese it! The cops!" and I ran. We all ran. The police!

I ran alone. Then I ducked into an alley and ran some more. At last I finally got back home and climbed up into my room. I got into bed trembling, and listened for the police. None came, so I felt safe and almost went to sleep. Then I sobbed.

The blond boy who didn't move. Who didn't seem to breathe any more. Had I killed him? I clutched my blankets in terror. Had I killed him?

When morning came, I made my plan. If that boy was dead, the newspaper would announce it. I would get a paper every day. If a boy about eleven or twelve years old was not listed, I would know I had not killed him. Day after day I ran way down to Hyde Park to read the paper and soon I knew just where to look for deaths. And then I read, "James, beloved son of . . ." Oh! I read farther. James was four years old.

Every time I found no boy about my own age reported dead, I felt more hopeful. At last I gave up and didn't look any more. The magazines didn't say how quickly people died after having been punched on the temple. For a long, long time, I woke up at night—clutching my blankets in terror.

I learn to drive a car

On Fräulein's day off one of the maids was supposed to look after me. Fortunately Delia, the maid who usually took on this duty, was in love with a truck driver.

Delia always suggested going for a walk after lunch. Almost invariably, a huge Mack truck was parked at the corner of Smith Road and Brush Hill Road. Delia put her big felt hat on my head, and shoved my hair up out of sight so I looked like a grownup. I sat in the driver's seat. A large, firm pillow was placed behind my back so I could reach the clutch and the foot brake. With much muscle, and both hands, I forced the truck into low gear. The driver sat between Delia and me, and when there was traffic, he paid attention to what I was doing. Brush Hill Road is hilly, and each time that I had to change gears, I braced my back against the pillow, and let go of the steering wheel to use both hands to shift. Truck drivers were big, burly men and could shift with one hand. We headed for the Blue Hills Parkway and I knew what was coming: I parked by the side of the road so that the driver and Delia could get out—and climb into the back of the truck. Then I

drove round and round in the parkway. I believe we were the three happiest people on earth.

Cars and knowing how to drive changed our lives. We had more *opportunities*. No longer did we have to settle for games like *Who can get thrown out of the movie theater first,* we could start borrowing cars. Borrowing was not stealing. None of us would have dreamed of stealing. We took cars from our aunts and uncles, and from our fathers— and we always brought them back . . . after rocking them, or maybe just skidding.

Skidding was best done on a large, wet lawn. Get up speed, slam on the brakes, and feel the car gyrate in magnificent, swoopy curves— each tire track clearly marked on the smooth, green lawn. Always plan how to get away, and get away before anybody comes. We never "skidded" lawns of people we liked.

Rocking caused no damage, but was fun anyway. Cars were high in those days, so they rocked quite easily. The trick was to drive quite fast down a road, zooming back and forth between the right and left sides till each time you hit the edge of the road, the outer two wheels left the ground.

Three boys from the Hingham area wanted to date me. One backed out when he found out that he would not be allowed to meet my parents, and that I proposed to meet him under an oak tree instead.

Another, Gordon Gauld, drove right up to the front door in his magnificent, ancient Fiat. He listened politely to my father, who showed him his workshop, and marveled when Father showed him how he could turn screws with precision down to three one-thousandths of an inch. *He* was allowed to take me to a football game.

The third, Laurie Parker, understood perfectly that under no circumstances was he to come to the house. He was of my blood, and not what I would call a goody-goody. I showed him how to rock cars, and on our first date we stopped near a country club. There was a row of wicker chairs on a long, high verandah overlooking the golf links down below. Laurie threw a chair over the railing so it would roll down the hill. Then I threw one, and we threw more. Just as we were getting into the spirit of this merry mayhem, an old man peered out of the club house, and then ran toward us shouting obscenities. We rushed to the far end of the verandah to escape. One look over the railing showed us it was too high to jump. Laurie swung with instant grace, to a gutter pipe and slithered down to the ground. Wasting no time at all, I followed.

Then we ran around the club house and watched the back of the old man shouting down to where he thought we were! At last he gave up and went back into the club house.

There were still a couple of chairs "unthrown." Not wishing to leave unfinished business, we sneaked back onto the verandah. Furthermore—to avert boredom—we shouted and made a lot of noise. Sure enough, here came the old man, again shouting obscenities. Down went the chairs! Down the gutter pipe we went.

We had parked the car well down the driveway. After we had driven a mile or so, Laurie suggested putting the top down. He drove back slowly. I sat quite close to him. And when we got back to our meeting place, he kissed me under the oak tree.

I thought of telling Fräulein about the kiss.

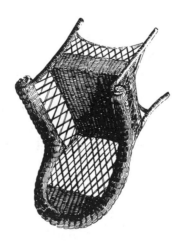

Good evening, Miss Flint

As I approached "sweet sixteen," Neddy asked me for a date. This struck me as so hilarious that I punched him in the stomach, gave him "the bird," and called him "Sweetie Pie."

It was the end of an era. Neddy and Winkie and Fig started treating me gently. Playing with them wasn't any fun anymore. And then, at Christmastime, Noukie Wright's mother invited me to a houseparty at her house in Hingham. None of the boys there knew about dancing school, and that I was to be shunned. Even Noukie's brother, who was at Harvard, danced with me over and over again, and Laurie Parker sneaked me away from the house and took me down to the beach. By the time the houseparty was over, I had several invitations—invitations to dance, to go to the theater, and to go to the Harvard-Yale football game.

I came home thrilled and told my parents all about the invitations, innocently thinking that they would approve. My father said, "Frances, you will accept none of these invitations." And when more invitations arrived he always said, "No."

Why always *No?* Other girls were allowed to go to dances, football games, and proms.

One day Jaime Moreno, a romantic South American boy, who had sent me countless orchids, invited me to the prom at Mitchell Military Academy. An engraved invitation came with his letter—as well as a printed letter to parents declaring that all young ladies attending the school for the prom weekend would be properly chaperoned; a dormitory would be emptied for their occupation; they would eat in the dining hall; and no girl would be permitted to come *without the permission of her parents.*

A weekend at a boys' school!

I could climb out of my window and meet boys to take me dancing—but a whole weekend!

It was Bertram who saved the day. Bertram was a year and a half younger than I. His voice was just changing, but he offered to telephone the headmaster of Mitchell Military Academy. "I will tell him only the truth."

We waited until the grownups were all out of the way. Then Bertram sat in my father's desk chair and gave the operator the number of Mitchell Military Academy.

"This is Mr. Flint. I would like to speak with the headmaster."

". . ."

"Mr. *Flint.* Mr. Laurence Bertram Flint." Bertram was trying so hard to keep his voice low that he was a little hard to understand.

Bertram leaned back in Father's chair and nodded his head ponderously the way grownups do.

". . ."

"This is Mr. Flint. Frances has my permission to go to your prom." Bertram's voice shot up toward the end of the sentence. Perhaps the headmaster hadn't noticed?

But Bertram had to repeat. "This is Mr. Flint. Frances has my . . ." Bert's voice cracked and cracked upwards again. ". . . *permission* to go to the prom."

When the prom weekend finally came, I packed my suitcase and put it in the Lexington touring car that Bert and I shared. I told the family I was going to the Austin Treadwell Whites'—where I was encouraged to go.

I went to the Whites' and spent almost twenty minutes there, after which I roared down their gravel driveway and headed for Mitchell Military Academy.

Bertram and I had a precise code of ethics: neither of us had told a single lie.

Climbing out of my window to be taken to the theater or dancing presented few problems. It actually got easier to climb out of my window because I was taller now. Some of my dates must have wondered why I asked them to meet me by the gnarled oak near the Hollingsworth gate—rather than coming up to the house and ringing the doorbell. Those who had the temerity to pay me a call in the usual manner never wondered again—if my father was at home when they appeared. One young man arrived on foot in a blizzard. He left his overshoes in the front hall and escaped through the back pantry door rather than enduring the terror of being confronted by my father face-to-face again.

There was always the danger that I would get found out. What if one of my father's friends recognized me at one of Boston's popular night clubs? After a year or two of this exciting type of dating, Norman Cutler, the son of the chauffeur of one of my mother's friends, asked me for a date.

Dating the son of a chauffeur struck me as a glorious disobedience—and besides, Norman was very good-looking. I did, however, retain just a bit of caution. "Norman, let's go where nobody knows us, shall we?"

Norman thought a moment. "I know a place near Walpole. It's called the Webber Duck Inn. Is that far enough away?"

"I never heard of it. It sounds just right."

Norman didn't need to be told that a chauffeur's son should never appear at our front door. He suggested we meet where Mother's friends, the Galbraiths, kept their cars. It was odd for me—in full evening dress—to meet anybody where servants met, but I soon got used to it. Norman seemed to have a variety of handsome cars from which he could choose and we wended our way to the Webber Duck Inn over and over again.

At first his dancing style bothered me. He moved my right arm up and down like a pump handle and he held me in a curiously affected manner. After two or three visits to the Webber Duck Inn, Norman, who was quick to learn . . . and a natural dancer, desisted from the pump handle, held me with style, and danced as though he had spent eight years in Mr. Foster's dancing class. The lights were low, the floor was large and well waxed. Food was the last of our interests, but Alphonse, the head waiter, graciously placed this striking couple at a prominent table near the dance floor.

Every time we went there our arrival was always the same. "Good evening, Alphonse."

"Good evening, Miss Flint." And Norman and I were wafted to the best table in the house.

So—before I was a debutante—I became familiar with most of the night clubs and speakeasies in Boston—and the Webber Duck Inn.

I had one narrow escape. Freddy Staples took me to the Coconut Grove—where we had a pleasant evening. The very next night it was raided by the police. All those dining at the Coconut Grove were pushed into paddy wagons and their names were published in the paper the next day.

The Webber Duck Inn seemed a remarkably safe place to sneak out to.

One day, my father said, "Frances."

"Yes?"

"I feel that the first time a young girl goes to a night club, she should go with her father."

I couldn't think of a thing to say.

"This evening I shall take you to a night club. It will be a formal occasion. We will leave at seven o'clock."

"Yes, Father."

My father wore tails and a top hat as though he were taking my grandmother to the Boston Symphony.

We headed away from Boston—out into the country. We headed toward Walpole. We headed toward the Webber Duck Inn. My father parked his enormous car and we walked into the Webber Duck Inn.

Alphonse, the head waiter, met us. He said, "Good evening, Miss Flint."

I gasped in terror.

Alphonse led us to a table, lit the candles with a flourish, and presented my father with the wine list.

"Frances," my father's voice was far from angry: "I haven't been here for years and years. Did you notice the head waiter recognized me?"

The judge who changed my life

Laurie and I invented some new games, like "Who can break the biggest plate glass window?" In many ways we were in total agreement, but one night Laurie shocked me. We were filching those red lanterns that are placed in streets where deep ditches had been dug for water mains, or something of the sort. Laurie said, "This is just what I need."

"You're not going to *keep* it, are you?"

"Sure."

Laurie's answer was offhand, but I was aghast. "But Laurie, that would be *wrong!*"

I finally managed to explain that if you took something for the fun of it, that was all right. *But* if you took something because you wanted to have it—that was stealing.

One night the police followed us. The squad car with flashing lights drove into our driveway just as I was climbing up into my room. I jumped into bed quickly with all my clothes on. My heart was going like a sewing machine. I could see the powerful beams of searchlights outside my window, and I could hear my father stamping downstairs. He must have told them it was a mistake, because everybody went away. The night was utterly still . . . just heartbeats.

Bertram sometimes went with us to dance halls. And then one night—actually it was so late that it was really early morning—Bertram was climbing up to his room when the milkman arrived. There was a loud crash: the milkman—convinced that Bertram was a burglar—had dropped his container with all the quarts of milk for the Flint household.

So the milkman got to a telephone, called the police, and they were at our door again.

The very next time Laurie and I went forth to cook up a bit of excitement the police must have had us pinpointed. They caught us. My father stormed and ranted. I couldn't possibly take in what he was saying.

I was arrested and had to go to juvenile court. I remember what I wore that day: a mauve sweater, quite tight, and a many-gored light gray skirt, quite short.

I was not allowed to see Laurie. And I had to write to a parole officer once a week for one year (my freshman year in college).

I shall always remember the judge at that court. He pointed out that we had been inconsiderate. He didn't scold: he explained. He told me that one of the windows we had broken was in a house where there was a pregnant woman who very much wanted to have a baby—and because of the terrible fright we had given her, the embryo might be still-born. He pointed out that the red lanterns were to keep people from getting hurt; they were warnings, and because of me somebody, perhaps a boy who was very much loved, might get killed or crippled for life.

He pointed out that storekeepers with plate glass windows often were poor, and had worked years to afford that big glass.

I shall never forget that judge. He explained, and he changed my life. I became considerate.

Advice from Cousin Tom

My cousin Tom was four years older than I, and I listened carefully to whatever he suggested.

"Tom, I'm going to the Brattle Hall dances this season." Tom looked at me appraisingly.

"Still going to dancing school?"

"Yes."

"Still spend most of your time being a conspicuous wall-flower?"

"Yes."

"Well, the Brattle Halls are cut-throat. Let me give you a piece of advice."

"Yes, Tom."

"Never, under any circumstances let anybody see you if you are not having a good time. Do you understand?"

"But how . . . ?"

"Hide, if you have to. Go home. Or hide in the powder room. Get out of *sight* if you're not having fun."

I saw things at the Brattle Halls that I would never have thought possible. Tom was right. I saw girls sobbing in the powder room; others just pretended to have a headache. These were the "pills"—the ones that nobody wanted to dance with.

There were about twice as many men as girls at these dances. The men stood in a great cluster in the middle of the floor and when they felt like it, they stepped outside of this cluster, which was known as the "stag line," tapped a dancer on the shoulder to cut in, and danced away with his girl.

Some girls were cut in on over and over again. Some of the most popular ones could just dance a few steps before another man cut in to claim them.

And then there was the other side of the coin. Some girls danced around and around the room—over and over again and nobody cut in—ever. The girl's misery, and that of her unfortunate partner, were plain for all to see. I watched Nita Tate—a girl I knew slightly—dance around and around the room with a man who was far too short for her. Nita was definitely pretty, but her predicament was utterly obvious. Her partner danced near the stag line, and he was holding something behind her back. It was a ten-dollar bill. Pretty soon somebody stepped out of the great cluster of men in evening clothes, took the money, and cut in to dance with Nita.

The chaperones, popularly known as "the lorgnette row," would have banished both men if they had seen this outrageous act. Having seen the money pass hands, I wondered for a moment if there might be a ten-dollar bill behind my back right now.

My partner, who danced nicely, looked down at me shyly and said, "I never know what to talk about at these affairs, do you?"

"That's been worrying me too," I answered fervently.

"Well?"

I did my best. I looked straight into his eyes and asked, "Do you like goldfish?"

He burst into delighted laughter; everybody could see we were having fun, and instantly somebody cut in. Then somebody else cut in—and still another! Nine years of dancing school was now but a miserable memory and in less than an hour, I had gone from the pill list to the belle list. And it was a year of the wildest luxury. Just about everybody wanted to dance with me and the family had pots of money.

Back to Miss Eldridge

Gradually my parents had given up having servants. At last there was only my beloved governess.

The next year the Depression was well under way when I spent a lovely year being a debutante. My family could not afford to give me a coming-out dance. They settled for a ladies' luncheon at the Mayflower Club. And my father stopped talking about buying a destroyer and converting it into a yacht.

It was Monday. I dressed carefully. A turquoise blouse and a smart black bouclé suit with a fashionable short skirt. Shoes were the problem. All my best shoes looked shabby or were worn out. My black pumps with four-inch heels would certainly look just right. They were elegant and looked almost new. The soles were worn through, but I could fix that.

First I borrowed tinsnips from my father's workshop. Then I rummaged in the trash barrel for two tin cans. These I washed, then I flattened them by jumping on them, after which I cut them neatly to fit inside my shoes. To protect my silk stockings, I put a layer of cardboard over my tin inner soles.

The last time I'd threatened to leave home, my father said, "You can't. You haven't been trained to support yourself. I hardly think anyone would hire you."

With these cheery words ringing in my ears, I headed for Boston and Miss Eldridge's Employment Agency.

The smell. How well I remembered the smell: mould, dime-store perfume and something else . . . overcooked cabbage. It was the smell of poverty—and here I was going up the very same steps to a room where I had first hired a cook.

Miss Eldridge looked tired—and much older. But she got up quickly when she saw who it was. Suddenly she looked so happy. "Miss Flint! How very nice to see you!"

We shook hands.

"And what will it be today? A cook? Or perhaps a waitress?"

"Miss Eldridge . . ."

We just stood looking at each other. And then I managed to say it. "*I* am looking for a job."

All the cordiality was gone. Miss Eldridge spoke in a tone I had never heard. "If you will come this way, please."

She led me to the room with the bench. It was crowded.

When I sat down I remembered to cross my legs carefully and to keep my toes down so no one could see the holes in my shoes. I watched the door. I hoped . . .

Suddenly—overwhelmingly—I knew what it was like to sit on that bench.

I learned that servants and other members of the lower classes were *people* who hoped, and feared, and fell in love. . . .

Who would hire you?

When I was a child I had two dreams: I wanted to live with wild animals, and I wanted to marry a tall, dark man. I did both.

When I became twenty-one, then the legal age to be deemed an adult, I could leave home without being a runaway, but I needed to make money. My father stormed, "You can't leave home. Who would hire you?" And then he raised his voice to his put-on simpering tone, "You can make lace, and dance, and play the piano. You can play tennis and ride horseback correctly. You speak three languages and know how to enter a ballroom gracefully, but" (he could be very condescending) . . . "Well, somebody might take you on as a governess . . ."

My recent encounter at Miss Eldridge's had scarcely boosted my confidence.

There were only a few occupations that I, Miss Frances Flint, could enter without disgracing the family.

I changed my name.

Professionally, I became Frances Flynn. I didn't have a profession, but it was a nice bit of family loyalty. I put on the same clothes, the same shoes with their tin-can inner soles, and I went job hunting again. I headed for Hixon's—the most expensive dress shop in Boston—where William Randolph Hearst bought his mistress her dear little frocks for astronomical sums and Boston bluebloods squandered their wealth.

I was welcomed: "What can we do for you, Madame?"

"I want to see the owner."

A stricken voice answered, "You mean the manager? That's Miss Callahan."

In a few moments a bossy, obviously able, Irishwoman appeared. "Is something wrong?"

"No, I would like a job as a fashion model."

"Have you had any experience?"

Fashion models had to be very tall. I drew myself up to almost six feet with the help of the four-inch heels on my precious black shoes.

I smiled, almost absentmindedly. "I have been accustomed to wearing beautiful clothes all my life."

I got the job.

Having just flunked out of Smith College—with three A's and three F's—I did not really seem very employable, but in less than six weeks I was making more money than my father had ever made and—more important—I was invited to a houseparty weekend at Dartmouth College. At the houseparty there were tea dances, evening dances, and there was a football game.

It was at the football game that I suddenly saw my tall, dark man, smoking a pipe and wearing a plaid jacket. I knew that I would die if I couldn't live with him.

That very evening he heard a girl's voice, "low, melodious, unforgettable." He followed it down the hall and there I was. We didn't get engaged until the third date. Frederick has always insisted, "We Norwegians are slow, we like to think things over."

Cool Cats

My dancing days always haunted me. I remember the evening we slipped into my green Essex roadster. Frederick collapsed his top hat and slipped it into the small space behind the front seat . . . and we laughed. We had just left an incredibly dull party without saying good-bye to our host and hostess.

The strains of a dreary string band faded as we purred down the long driveway to escape. The night was still young.

"Let's go to Nantasket."

"Nantasket?" What would my father think? His daughter slumming that night at a beach—a beach sprinkled with ice cream cone stands, spun sugar stands, hot dog stands, and roller coasters—slumming with a college boy who scarcely had a penny to his name, but whose formal evening wear was impeccably tailored.

We moseyed along the waterfront. No waves, brightened by moonlight, drew us to the beach. We moseyed exploring—and then we heard a faint sound: drumbeats and the sweet moan of a saxophone. We were drawn as though by an invisible thread to a cheap little cafe. We sat at one of the many small tables covered with oilcloth and Frederick absentmindedly ordered something to justify our presence in that seedy, small establishment. The band was silent.

And then they played again. Six black men made music. We got up slowly, walked to the tiny dance floor, and danced. The band gave us about sixteen or twenty bars of dance music and then they broke the beat.

Then they lured us into a swimmingly syncopated rhythm that we had never encountered before. It was heady and I floated in the arms of the man I loved.

Discord: They broke the beat again. I realized later that they were trying to smash the mood and run us out of there.

There was a glass cabinet with pies, doughnuts, and sweet rolls stuffed with some sort of dyed-sugar mixture. The glass acted as a mirror and as we danced I could see Frederick's well-tailored trousers and his patent leather shoes—and I could see my long ivory satin dress swirl around his legs to the absolute beat of the ever-switching music.

Those six musicians had decided to get rid of us—not by pointing out a sign that said NO DANCING, but by breaking the beat and shifting the rules from minute to minute.

All I knew was that I was dancing in the arms of my love, and that he was dancing as I had never known him to dance before. Later it seemed to me that it was flexible perfection. At the time it was a type of delight that I never expected to be surpassed.

The orchestra took a break. Then the mood changed . . . it was electric. No longer had those six men decided to shag us out of the place. They started to play just for us—to draw us out. And perhaps the best band we have ever listened to played just for us and our dancing. Delight. And they played with delight. And our whole beings— absorbed by such music—danced as we had never had a chance to dance before.

"Cool Cats." The orchestra was singing and making up words to a song. As we danced we realized that the song was directed toward us. We were the "Cool Cats."

An elderly waitress came to present our bill. She pointed to a sign: NO DANCING. And I noticed another sign CLOSING HOUR 12 PM. It was after 3:00 . . .

Frederick paid our bill. Then I said, "Darling, I've got to talk to them."

I overcame my shyness and went over to the orchestra. "This was the most wonderful evening of my life."

I try to explain my parents

The first part of this book was written from the viewpoint of a child. Now, as I look back on the grownups who ruled me, I might well be more tolerant.

I know my parents loved me. They had a dream of what their beautiful, gifted daughter was to become: an international hostess, and a gracious "Lady Bountiful."

My father married an heiress; and this may have accounted for some of his frustrations and subsequent behavior. My mother wanted him to go to "his office" daily as her idolized father had done. My father—I think very sensibly—did nothing of the sort. With plenty of money at hand, he pursued worthwhile interests of *his* selection: criminology, photography, the French Revolution, and making parts for his expensive automobiles. He became an expert in each of these fields.

My father liked jokes about policemen. My mother liked puns. I never once heard them laughing together.

My father could whistle, and he could sing: Coming down our long staircase seemed to stimulate him, and his magnificent baritone carried throughout the house when he was in a good mood.

One could hear my mother's soprano all over the house too. It had a surprising amount of volume. She had no ear for music and without fail—sang off key.

My father was known as "the fire-eater" behind his back. I know of no one who was not afraid of him and his violent temper. People were afraid of him, not only face to face, but over the telephone too. When he answered, the men who wanted to ask me for dates—just hung up. Some of these had considerable poise. An Englishman, who had been an officer in the army and had fought in the Russo-Japanese war, was one who routinely hung up at the sound of my father's voice.

Then Father would bellow with rage and blame the telephone company for cutting off the call.

"That is nonsense and inefficiency," he would shout into the telephone. "Put on the supervisor. Who is in charge there?"

111

My father, the criminologist.

Listening to whoever was explaining that the fault was not the company's, added fuel to his rage.

Meanwhile I listened and wondered: who is it that had wanted to talk with me?

My mother's example may have had a pronounced influence in making me a scientist. She wore a brave smile and was forever and ever determined to present any and all situations in "their best light." That rosy glow of happiness that she insisted did permeate our lives was wishful thinking and nonsense. I deemed it outright dishonest—and I still do—but now I can see it wasn't just weakness; it took a certain type of courage.

112

*Fran and Mother by the big
brick house where I was born.*

When I was a very small child I made up my mind. Never think the way Mother does. Think for yourself, and if something is unpleasant, remember it accurately—don't gloss it over. Perhaps that is why I remember my childhood so well.

My mother was an omnivorous reader. She had excellent taste in art, literature, and gardening. She knew plants and had no hesitation in keying out unfamiliar species in Gray's *Manual of Botany.* She had no fear of heights and was a natural climber of trees. She had little interest in food (unlike my father), and didn't even like to talk about good things to eat.

My family seemed to believe that children and servants were not people. They were to be molded and disciplined, but who cares what they think? This had a strong advantage for me. The grownups would

113

have been much startled to learn what I thought—and many of the things that I did.

My family was sure of itself. These grownups knew that they were right. They were well-born. Their ancestors had fought in the Revolutionary War, and they proudly traced their roots back to families and places in the British Isles. Above criticism? Yes, they thought themselves above criticism.

My governess, Fräulein Anna Emelia Aida Taggesell, "gentled" our household. My father didn't shout so loud, my mother didn't sob so often, and the children behaved better when she was around. Her fiancé had been killed in the Boer War, so she became a governess, first for Admiral Parry's daughter, Joan—in Tasmania, Vancouver, and other far parts. Her next pupils were Russian, so she taught them English, German, and French in Russia. Then came Phyllis and Doris Tyser of Tunbridge Wells near London, after which she became my governess in America.

Now that Frederick and I have pursued an eclectic career together for fifty-nine years, and have published 168 papers and countless reviews together or separately, and have been honored both at home and abroad, and now that I have written ten books, won prizes for my paintings, and have been on innumerable committees and directorates, as I look back over the years—I sometimes think of Fräulein. I wish she could have known how her pupil turned out.

My childhood gave me some strong advantages: I learned to cir-

Fräulein, who gentled our household.

cumvent grownups to get what I really wanted. Both slum kids and I were precipitated into a system in which we had to keep alert to strive for our futures. I'm glad I didn't try to write this book any earlier. It might have upset me.

I hope now that those teenagers who feel alone and desperate as I once did, will take hope from this book. Finally, I turned out all right as a person, as a wildlife biologist, as a wife, and as a writer.

The four Flint children: Bertram, Putnam, Vasmer, and Frances.

115

And then there were none

I vividly remember the first time in my life when my courage failed me: May 12, 1916. The wind blew hot and dry. It roared through the treetops near the tennis courts at West Chop on Martha's Vineyard island. It was the day of the junior tennis tournaments. Older children were playing on one court and the little ones, including me, were playing on the other. The roaring wind was my friend; it threw the boy I was playing against off his game and I was winning.

The wind roared strong and dry that day. A few miles away a fire raged over some twenty square miles of the last stronghold of the heath hen, the prairie chicken of the East. The wind rose to gale proportions. Several hundred men and women, and I suppose even children, rallied to fight the fire. According to the *Vineyard Gazette,* May 18, 1916, "The buildings on the state heath hen reservation were saved by desperate work of the fire fighters. Some of the heath hen were burned—perhaps a tenth of the number of old birds—and all the eggs for this year's crop of young were destroyed. . . ."

There were roughly 2,000 heath hens in 1916 and the next year the population was down to about 175. It never recovered. In 1928 only three birds were reported and in 1932 the heath hen was declared extinct. I remember the wind roaring over the tennis courts.

And I remember a truck that veered off the road and drove right across the lawn to where we were. It was so sudden and peculiar that we all gathered around and the driver, an old fisherman, shouted, "Fire! The Great Plain's afire!" He pointed at the empty back of the truck, "We need help."

We—the city kids—stood perfectly still, gathered around the truck. I looked at the big boys, but nobody said a word. I tried to speak—to say I'd help—but no words came. And when the truck drove away empty, I was ashamed. The wind swept hot crackling fire over the nests and eggs of an endangered race; it roared in the treetops by the courts. We played tennis.

Perhaps the shame of that episode left its mark on my life. At any rate I learned so young about the impending doom of a species and later

116

when I had grown up I helped to avert another doom. By a strange quirk of fate I have spent most of my life working with Frederick my husband—to understand and preserve the greater prairie chicken whose ancestral home is in the prairies of the West. We have gotten up over and over again (actually about 1,044 times) before the chickens left their roosts, to learn their ways. We devised traps so we could catch them unharmed and band them to study individuals (and we kept our babies in prairie chicken traps instead of playpens). We invented a way to restrain a prairie chicken gently while it was being weighed (put it in an old wool sock). We built blinds so that we and countless other observers could study behavior during the booming season. Booming is the fantastic mating display in spring, when the cocks blow up big orange air sacs on their necks and make sounds like low-pitched organ music.

We fixed up and moved into four abandoned farmhouses to be near the chickens. Each time we moved we put our worldly goods into a roadster and a trailer.

I had thought of writing a book called *The Things One Doesn't Say.* Not that these things are hush-hush. But what lies back of scientific work seldom shows in a technical paper or book; the viewpoints of the public, the adventures of the investigators, and the fascinating struggle to find out more.

Two worlds

The onset of the winter of 1935–1936 north of Necedah, Wisconsin, probably struck our widely scattered neighbors as normal: a bit more snow and colder than usual, but essentially normal. Frederick takes things more calmly, but for me each day glowed with the sense of wild adventure. Sailboat racing, riding in horse shows, tennis, dancing all night, and even what camping we had done had not prepared us for survival in central Wisconsin: nor for our first job in prairie chicken country.

The kitchen end of the abandoned farmhouse we rented for five dollars a month sagged away from the rest of the house and the opening was stuffed with rags and old quilts. We pulled out and burned all this rubbish and plastered the gap. I know now that the rags were better insulation than our plastering job, but our families and teachers had never taught us anything like this. I had, however, gleaned a useful hint from an unexpected source. My governess, who had tutored Sir John Parry's daughter Joan before coming to look after me, told me about a ghastly fright she once had. Admiral Parry and his entourage were in Tasmania; Fräulein was upon the toilet seat in the outhouse and a sailor opened the back to take out the buckets! I loved to hear her tell this story. It didn't seem proper and Fräulein's stories were seldom as risqué as this.

So one day when Frederick was not at home, I managed to find two buckets and place them on planks beneath the outhouse holes. I thought this was nicer and it gave me great satisfaction to get everything shipshape for the winter. But Tasmania has a milder climate than central Wisconsin: I had a surprise in store. Both buckets filled up with alarming rapidity. Again I waited until Frederick was away because he would have insisted that the outhouse was *his* job. I put on my boots and outdoor clothes and went out to empty the buckets by our dump heap. The contents were frozen solid! No amount of banging against trees would dislodge them.

Our woodpile was pitifully small so an outdoor fire was out of the question. I lit two burners on the kerosene stove to heat the buckets. From time to time I tested with a stick to see how the thawing was progressing, muttering wise sayings like: menial work is honorable, manual labor is not demeaning. At last I was able to empty the buckets, and in spite of the bitter cold, I aired the kitchen. Then I washed my face, my hands, my hair, my shirt, my trousers, and my socks.

One of our treasured possessions, an oval mirror with a gold patterned frame, hung in our living room. As though drawn by an invisible thread I went into the living room to look at myself. I looked at my face a long time, and then I spoke to it: *"Anyway, I'm me."*

It made me feel much better. I practiced court curtsies in front of the mirror for a while. Through no fault of my own I was born with a silver spoon in my mouth and my grandmothers had fully expected that I would be presented at court some day. Twelve years of dancing school and dancing masters had perfected my curtsies. Now the world of cities, of dancing, of theaters, and servants seemed thousands of miles away and eons behind me.

Not for all the capitals in Europe and the wealth of the Indies would I give up what I had now: love, adventure, and public service in the unmapped wilds of central Wisconsin.

Frederick and I made the first real road map of part of central Wisconsin. Our instructions were: any trail you can travel by car is a road. The vastness of the area was staggering. Interlocking trails seemed to lead nowhere, but now and again led to a house rather like ours. We saw very few people. Finally, late one summer I saw my first American Indians. I'd been looking forward to this for a long time. They were in a sky-blue Pierce-Arrow touring car and they all piled out of it and came eagerly toward me. The driver asked, "Say, can you tell us the way to town?" Later, I met and worked with Jimmy Blake, an Indian who slid silently through the brush and didn't get lost, who could walk right past our campfire without our noticing him, and who taught me much of the woodlore that I know today.

We tried to explain to our neighbors, to Indians, to everyone what we were doing and why: that this great region was to become public domain and that the wildlife would be managed so the sandhill cranes (then rare) would trumpet over the marshes each spring, the prairie chickens would boom in the early mornings, the fur harvest would be planned, and the deer would be held down so they would not overbrowse their range. We tried to teach conservation.

One day we encountered two boys about sixteen and eighteen years old herding cattle. Frederick brought out his best one-syllable words and gave them a splendid explanation of game management. Both listened without a flicker of expression. At last one boy's lips moved a little as though he might be about to say something. Frederick paused expectantly, but the boy turned to me. He asked politely, "What good does it make to paint your lips for?" And again I was reminded of two worlds.

Flame velvet

Together, joyously, but not without trepidation, we had made the decision to burn our bridges behind us, cross the Rubicon, and take to a life as biologists in the wilderness. Such decisions are rather glorious, but somewhere, way in the back of my being was a small impish flame that gave me the impression that if we really wanted to, we could unmake our decision and go back to the old, easy, rather charming mode of life we had known before. In my case it was an episode, which now strikes me as rather silly, that doused that small flame—that odd little half-hope that we might combine the old with the new. Thawing and emptying those two outhouse buckets brought me bang! awake! My interest in any wan hope of going back was as thoroughly extinguished as though an irreversible chemical reaction had taken place. Frederick's episode was yet to come, and always bothered us both a bit.

My episode involved just me. And it seems odd to me now. Imagine a sensible woman in her mid-twenties getting so keyed up at cleaning an outhouse that she had to go stare at herself in a mirror afterwards and draw strength from past glories.

Now that I look back on it, I think what a blithering idiot I was to make such a fuss. And then I remember the way I was brought up: well-bred girls always wear hats and gloves when in the city, they wear gloves when cutting roses in the garden, and they make sure to wash their hands after patting the head of a dog.

I reckon that some women just naturally whistle when they have an unpleasant little job to do with their hands; others learn to whistle while getting it done neatly, and still others shrink delicately from such situations, convinced that they are the really true ladies. Frederick scolds me if I beat him to an unpleasant job, but he has never accused me of not being a lady. He simply announces, "You should have let me do that."

We cut our firewood with a two-man saw for the first time that winter, and the snow piled out of the sky and drifted until some of the drifts reached two-thirds up the telephone poles. Then the roads drifted shut and we subsisted on what we had in the house. Snowed in. We did our work daily, trekking on snowshoes to census game; we cut more firewood and learned to heat only one small room, the kitchen— and of course, only when we were there.

Day after day we counted flocks of prairie grouse and learned to distinguish between the dark bellies and square tails of the prairie chickens and the light bellies and pointed tails of the sharp-tailed grouse.

We counted quail too, and as the temperature kept dropping, the coveys got smaller and smaller. Finally, we, on snowshoes, were able to pick up emaciated starving quail that no longer could fly, or even run. Their breastbones stuck out in sharp fleshless keels and we gave a few of the thousands of quail a swifter death than the slow starvation that took the rest of them that winter.

We got "snow stupid." Outdoors, we were alert and awake, but all we wanted to do when we got home was to get warm, to sleep, to sit, or to eat. Quite often I fell sound asleep during supper with my head on the table next to my unfinished meal.

Our chores at dusk were always the same: start the fire in the kitchen (a room that went from 20° below zero to fairly comfortable in about half an hour), pump water, cook, eat, write up field notes, and crawl into bed.

Snow stupid, alone together, we were content. We spoke very little;

it seemed that each knew what the other was thinking. Our vocabularies dwindled and unplanned sign language took over. There were good books in the house for "the long winter evenings." They stayed on the shelf unread. We were content.

Suddenly, late one afternoon, our chores multiplied. At first neither of us realized that just one change in our relatively smooth schedule could cost so many extra hours of work and use up so much energy. The pump froze.

The kitchen was just getting warm enough so I couldn't see my breath. I had taken off my mittens to chop apart some frozen meat for supper when Frederick burst into the house saying, "We need boiling water—lots of it."

Both of us filled the washtub and two buckets with snow. We set one on the wood stove and the others over the two burners of the kerosene stove. Snow melts *very* slowly and huge quantities of fluffy snow produce only about a glass of water.

I lit the two burners under the oven to thaw and cook some meat, but thawing meat seemed disloyal to the present emergency, so I filled the oven with pie plates filled with snow.

We ate some dried prunes and bread. From time to time we left the steaming kitchen to get more snow. Stars sparkled in the still black night and sporadically the ground cracked like a pistol shot as the frostline seeped lower. It was probably about 35° below zero.

Long past our bedtime we were ready to thaw the pump. Frederick jiggled the long pump handle and I poured boiling water into the little hole at the top. It didn't take long: in a moment or two we succeeded in filling the whole inside of the pump with solid ice. A collar of ice formed around the top of the pump and thick vermiform icicles exuded from the collar. There was still a little lukewarm water left. We stirred in some powdered milk, and drank what was left of what I believed to be the end of the great snow-melting episode.

But day after day we melted snow. Snowmelt for drinking, snowmelt for dishwashing, snowmelt for baths, snowmelt for washing clothes, and snowmelt for rinsing the soap out of them. We had to cut extra wood to keep a fire going strong, for kerosene was expensive and besides our supply was rather low.

At last help came. Two neighbor boys, Alex and Andrew, who had walked through the woods in autumn carrying us sacks of potatoes and a citron when we had first moved in, came by to see how we were doing. Andrew scratched his neck with his mitten and took a good look at our pump. "Got some rags an' some kerosene?"

Frederick produced a can of kerosene and I went to hunt up some rags. I poked about in odd, cold corners of the house and barn, but I had been taught that rags are filthy and had burned every single one. Then I rummaged among our clothes to see what could best be spared. By the light of a kerosene lamp, I unpacked our suitcases and boxes in the cold upstairs storeroom, and one by one I threw things to keep on the floor behind me.

There was my tweed suit, made for me by a Boston tailor—might need that again someday; the underwear from my trousseau had very little bulk, and I had a feeling that pure silk wouldn't burn very well anyway. There was a real find: a pair of flannelette pajamas. Each night we both wore two pairs of pajamas, two pairs of bedsocks and mittens to bed. And pajamas were essential in daytime too—for field work. We wore them under our clothes because we didn't have money enough for warm winter underwear. With increasing desperation I emptied boxes, and my little pile of potential rags hardly grew at all: we needed everything.

At the bottom of one wooden box I came on a specially wrapped container, large and white and tied with narrow mauve ribbons. It was from Saks Fifth Avenue. In it was my flame-colored velvet evening dress. Flame-color that picked up the golden glints in my hair; the low, soft cowl neck that Frederick considered so becoming; and the full, floor-length skirt that had floated in undulating swirls as we danced together under crystal chandeliers. I would never wear it again. I hurried downstairs whistling and handed it to Andrew. His big hands felt the bulk of the material. He nodded and wrapped my dress around the pump. Alex poured kerosene, soaking the dress again and again. Then he reached in his shirt pocket for a match.

I went back into the kitchen and watched the flames leap high, almost as high as the branches of the jackpine by our back door. I looked at the men. Alex and Andrew, heavyset, with rough-hewn, strong features, warmed themselves by the fire, secure in a job well done. Frederick stood a little apart, aristocratic and elegant, even in his worn field clothes. I could see his fine black eyebrows and his small straight nose. He wasn't watching the flames. He watched my dress, and when it was gone he still looked at the pump. His face was inscrutable.

Be alone when you talk to yourself

By the time we knew how to catch a prairie chicken and how to thaw a pump, we felt ourselves more or less seasoned wildlifers. We had had our introduction to attitudes toward female biologists, and idealistic ideas from Washington, but we were to learn more about local politicians.

The first time we ever voted in a presidential election we voted *against* Franklin Delano Roosevelt although his resettlement program was our source of bread and butter. We drove to town and went into a cheerless building. Our names and addresses were recorded and then we stood in between some little partitions—each arranged in such a way that you could pull a small cotton curtain behind you and nobody could see what you were writing. Next, having checked off our presidential choice, we folded the ballot and put it in a slit in a rather large wooden box. We did not look to see whether or not the box was locked.

Frederick and I left our booths feeling rather noble. We had voted against Roosevelt and against our own personal interests as well. Arm in arm, we walked down the street feeling pleased with ourselves.

Presently we heard a man running behind us; he grabbed Frederick's arm. "You made a mistake!"

"A mistake?" Frederick inquired in mystification.

"Yes, you didn't put the 'X' in the right place. You didn't vote for Roosevelt!"

Frederick looked at the distraught town chairman, or whoever he was, and uttered just five words. They were final. "We did it on purpose."

Those who are distressed by government spending nowadays are plunged into a welter of confusion. We were not: the problems where we were covered only a measly 100,000 acres, and Frederick had been told by the Resettlement Administration of the United States government that he was in charge of the whole Central Wisconsin Game Project: Necedah.

There was an office in town. He didn't spend much time in that faraway office, but on December 29, 1935, he was informed that he would have 500 men working under him in five days! He announced he would be in the office every day, including Saturday and Sunday, and that he would hire foremen.

Frederick had never directed more than two or three people in his life before and one of them had always been me. How to keep 500 men busy? Three of the foremen hired that day became leaders of special game projects and worked with us in the field. Frederick's instructions were to put thirty-man crews to work. This he did. Thirty-man crews were easier to transport in a truck, but he stubbornly kept those three foremen, not to direct others, but so that he could have his own research crew.

The workers were on the relief roll. They were hired whatever their capabilities were, but he could hire anyone he pleased as a foreman. When interviewing Bud Truax, one of his three foremen, Frederick discovered that Bud's father had a good job with the railroad, his brother was a school teacher, and Bud himself was far from destitute. But Bud's application stated he was on relief.

"How is it," Frederick asked gently, "that you are on relief?"

"Why I'm not on relief, sir." Bud was soft-spoken and blushed easily.

Frederick pushed Bud's application over to him. "Is that your signature?"

"Yes, sir."

"Didn't you *read* what you signed? This states you are on relief." Bud shook his head sadly.

Frederick grabbed the application and went straight to the office manager. "There's been a mistake here. This man is not on relief."

Mr. Gaffney, a ruddy-faced, silver-haired politician, gave Frederick a broad wink. "That's all right. We'll let it go. We're helping *lots* of people."

As the months passed Frederick and Mr. Gaffney got into numerous disputes: over and over again one gave an order and the other countermanded it. Just as Frederick thought he had the office running smoothly, with the furniture where he wanted it and each girl working to the best of her abilities, Gaffney rearranged everything. Frederick put Isobel, who was a marvel at typing technical papers, in a quiet corner where she could work without interruption. Mabel, who could

129

neither type nor spell, was moved up front to answer the telephone and field questions, which she did very well. That was on Friday. On Monday Isobel's desk had been moved up front again.

Frederick sent Bill's crew out to repair the dike road and when Bill reported in, his crew had trimmed some Norway pines instead.

This type of thing went on daily for months and it is a credit to both men that unpleasantness was always kept below the boiling point. Frederick is always polite and almost always reasonable. Gaffney was an outstanding manipulator, as most good politicians are. The situation gradually became more and more impossible. One day after another merry little turmoil, Frederick said quietly, "After all, I'm in charge of this office."

Gaffney sputtered, "*What?*" He stomped to his desk and produced a document that clearly implied that he was in charge of the *whole* project. Frederick produced an almost identical document! Eventually a long-overdue directive from Washington clarified the division of duties: Frederick was to direct game management and specify the work to be done, and Gaffney was to run the office—to attend to the details of hiring and firing, time sheets, payrolls, and the like.

I had nothing to do with the big crews. Not all 500 men showed up, but there were hundreds and no equipment for them to work with. For months there were no shovels, no axes, no wheelbarrows. To keep them busy, William Schuenke invented something called "The Continuous Game Inventory." Lines of men walked through the woods and marshes counting flocks of prairie chickens, sharp-tailed grouse, quail, rabbits, and deer. Crews often got lost, and if they encountered me—a girl cruising the woods alone—they not infrequently had to ask just where they were. Later, after most of the men had gotten work elsewhere, or disappeared for one reason or another, crates of brand new equipment arrived—shiny new shovels, axes, and tools, some of which none of us could identify. The forester's shed was used to store them in.

So much for big crews. Frederick put me in charge of a crew! My position on this federal project was distinctly shaky because of my sex. We both felt fantastically lucky because Frederick had wangled an agreement—although he never could get it in writing—that I was to be permitted to work full time—without salary.

And now I was to have a crew! To be sure, my crew consisted only of two men: Bud, who blushed so easily, and Os, who carried a huge thermos bottle of coffee wrapped in a blue blanket wherever he went. I had never directed a crew before and was determined to do it well.

Frederick brought them to the house, announcing, "We need owl pellets." Then he jumped into the car and drove off.

First, I told my crew, "Owls gulp much of their food down whole." I added, "As they can't digest bones very well they cough up pellets with fur or feathers outside and the bones are inside."

Bud leaned forward. "You mean that this comes out of their *mouths?* They are trying to . . ."

I could see him trying to form the word "vomit" and quickly said, "Yes, we'll pick up all the pellets we can find and later we'll pull them apart to see what the owls have been eating."

Silence.

"The horned owl's pellets are about half the size of a cigar. They are grayish and you'll find them under pines and leafy oaks where the owls like to spend the day."

I cut off further discussion by getting out a map. It was marked off in square-mile sections. "I'll take this middle section, Bud can take the section to the east of mine, and Os can take the section to the west. Everybody will work his own section thoroughly and we'll meet at the truck about sundown."

Each of us carried a big paper bag to put the pellets in. I moseyed along from one likely looking roost to another, finding none. Just outside my section to the west was a fine-looking stand of old pines, but they were in Os's section and it wouldn't be fair to trespass. Shortly

Os and Bud.

before noon I ran into a horned owl winter territory and knew I wouldn't come out of the woods with an empty bag. I ate my lunch of a cold meat sandwich and raisins and continued on my way. Then I hit the jackpot: countless pellets under one great white pine.

It is my custom, when alone, to talk to myself, or better still to argue with some distinguished character—real or imaginary. Furthermore, I tend to talk in French or German so I won't forget these languages. I had recently translated M. Guérin's splendid book on the food habits of the tawny owl. Of course, I had never met the author, nor did I have the slightest chance of ever doing so. There were, however, a few little points in his book with which I disagreed.

I dug among the pine needles, pulling forth more and more pellets; then shifting on my knees to a new spot, I dug for more. The flow of conversation never ceased, for M. Guérin was not there to answer or to interrupt. From time to time I paused to elaborate an especially telling point with both hands, and then again I stopped to indicate the size of a small pertinent detail, smiling with animation at my invisible listener.

It could be that a twig snapped or perhaps a shadow moved. Suddenly I had the distinct impression that I was not alone.

Bud had been standing behind me and apparently for some time. He blushed deeply, and so did I. He tried to speak, but it seemed to strike him as hopeless. I showed him my bag of pellets, but the scene he had just beheld rendered him incapable of recognizing what was in the bag.

Finally I pulled myself together to explain, but I started my explanation in French!

Clearly, it is important to impress one's crew *favorably* on the first day. It is now forty years later. Bud has had ample opportunity to forget a great many things, but he has never forgotten his first day on Fran Hamerstrom's crew.

The wildest animal

"What is the wildest animal you have ever handled?"

Sometimes I answer, "Bald eagles not only sink their talons into you, but bite as well. Golden eagles are strong and sometimes unpredictable. I've handled a fresh-caught adult badger, and been bitten by raccoons, dogs, cats, muskrats, mice, and an adder."

Most people seem to associate wildness with danger to themselves. Having handled a variety of wild and domestic animals since I was nine years old, my concern tends to be for the animal itself, rather than what it might do to me. By my definition of wildness, by far the wildest creature is the prairie chicken. No other animal that I have handled is so apt to fight constraint and injure itself. They are *wild!*

We have learned to handle hundreds of prairie chickens without injury and have passed on this information to others.

At first we thought that trapping prairie chickens for banding would be rather like pheasant trapping. Pheasants are phlegmatic creatures and walk calmly into funnel traps and feast on the grain within, seldom injuring themselves in a properly constructed trap.

We patterned our first prairie chicken traps after pheasant traps. They were six feet long, four feet wide, and three feet high.

We covered the traps with chicken wire and fashioned a funnel at each end. We placed the traps in a likely looking field, where the snow was well laced with chicken tracks. The bait was yellow ear corn. We arranged it with careful deliberation: some ears stuck up out of the snow, some lay carelessly on the snow inside the trap, and we knocked kernels from a few ears and spread them in a little path leading through the funnel entrance and right into the trap. This last strategem served a double purpose in our minds because the partly denuded ears looked as though prairie chickens had already pecked kernels from them and surely the birds would gladly enter where other birds had already fed.

That night I dreamed of traps full of chickens, and as though Frederick suspected how high my hopes were, he tried to fend off disappointment. "We'll be very lucky to catch one or two."

But I knew: I just felt it in my bones that we were going to make a good catch. I was right. We got out of the car, put on our snowshoes, and set forth joyously. Even from a distance we could see that we had caught quite a lot more than one or two.

Joy turned to horror, to despair. The birds had thrashed and beaten their way all around the edges of the traps, they had poked their heads through the wire mesh, and some had torn the skin across their scalps, exposing bare skull. There was a blood line about nine inches above the snow all around each trap, and the snow was spattered with blood. It was somehow like coming upon an automobile accident suddenly. It looked awful.

I know now that it wasn't nearly as bad as it looked. Most of the injuries were superficial. The abrasions on the wings would have healed nicely by themselves, and all the head injuries needed was three to five stitches to bring the skin back together. There really isn't much of a trick to suturing a scalp cut. After all, the skin is there; it just has to be pulled back into place and sewed up. If the edges of the skin are dry, I moisten and loosen them with my tongue; if the skull is dry I get plenty of spit on it and then I am careful to line up the edges of the wound when I put in the stitches. I minored in veterinary medicine at Iowa State College, but no one ever told me to use my own spit when the temperature was 20° below zero. My teachers did tell me that upon occasion it is best to operate promptly and on the spot.

On the spot was right there, miles from any town, and we weren't seasoned. We killed those chickens that looked hopeless and banded the rest and let them go.

It was a bad setback in our trapping attempts—just our first setback. The next one was equally unexpected.

Of course we hauled the traps home and pried off all the wire. Then we tried to get some netting to cover the traps. There was none to be found and no money to buy any. By sheer good fortune one of the books we had with us was my grandmother's *Encyclopedia of Embroidery.* I wonder now whether I actually supposed that I might have time for embroidery, or whether I brought it along for sentimental reasons. On page 397 there are explicit instructions for making netting, illustrated by a helpful line drawing.

We found string. The local bank and especially the offices of the Resettlement Administration supplied rather a lot. We asked people for string and we helped ourselves to string out of wastebaskets. We knotted the pieces together and then we sat on our kitchen table evening after evening and made netting, circumventing the knots. Sometimes it occurred to me that a future Ph.D. candidate could better employ his time, but it didn't take a Ph.D. mentality to figure out that we'd better sit *on* the table rather that *at* it. The floor was so cold that even in heavy field boots our feet got numb near the floor. I knocked a cup of hot coffee over one day and took the coffee up with a knife. It was frozen solid before I could reach a mop.

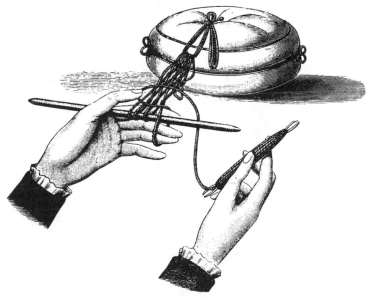

FIG. 614. FIRST POSITION OF THE HANDS.

We sat on the table and netted. It was peaceful: no TV, no radio, just the crackle of wood in the stove and, in February, great horned owls called on still nights.

Our string, coming from so many sources, also came in many colors: stout white butcher's twine, black and white twisted string, green string, yellow string, and quite a lot of red string because Christmas was not far behind us.

Because prairie chickens can distinguish between yellow corn and white corn (they prefer yellow), we correctly assumed they were not color-blind. But we were incorrect in assuming that they would shun bright-colored netting. Frederick bought some olive-drab dye and I dyed all the netting in our washtub. I followed the instructions on the package carefully. I boiled the netting in this dye bath and then I set it with a mordant. The recommended mordant was not very expensive: it was salt. Even after all our work we had only enough netting to cover two traps, but we set these out near the edge of a likely looking field. Again I dreamed of a big catch, and we looked forward to checking our traps. The next morning there were no birds in the traps. But the snow near both was fairly stamped down with a multitude of tracks, and fragments of our netting moved lightly in the morning air. It appeared that all the squirrels and all the rabbits and all the deer in the county had come to feast upon that precious salt.

Jack wants to shoot

In the 1930s the area north of Necedah was a sparsely settled and sometimes violent land, described by many as desolate. Shortly before we moved in, a game warden had been shot and the general feeling of the country was against law and order, especially as far as game laws were concerned. Whole families were able to subsist on a cash income of $150 a year. Most grazed their scrawny cattle on public land, canned quantities of wild berries and bracken fern, found bee trees for honey, and supplemented their diet with deer meat. I didn't like the story about the game warden and made a point of telling everyone that my husband was *not* a warden—he was a *game manager* and had nothing to do with making arrests.

Central Wisconsin was also a country where the conversational art of telling complicated lies was developed to a high degree. There were strict rules—the lies had to have at least a kernel of truth. The neighbors were kind to us and brought odd and useful presents like a kerosene can that didn't leak because they had soldered it for us, food, two window panes, a year-old copy of the *Woman's Home Companion,* and a huge roll of felt that the paper mill didn't need anymore. (After I had converted the felt to hide our worst floor, I learned that 'everybody' made clothes out of paper mill felt.)

Especially Alex and Andrew, who lived a couple of miles away, brought us stories and gave us advice. Some of the advice was bizarre and some of the stories were innocuous.

"You gotta keep pigeons to attract away the lightening. Look," Andrew added, "see this gash onna floor? That's where lightening hit oncet."

Alex said that this was the bedroom and that the previous occupants had had an axe, a shovel, and a plowshare leaning against the bed at the time the lightning struck, but they tried to get us to believe that it would never have happened with pigeons around.

"If a hoss dies, bury it under the barn door an' no more hosses'll die in that barn."

"There's monkeys breeding in the river bottom." We traced that story. Opossums had only just extended their range so far north and their long prehensile tails gave the boys a fine chance to test our gullibility. They must have been having a very good time at our expense, and I'm sure they considered us stupid and often ungracious. How was I to know that when a polite Pole comes to your house, it is his duty to refuse any food offered? He must show that he came for the pleasure of your company, and it's up to the host or hostess to make the same offer again after a short period of grace. I offered from our scanty supplies, and when they said, "No," I believed them! They waited for me to offer again and I let them down.

It took a long time to learn local etiquette and even longer to evaluate and decipher the rules of telling lies.

We were unprepared when Alex and Andrew arrived one day, sat down comfortably in our kitchen, and Andrew announced, "Everybody knows you're not a game warden." I breathed a sigh of relief. "They all know it's *her*." Both boys looked at me. "They know *she's* the game warden."

"And," he continued, "you went past Jack Becker's barn, didn't ya?"

I *had* gone fairly close to the barn of our nearest neighbor while following the tracks of a covey of quail.

"Jack Becker knows," Andrew continued sadly. "You saw that deer

hangin' up in his barn, and both his son an' his son-in-law had to leave out for Chicago."

"I never saw a deer in that barn!"

"Don't make no good to say that. Jack says as soon as he gets the chanct he's goin' to shoot Fred there."

Why Frederick? Either way it wasn't very pleasant. We made a few inquiries, "Have Jack Becker's son and son-in-law gone to Chicago?"

"Yes, two days ago."

I asked in the hardware store, "What's Jack Becker like?"

"He's all right . . . pays his bills, an' a good farmer. I wouldn't want to cross him though . . . quick tempered."

"Has he got a gun?"

" 'Course he's got a gun."

In the evening Frederick announced, "I'm going over to see Jack Becker."

"And I'm coming too."

"No, I'm going alone."

"Please, darling, let me come too. Ladies have a softening influence."

"I have made up my mind to go *alone*."

"I'll wear a skirt—my green tweed skirt."

"Fran, the matter is settled. I'm going alone and on foot."

"But he wants to shoot *you*, not me!"

We argued far into the night. Breakfast was a quiet, miserable meal. Then Frederick put on his jacket and started for the Beckers' house. It was the only farm in sight of ours in that lonely country, and it was half a mile away.

I took our binoculars out of the case and went upstairs. Kneeling on the floor by an open window, I watched Frederick walk. His arms were swinging freely to show clearly that he was not armed.

We had agreed on one thing: walking was safer than appearing suddenly in a car, but now I couldn't help feeling that a car might have given some protection.

I watched the figure of the man I loved getting smaller and smaller, fearing that at any moment it would suddenly lie crumpled on the road. Time stretched like an enormous elastic—toward the breaking point of eternity.

I heard no shot and thought, but wasn't absolutely sure, that he had made it to the house safely. One thing I knew for certain: there are people around here who have shot a game warden. The only *fact* I had didn't make waiting any more reassuring.

139

Frederick came back down that long road alive. His account of what had happened was somewhat bewildering. "Jack Becker just laughed and laughed. He said, 'There wan't a word of truth in it—our boys didn't light out. They went to Chicago looking for jobs.'"

We became fond of Jack Becker. He had a job somewhere and managed to farm too. When corn-planting time came, he rode his tractor by moonlight and sang above the roar of the tractor. His songs were like a paean of praise to the world and the stars. We could hear his magnificent baritone when we were lying in bed. It was the voice of the man who didn't shoot Frederick.

The next year we were graduate students and lived near the suburbs of Madison, far from the mellow sound of booming prairie chickens and far from Jack Becker—singing on his tractor beneath the light of the moon.

Moving day.

But it's already done

Aldo Leopold was known by many of his students simply as "The Professor," as though there were no other professors on the University of Wisconsin campus. His office in 1938 was a small, badly lit room in the basement of the Old Soils Building. To enter it one passed through a sort of vestibule, used by the campus gardener as a potting shed. The potting shed was also the only "office" of The Professor's six graduate students. We kept a bannister brush hidden under the big table we used for making graphs, preparing specimens, and studying, so we could brush away begonia leaves, wet earth, and the fragments of flower pots that the gardener left behind.

Leonard Wing, one of the students, refused to work in the potting shed and tried to get the rest of us to keep it picked up so the entrance to The Professor's office would make a good impression. Late one afternoon, Wing, his dark eyes sparkling with suppressed excitement, whispered, "I've found a whole empty building on the campus. We are going to move The Professor. Bring your car at 8:00; it will be dark by then. You tell Hawkins, and I'll tell Wade."

We met at 8:00. Wing said, "I've found two wheelbarrows. Let's get the top of the Hamerstroms' car down right away; the big things go on the car. I'll keep an eye out for the night watchman and the campus cops. If you hear the call of a barred owl, it's the signal: watch out. . . . And you, Hawkins, take off that white sweater. It shows a mile away."

I hung the sweater over Leopold's desk lamp so passersby would be less apt to see what we were up to. We packed and moved all the books, all the reprints, all the maps, the duck decoys, and the furniture into a roomy empty building that had once been a dwelling. We moved everything and then, to convert the whole ground floor into Leopold's possession and fill the place up, we moved tables and chairs and bookcases from our own quarters and arranged them to "occupy" as many rooms as possible. As a final touch I picked some flowers from the campus gardens and put them in a mason jar on Leopold's desk.

Exhausted and somewhat grubby, we waited for Leopold's arrival the next morning. The Professor came down the path at a brisk pace. Leonard Wing, whose sense of the dramatic far surpasses mine, announced, "Your office isn't here any more. Follow me."

Wing led the way to 424 University Farm Place. He threw the front door open and announced, "This room will be for seminars. It has a fireplace for winter seminars and it can hold forty people."

Wing moved to the adjoining room. "Your office!" Sunlight poured in through big bay windows. All the books were in position on shelves that left room for more, and Leopold's pipe rested on the ashtray on his desk.

Wing let Leopold take it all in for a moment or two and then announced, "There's more. This room is for graduate students. It needs more desks."

He moved us on to the former kitchen. "This is the laboratory, it needs painting. We'll do that this afternoon."

Then he led the way to the pantry. "This is the darkroom. We'll paint it black. It has running water too."

Finally, he opened a door leading to a room almost as big as The Professor's former office. "We could use this for storage, and there is plenty of storage space in the basement too."

Leopold asked, "How did this come about?"

Wing's deep voice answered pompously, "The other office was not suitable for you."

The rest of us explained how we had managed the move with two wheelbarrows and one car "between two days."

Leopold sat on the edge of his chair and telephoned the authorities. We could hear only his end of the conversation. "You say that the building has already been assigned to another department? . . .

"Yes, I understand perfectly. What I'm trying to explain is not that I wish to move my office. It's already *done* . . . !

"No, just the ground floor. The whole ground floor." . . .

At last Leopold settled back in his desk chair, reached for his pipe, and lit it slowly. He didn't need to say a word. He was smiling and so were we. In those days not everybody knew that Aldo Leopold was a great man, but his students did.

Aldo Leopold.

143

"424 University Farm Place" was the address of Leopold's department for the rest of his life.

And sometimes, when I hear a barred owl call, I remember that night and the dread with which we listened for footsteps, police whistles, and for the warning that never came.

A letter from my mother-in-law

When Aldo Leopold assigned us both to work on prairie chickens, we could hardly believe our good fortune. I knew that Frederick would be accepted, but I never graduated from high school, and flunked out of Smith College in my sophomore year. To be sure, my scholastic record shot up after my marriage. I straightened out, graduated from Iowa State College, and even received a prize for the woman most likely to succeed in research. To work with Frederick as a team, rather than as a tag-along wife, I needed a chance to work for my Master's degree. Leopold never held my sex, nor my early scholastic record, against me.

And now we were about to head for our first field assignment on prairie chickens. Leopold arranged for us to move into a farmhouse in Waushara County. Clyde Terrill, the kindly owner, said, "Tell your students they don't have to pay rent. There are some broken windows upstairs; I hope they'll fix them. And I left some food up there once. Tell them they can eat it." He added, "I wish they'd paper the kitchen too." It was plain that —someday—he hoped to come back to a ramshackle old building that he had named "Paradise Found."

Frederick had a toothache.

He was cutting a wisdom tooth. I drove the last part of the way so he could hold his scarf against his jaw. We bumped through snowdrifts and at last the headlights picked up our new home. It was New Year's Eve, but for a fleeting moment I wondered whatever had possessed us to come straight from a party to move into a strange house after dark— and in city clothes. I could see the rusted screen of the front porch flapping in the wind. Frederick was crouched low holding his cheek. "You just stay in the car. I'll go in and get the house warm."

The key, we had been informed, was under a rock by the front door; in high heels I fumbled around in the snow, which was getting deeper by the minute, to find rocks. There were several—all frozen down. I let quite a blast of cold air into the car looking for the jack handle.

145

"Want me to help you?"

"No, I can do it. You just sit there."

Using a chunk of stovewood from the shed back of the house as a fulcrum, I tried to pry the rocks up. It was hopeless; they might as well have been set in cement.

Returning the jack handle to the car, I shouted, "I'll have to break in."

Frederick nodded without answering, but in a few minutes he joined me and together, without splintering too much wood, we jimmied the door open. I'm sure that if he hadn't had a great deal of self-control he would have been uttering little moans of pain. It didn't take much persuasion to get him back in the car to wait for the promised warm house.

I built a fire in the kitchen stove. All it did was belch smoke, so I had to open the doors and windows to let the smoke out. Next I tried the living room stove, an ornate heater with isinglass windows. The result was the same. Coughing and with stinging eyes, I aired the house thoroughly. There was a kerosene cook stove. We would have to make do with that. There were numerous cans that might have held kerosene; they were all empty, even the one with a frozen potato stuck over its snout.

Dejected and thoroughly chilled, I went out to the car. "Darling, do you think we can make it back to that last town? We have to buy some kerosene."

"We can try."

The drifts were piling up, but we made it back with a big can of kerosene. We lit the stove for a few minutes to warm up our hands. Then we felt our way up the narrow stairway and found a pile of quilts. Acorns tumbled out when we lifted them, and they smelled like mice. But we put the pungent quilts on a creaky bed and crawled between them. Slowly, slowly, the aching cold left our bones and we were warm. The next morning frost tipped Frederick's eyelashes. They were long and black and curved, and frost tipped every lash. He smiled in his sleep and I knew the toothache was gone. At last he stirred and woke up.

We dressed quickly. I had to get back into my finery because my field clothes were still in the car, but Frederick soon produced the duffle bags so I could change in the icy kitchen.

Again smoke belched from the stove. Frederick adjusted the doors and the damper and tried all the tricks he knew to get a fire started. I tapped the stovepipe with a high-heeled shoe. We fought that stove with all the skill we had. Suddenly the smoke went up the chimney instead of out into the kitchen; the fire caught and crackled.

The house was full of food to augment our supplies: flour, prunes, raisins, sugar, syrup, pancake mixes, tea, coffee, dried milk, and unidentified pastes and mixtures. Only the coffee was labeled correctly. The flour was in a huge cookie can; cookies, raisins, prunes, and some mouldy bacon emerged from a fishing tackle box; I didn't find the jams and jellies for a long time. They were stored in milk bottles inside two big potato-chip cans marked "Machine Oil." The remains of a package of cornflakes contained more mouse and squirrel droppings than cereal. We, too, soon learned to protect all food from marauding rodents.

Daily we explored the vicinity of our house on snowshoes looking for prairie chickens, and we finally found a few tracks in a rye field where the wind had exposed pigeon grass and ragweed. Then we asked our neighbor John, where we could find chickens.

"They's went . . . all went . . . used ta be some 'round here . . . they's went."

Then he gave us the local news. It was said that Charlie Pratt was going to put in electricity! "And you know what Pete did?" Pete was our neighbor on the other side and we hadn't met him yet. "Pete found an electric bulb onna dump an' he clumb the phone pole to hook it in, but he never got no yard light. He got nothing!" John laughed hugely and offered us a drink.

We drank some stinging whiskey out of big white cups and took our leave. We headed for Pete's. There *was* an electric light bulb, fastened in some mysterious manner to the phone pole nearest Pete's house, and we didn't expect to learn much.

Pete may not have known much about electricity, but he knew where the chickens were. "There's corn on the marsh," he waved his arm expansively toward the west. "Too dry here, but the corn on the marsh grew good an' that's where the chickens are."

He was right. We never saw any chicken tracks near our house again, so we hauled our traps to the Leola Marsh miles away and made some pretty good catches.

Our house was in the hills. They weren't big hills. Chunks of ice had become embedded in the moraine left by the last glacier and, when the climate became warmer the ice melted, leaving innumerable small ponds surrounded by hills. It was as though the landscape had been designed by some devil to catch snow and plug up the roads in the Year of Our Lord, 1939. The winter landscape took on an unreal quality. The tops of telephone poles looked like fence posts in the drifts. We never met anyone who had a telephone and I wondered where the poles led, tall on the hilltops and short in the valleys. Finally, we were snowed in with no way to get to the marsh where the prairie chickens were, some seven miles away.

The mailman came by our house. He had invented a *snowmobile!* And this was almost surely the first snowmobile in the state of Wisconsin. This contraption had proved untrustworthy and was soon replaced by a factory model with six back wheels—three on each side—and runners in front. He romped across the top of the drifts followed by an enormous whirl of flying snow. The first time he came by, we thought the road must be open again; a machine that rode on top of the snow was beyond our imagination.

The snowmobile let us know that the road was still unplowed, and if the whirling cascade subsided at the end of our drive, we knew that the mailman had stopped and that there was something in the box for us. We rarely received mail; we had no bills to pay by mail, and no one consulted us professionally.

Our mothers kept writing us. Frederick's mother wrote me, I remember: when entertaining at luncheon use doilies instead of a tablecloth. It happened that I read the letter when sitting at our dining table. The decor consisted of a battered kerosene can and funnel; a lamp with a smoky chimney; an axe, saw, and hammer; two recent copies of the *Journal of Wildlife Management;* and a partly consumed can of sardines. The table was covered with patterned oilcloth; the pattern consisted of flowers in pots, and the cloth was cracked. . . . "Use doilies. . . ."

"And remember, dear" (she advised me on various matters as long as she lived), "to have your mink coat lined. It's just wrong to wear it the way you do."

I paused for a moment to recall an evening in New York and the face of the head waiter in the Stork Club. Even when I was a debutante I had made my own mink coat from an old one of my mother's, plus furs rescued from trunks in my parent's attic and road-killed mink that I had skinned and tanned myself. It was floor length, and its voluminous folds moved with grace when I walked because I had refused to line it. The inside of the coat consisted of the undersides of mink skins neatly sewn together. Some of the furrier's skins had little punch marks for coding the color and grade, a few of mine showed bite marks at the back of the necks of some females—wounds inflicted by the rough and tumble matings of big males with small females—and some of my hides were discolored.

Anyone who has been a fashion model and worked the East Coast circuit from Boston to Palm Beach well knows what sort of an impression her clothes are making. My escort and I had swept into the Stork Club slowly. No one needed to tell me that heads were turning. The head waiter, with a little nod to my escort—so to speak, asking permission—seated me and lifted my coat with slow dexterity from my bare shoulders. As he exposed the inside, putting it over the back of my chair, I heard something between a gasp and a wheeze. For a moment his aplomb has been shaken.

Now I had forgotten my mink coat and the mousy quilts had not been warm enough last night. I dug around in our boxes and found it. I spread it skin side down on our bed. It looked just beautiful.

Then I hurried down to the warmth of the kitchen, pried a couple of sardines out of the can with my fingers, and nibbled on them while continuing to read Mrs. Hamerstrom's letter.

"Frederick writes that you are living in a little wooden farmhouse. Window boxes are very attractive, dear Fran—window boxes abloom with geraniums and petunias—and often set a small house apart and give it a pleasant cottage look.

"And remember, dear, don't spoil Frederick. There are times to be firm."

Communicating with my mother-in-law was always something of a challenge.

"Dear Mrs. Hamerstrom,

"Thank you for your nice letter and for reminding me of my mink coat. Our house would seem small to you, but it is just right for us. It has three bedrooms, a living room, a kitchen, a well-stocked pantry, and a woodshed. It is pleasant to have the woodshed attached to the house; we never have to bother with wet wood and sit by a snug, cozy fire every evening after the day's work is done.

"Our house is nestled amongst exquisite wild pine trees. It has beautiful simple lines and the well-weathered wood fits beautifully into the landscape, which is somewhat hilly.

"So far we have not entertained here."

I pried the last sardine out of the can and drank the oil (those who have worked outdoors in cold climates know that the craving for fat and oil in the diet is intense, but I didn't think I'd tell her that).

Then I came to the part about not spoiling Frederick and I wrote exactly what I believe. "I have every intention of spoiling Frederick." To soften it a little, I added, "Men are to be spoiled."

We both loved Frederick, but we saw him with different eyes.

149

Geraniums... red comforters... sleep

We thought it was impossible to snowshoe seven miles and back to tend our traps, but we were mistaken. At that time we had no real feel for prairie chicken trapping and set two or three traps out wherever we saw some tracks. Instead of waiting until a flock of chickens had almost exhausted a food supply and then moving in with a couple of dozen traps, we spread our trapline over many, many miles. Over and over again, we unset all our traps, lest an oncoming storm block the roads. Prairie chickens can probably spend a day or two burrowed under the snow without food, but we weren't taking any chances at finding dead birds in our sets. We checked each trap two, or even three, times a day.

We had no radio, no news of the outside world, and no weather reports. We had to take some chances on the weather, or we wouldn't have caught any chickens at all. Each time we holed up, snowed in at home, we savored the comfort and solitude. Then when the plow got through, we drove to the marsh and had to find our unset traps and dig them out. Some were completely covered by drifting snow.

Stuck... and again.

Once, in February, we failed as weather prophets. We drove home to a warm supper and creature comforts after a nice catch and careful baiting of all our traps. The next morning the roads were blocked solid!

I fried some meat, sliced some bread, and stuffed some sandwiches into our pockets. We ate a hearty breakfast and set out for the Leola Marsh. Our nearest traps were seven miles away, and the weather was a bit nippy for outdoor recreation.

Frederick laid out a plan: I was to unset the traps on the east side of the marsh, and he would take the west. Each knew exactly where the other was going and in what order we would unset the stations. Whoever got through first was to continue until we met. We met just before dark about nine miles from home. Scarves wrapped around our faces had saved them from frostbite, but the wind, if anything, had picked up.

We could see the dim light from a farmhouse lamp and headed for it and asked it we could come in and get warm. Mrs. Strattinger laid out a lavish supper for us, and Mr. Strattinger asked, "Where's your car?"

"Over at Clyde Terrill's. That's where we're living now."

"Well," he said, "you're going to spend the night right here."

Mrs. Strattinger took us upstairs to a room with geraniums on the window sill. She piled warm, red, feather comforters on the bed. It was just lovely, but neither of us can remember the room very well. It was like a moment on the TV screen when one button is pushed right after the next. Geraniums . . . red comforters . . . sleep.

She called us early the next morning, gave us a good breakfast, and we snowshoed home. The back door of the kitchen had blown open and I looked at the thermometer: it was 20° below zero in the kitchen.

Every house has something special. Clyde's, to be sure, had a back door that blew open in winter, but there were unexpected delights. There was a lake for swimming and for watching geese swing past dark oak woods to alight on the water. The lake was handy too. In summer I took a washboard to the beach and scrubbed the laundry clean. Then I rinsed the sheets by rushing along the shallows, avoiding the rocking grebe nests, and when I paused for breath, the wild laughter of the loons echoed around me. There was an organ in that old house too. It was out of tune; but when Frederick was gone, I sometimes played *Oh dem Golden Slippers* or *Lavender's Blue* as loud as I could. And pasque flowers bloomed not far away.

Frederick reached a conclusion that I had almost arrived at by myself. "We're going to have to move. It's just too chancy trying to trap from way out here."

"Too chancy." Yes, it was too chancy to stay in this wonderful house. The chickens might hurt themselves—or even die—if we couldn't get to our traps regularly. The decision to move was made; but the chickens would be booming soon, and we had our hands full.

Anyway, we wouldn't be leaving till summer.

The open room

When spring came, visitors arrived to watch the prairie chickens. We hastily built more blinds and warned everyone to bring his own bedding. The help of volunteers augmented by our own industrious efforts made it possible to read the band numbers of many of the booming cocks.

Most of the visitors liked our warm untidy kitchen and rural setting, but one woman furtively wiped her silverware with a towel as though we hadn't washed the dishes, and looked at each chair before she sat down as though she might find a worm on the seat. When she found that we were moving soon, she took me aside and in a voice pent up with emotion, said, "I'm very glad for you."

Fortunately she didn't come to our next house. We never saw her again.

We found our next house by chance. Bill Feeney, a distinguished falconer and biologist, was with us. He had come to look our marsh over with us to see whether it would be any good for hunting with his birds. On our way home, out of curiosity, Frederick drove down a long, unused driveway and there was an old, old house with beautiful lines, and cut off from the rest of the world. We explored it. Most of the windows were still in and some of the floors were sound. But the roof leaked over the west end of the house, and one wall teetered in an inconsequential manner like a set on the stage.

The living room looked out on an ancient walnut plantation, tall elms framed the house, and mammoth white pines grew in the woodlot and along the driveway. We found out later that Walter Ware, the pioneer who built the house, had planted the pines by digging up frozen "root balls" and pulling them home on a sled with a team of oxen. It was Wisconsin's first pine plantation.

"This is it. We're going to live here."

Feeney had knocked about in the jingweeds and had undoubtedly spent some time in some pretty awful shacks in the backwoods. Sure that we were going to come to our senses, he simply said, "It must have been a nice place."

Feeney came to look for us in the autumn, knowing that we were living somewhere up in the chicken country. It took him a long time to find us, because he really hadn't believed for a moment that we seriously considered moving into *that* house.

Aldo Leopold was with us the first night we slept under the leaky roof. It rained and water beat on the windows and broken shingles outside and dripped through the roof into containers indoors. We set up a bed for him in the living room under the sound part of the roof, and set ours up in the kitchen. Pots, pans, and bowls filled up from time to time, and one large pan on the foot of our bed kept the water from drenching our bedclothes.

The next morning Aldo helped me dig a new hole for the outhouse. We dug through water-washed sand and hit a darkened layer.

"Must have been timber then and fires too. Drift sand can blow and build up fast, so we can't date it very well."

As we dug deeper and deeper, Aldo speculated on the ancient history of Glacial Lake Wisconsin, and I began to sense why the Leola Marsh had become one of the remaining strongholds for the prairie chickens. The glacial lake bed was colder than the surrounding country—too cold for many kinds of farming—so there were vast expanses of pasture and hay.

After about an hour of digging together, Aldo commented, "Interesting, isn't it? People make outhouses and such much bigger than they need to be." We agreed.

Aided by friends from the university, Frederick and I rebuilt that

The open room.

154

farmhouse. It is my impression that the roof was shingled by more Ph.D.'s than any roof in history.

We tore down the wobbly wall of our future bedroom—at that time we just called it "the open room."

When Aldo commented on the water-washed sand from the glacial lake bed, we had both rolled the smooth surfaces between our fingers. Neither Frederick nor I knew anything about mortar. We rebuilt the foundation along the north end of the open room. It was an enormous undertaking; we bashed apart the old rocks and mixed up mortar from the sandpile by the outhouse. Frederick wielded a borrowed trowel, set each rock in mortar, and used a spirit level to get the top straight. We went to bed exhausted, but very pleased with ourselves.

The next day it was plain that something had gone very, very wrong. Mortar poured in little trickles from between the rocks; it was dry, but we could pry any part of the foundation apart with our hands. Frederick asked, "Do you still have the bag this stuff came in?"

I had torn it up for lighting fires and stuffed it back of the woodbox. As we never subscribed to newspapers, each bit of paper was precious. I helped piece the torn edges together and Frederick reread the instructions. As I had suspected, the piecing together was a waste of time. Unlike me, he can read complicated instructions once and then *follow* them. He had followed them exactly.

The failure of the mortar could be a serious blow to our pocket book. We had $50 a month between us and had to run a car, and a trapline, and get to Madison 100 miles away for seminars, and eat—without any expense money. Frederick suggested he take the whole foundation down and that I go to town for more cement. The division of labor was well planned. Unlike Frederick, who is far too polite to argue, I can put up a good fight if anyone has sold us defective merchandise. By the time I had driven five miles over a bumpy road to the lumberyard, my righteous indignation was at perfect pitch. I never rehearse what I'm going to say; I just get in the right mood.

"The cement you sold my husband is worthless."

An old man peered at me over his bifocals. "Worthless? You mean it was caked?" He sounded incredulous.

"No, it was not caked. It just comes apart."

He sat back in his chair and looked at me through his glasses. "You fixing up the old Walter Ware place?" he asked conversationally.

"Yes." *I* wanted to be asking the questions, and matters were getting out of hand. "We are rebuilding a foundation and we need some good cement. There is something wrong with what you sold us."

"Where'd you get your sand?"

I longed to tell him it was none of his business, but instead, blushing violently, I stammered, "I got it from near the outhouse."

"Sand out that way is round. You've got to get your sand in the hills."

"In the hills?"

The old man rolled imaginary sand between his big knuckled fingers. He shook his head sadly, deploring my ignorance. "Sand in the hills is sharp-pointed and the cement will hold. Tell you what I'll do." He eased himself out of his chair and stepped out of the loading platform. "See, you go north two miles and west one mile, that's Manzer's Corners. You get your sand there. You got bags to put it in?"

I shook my head.

"Tell you what I'll do. I'll *give* you some bags."

Paying for cement a second time bothered me and almost emptied my purse, but I couldn't help protesting when he dumped a big armful of bags into the car. "I won't need all those!"

That old man didn't say anything. He just looked at me and somehow he managed to make me feel stupid.

Other people had been digging at Manzer's Corners. I pulled the shovel out of the back of the car and filled two bags in no time at all, opened the car door ready to put them in, and found I couldn't move them! Feeling an awful fool, I dumped most of the sand back on the ground and filled every bag up just a little so I could lift it.

Frederick had the foundation apart and the rocks washed clean when I got back.

"Darling, I had to pay for the cement!" In my own eyes I'd lost face, but I'd excused myself. "It was really only reasonable. The cement was all right; it was just that we used round, water-washed sand. Everybody goes to the terminal moraine to get sand for mortar."

Frederick was amazed. "Is *that* what the man at the lumberyard told you?"

"No, Aldo told me part of it, and I put two and two together."

"Did you get the potatoes?"

"I didn't have enough money," and then I added softly, "in my purse." That "in my purse" didn't fool either of us. A 100-pound sack of potatoes cost a dollar, but we didn't have a dollar anywhere.

"I hope there'll be some cement left so I can fix the chimney."

There was. I pulled every loose brick off the crumbling chimney, cleaned it, and mortared it back in place. It was almost dark when I finished. Then I heard a screech owl calling. Herb Stoddard, the orni-

156

thologist, had just been up to spend a few days with us and had taught us how to call screech owls. You lie on your back and get a lot of spit ready; then you whistle low and falling and the spit rolls on your tongue trilling like an owl. I lay next to my rebuilt chimney and called. Before I could call again, a screech owl lit on the peak of the roof next to me.

The evolution of the chicken blind

Nowadays birdwatchers—especially prairie chicken watchers—sit comfortably in four- by four-foot cubes, or even bigger blinds. Some actually bring their own dome-shaped blinds and can zip windows and camera ports open and shut at will.

After a heroic morning sitting in a blind watching prairie chickens, the normal man complains, "Cramped, I was—my teeth chattered—couldn't stand up—wind howled...." I suppose hundreds have returned to the warmth of our big stove and complained in many a picturesque manner. People like to tell me their troubles so they tended to complain to *me,* and I gradually developed a series of small,

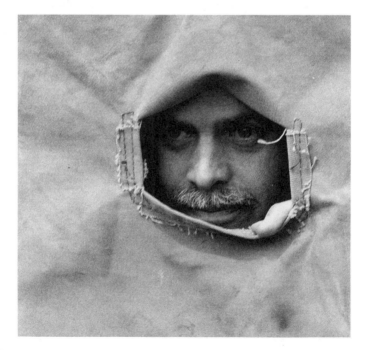

soothing mumbled phrases: "Must have been beastly . . . um . . . what a pity . . . um."

I could have told them a thing or two. I could have told them about the booming ground that was so wild that the chickens refused to accept any sort of blind and I had to lie in a ditch—without *any* shelter—in the dark and wait for daylight and then wait again, without moving a muscle, head down in last year's pigeon grass, until my ears told me that the hens had finally flown away and at last it was time to jump up and count the cocks.

Later Frederick would ask, "You say you flushed *eleven* cocks? Are you sure the hens had all gone?"

"Yes, the 'ladies present call' stopped at 7:16 and then I waited about five minutes. I flushed cocks only and got the count."

"That booming ground wastes a lot of time." Frederick shook his head sadly, "Took all morning for you to get just one count."

All morning with my head in last year's pigeon grass, but it would never have occurred to me to answer, "Cramped . . . lying in that ditch head down . . . the wind blew the back of my jacket up . . . my feet are still numb."

Year after year we had to check that booming ground without using a blind. When I think back to our earliest blinds, I realize that some of them were almost as bad as having no blind at all.

Our first blind and our approach to the art of watching prairie chickens was incredibly naive. The game warden told us where to put the blind, and in March 1939 we set up a folding card table on a little knoll on the Leola Marsh before daylight. Frederick sat on the ground, knees up, head down, and I put the table over him. Then I covered it with some old blankets so that the "tablecloth" reached the ground and was lashed down to keep it from blowing and flapping in the northwest wind. And I arranged peepholes so he could watch the prairie chickens when—and if—they came.

By rights I should have been inside and under that card table, as I am considerably smaller and fold up far more comfortably. We planned it otherwise: my job was to flush the prairie chickens toward him. Perhaps if we had read the literature more carefully, we would have gathered that prairie cocks select a booming ground and only go to it if they want to.

I walked and waded the marshland; and every time I saw a likely spot for chickens to be, I detoured to flush any potential birds *toward* him. I persisted in this unprofitable undertaking with increasing, quiet frenzy for I knew that Frederick would stay put where he was, without

159

moving, and never let me down. He'd stick it out under the card table until I flushed those birds toward him. The raw wind moaned above me as I ploshed through popple woods. I went in over my boot tops, and continued to plosh on as silently as I could, circling each grassy opening with what stealth I could muster.

Now and again I walked back to the edge of the vast opening—in part to make sure I wasn't lost—but it was also practical to know exactly where the card table was so I could steer any chickens that I might flush in the right direction.

After about two and a half hours of waiting, prairie chickens suddenly put in within sight of Frederick's card table of their own volition.

They stayed seven minutes.

The blind had worked! We were jubilant. Frederick said, "We'd better build another blind so we each have one." We constructed some wooden frames, covered them with old burlap bags, and allowed ourselves the luxury of an upside-down bucket to sit on. But the wind howled through the burlap and, worse still, so much light came in that whoever sat in the blind dared not move. Just opening a notebook and reaching for a pencil sometimes spooked the birds.

A trip to the town dump helped solve this problem. We found a soggy bedspread printed with pink roses, under a heap of tin cans; and we found a discarded circus poster blown against a battered car body. So much wealth gave great encouragement. We built two blinds and, as far as our material would last, we partially covered each: one with the pattern of roses shielding us from the sunny side and the other showing part of a lady riding part of a horse. Because we had our minds on the end product rather than on the ultimate effect, they were both upside down. Her legs in flesh-colored tights extended skyward and a little to the southeast; her toes barely touched the rump of a swiftly moving chestnut horse. If the neighbors started to talk we were unaware of it; our concern was with the prairie chickens. Both the lady and the roses were accepted by the birds, especially when the wind didn't cause the covering of our blinds to flap wildly and and spook them.

The wind still roared into our blinds and we kept trying to tighten up loose edges of burlap, bedspread, and circus poster. At last Frederick said, "We need something better. We need a good, solid, dark blind. The worst thing about these is that they let in too much light."

"I'll take care of it."

Frederick looked at me in surprise. "How?"

160

"I have an idea. I think I can get one in Wisconsin Rapids." Then I asked, "Do you want me to bring back anything else?"

"We need excelsior. It's high time we stuffed those birds." Every dead prairie chicken we found was autopsied and either made into a museum skin or otherwise stuffed.

That very afternoon I hooked up our eight-foot freight trailer and started off. There was a big store in town that sold furniture, refrigerators, and other large items; and such things were shipped in wooden packing boxes in those days. A piano crate would be too big, but a nice big refrigerator box would be perfect.

I drove into the alley behind the store and hesitated a moment; one could get into the store the back way, but it appeared to me that my chance of success might be improved by walking right in the front door like a customer. I combed my hair, added a little lipstick to my chapped lips, and turned the frayed cuffs of my jacket up inside the sleeves where they wouldn't show.

I walked right in the front door and sure enough a clerk came to welcome me. He had a pale face, thinning reddish hair and wore a cordial toothy smile. "Good afternoon."

"Good afternoon. Could you let me have a big box? I realize you must throw some away?"

He departed obligingly.

The store was big and dark and far from busy. It looked as though no one had shopped there for a week. Finally my friend the clerk returned still smiling and carrying a little box that could at most have contained a dozen blankets.

"Oh no," I exclaimed, extending my arms to give the impression of a huge box, "that won't do. You see my husband is going to be in it. He's big."

The clerk's pale face became, if anything, paler. His smile faded to

a look of toothy terror and he backed away from me, feeling his way between the sofas and chairs in the gloom. He pulled away until he reached a small door and fumbled for the knob. Suddenly he was gone. Perhaps I imagined it, but I thought I heard him turn the key in the lock.

Kindness prompted me to go knock on that door and explain, but common sense won. I don't think that man ever wanted to see me again.

Somewhat dispirited I left and went down the street, into the alley, and back to the car. I glanced sadly at the empty trailer and then looked once more at the big back door of the store.

The door was ajar! I jumped up onto the loading platform and peered inside. There, recently pried open and empty except for some fine excelsior, was a sturdy big box. A huge man in overalls emerged from behind some machinery and said, "What da ya want?"

"I want the box, can I have it?"

"Yup." He offered to dump the excelsior, but I said I could use that too, so he just helped me load the box into the trailer.

"What da ya want the box *for?*"

"It's for watching birds."

"Yeah, and what's the excelsior for?"

"To put inside birds."

Suddenly he laughed with boisterous appreciation. He plainly cottoned to a girl with a quick tongue who liked to tell tall tales.

Rather anxiously I asked, "Could you tell the man in the front of the store what it's for?"

"Him? That fraidycat?" I was treated to a solemn wink, "You told *him* and he didn't believe you? I'll fix him!" he chuckled.

My burly friend headed for the front of the store, little suspecting that "fraidycat" was hiding back of a locked door—a door locked against a woman who was about to put her husband in a box. I had plenty to think about on the way home.

Frederick, bless him, admired the box and my neat haul of excelsior as well. "Did you have to pay for the box?" he asked.

"No, it was free. I got it for nothing."

"You sound a little subdued. Where'd you get the box?"

"In the furniture store. Nobody believed me there."

"Nobody believed you?"

"No, and the clerk thought I was going to put *you* in it."

Frederick looked utterly mystified. "I hope this box is not going to be exclusively for *your* use? I *will* be in it, won't I?"

162

"Yes, darling, but you see he thought you were going in piecemeal."

"What?"

"There's a man in that store who is very afraid of me."

Frederick can be wonderful. He simply studied my face for a moment or two and then spoke softly. "It's been a long day, hasn't it?"

He has a beautiful voice like dark chocolate.

Diseases, not only shock but sack and sock

Finally we built ourselves several good blinds covered with canvas. The chickens we had banded in winter wore aluminum bands on which remarkably small numbers had been stamped. Hunched in our new blinds, we tried to read the numbers of displaying chickens. Furthermore, we used binoculars. Spotting scopes were not yet in common use. Reading band numbers on cocks was not easy; as the hens spent most of their time low in the thickest vegetation, it was essentially impossible to read their numbers. We decided to settle for the cocks. Our hope was to read every cock's band on every booming ground to see where the birds we had caught in winter had gone to display in spring. The only way we could accomplish this was to spend very few mornings on each booming ground and then move the blind to another. To my chagrin, I had spent almost a week on one booming ground because one lone cock persisted

The chickens wore aluminum bands.

in booming on a faraway knoll. I couldn't even tell whether or not he was banded—much less read his numbers!

On Easter morning a huge white bird flew right in front of my face, and I peeped cautiously out of the blind window. I thought it was a gull. Then I lifted the flap of another window and beheld that this monstrous bird wasn't a gull at all. It was a snowy owl—the first that I'd ever seen—and it was sitting on top of the very chicken I needed to check for bands.

Without a moment's hesitation, I pushed my way out the door flap of the blind and rushed to grab that chicken from her. The owl hopped only about three or four feet away, unwilling to relinquish her quarry. I seized the incapacitated cock, and the owl started to follow me back to the blind. Maybe I could catch the owl too!

Quickly I unlaced one of my tall boots and tied the chicken's legs together. Then I held the fluttering chicken out of the door slot. The owl bobbed its head and walked a few steps toward the blind. It moved faster, almost flying to reach this delectable meal again. I lay on the floor of the blind ready to grab its legs. Victory was within a few yards when this unusual activity attracted a flock of crows. They dive-bombed

Deciphering notes at the end of the morning.

165

and harassed the owl until it gave up and took off in the pale rosy light of the sunrise. By then the prairie chicken had died of puncture wounds. It was unbanded; but anyway, I almost hand-grabbed the first snowy owl I ever saw and I did not toss the chicken carcass into an incinerator!

In 1940 it was neither bad form nor illegal to eat what unexpectedly came our way (out-of-season deer meat was the only exception). Nowadays if a biologist has no scientific use for a carcass, he must turn it over to a public institution "through channels," bury it, or burn it. I was very careful not to burn the carcass of the prairie chicken killed by the snowy owl. I roasted it in a hot oven for exactly twenty-five minutes. Joe Hickey, a fellow graduate student, was helping us out for a few days. Luncheon on Easter Sunday was the best meal any of us had had in some time.

I would like to add that the very idea of killing anything out of season for our own selfish use as food was inconceivable. We had too high a regard for our profession.

Having a prairie chicken in our hands during the booming season cemented our determination to color-mark the cocks on our booming grounds. We made bow nets, stapled them down carefully in the heart of what we believed to be individual territories, and ran a long string to the blind. It was hard to tell when the cock I was after was well centered in the bow net, but I gave a mighty pull when I figured he was in position and netted my bird. I put him into a sock and reset for another.

The next cock I tried for simply stamped along the edge of the bow net and never got inside the magic circle.

At the end of the morning's work I ran jubilantly toward Frederick shouting, "I caught! I caught!"

Frederick seemed a bit subdued. "I caught too, but my bird is dead."·

I handed him the sock heavy with my bird, to raise his spirits. It was strangely inert: my bird was dead too.

We called it "sock disease" and decided that prairie cocks are more sensitive during the booming season and cannot be left lying around in socks as they can in winter.

R. K. Meyer, the endocrinologist, autopsied those birds for us and could come up with only one tentative conclusion: hypoglycemia—shock disease.

He gave us each a vial of sugar solution and a syringe. "Next time just inject warm sugar solution quickly, and maybe the bird will come out of it all right."

For some years thereafter we each wore a vial of sugar solution next to our skin to keep the solution warm, and we each carried a syringe. There never was a next time. We encountered this unhappy phenomenon just once. After the double accident, we processed and released booming-ground birds far more quickly than winter birds. Now that I look back on it, it seems that our early diagnosis of sock disease was correct.

Sack disease is not the same. We soon learned that in winter if we had a good catch, we'd better not put more than five birds into one burlap bag, lest those on the bottom smother.

Imping

Early in the spring the prairie cocks rush about on the booming grounds and fight. Usually the fights draw no blood. Prairie cocks have no spurs, but they fight each other with their feet and wings—and they bite. Feathers are strewn all over the booming ground and sometimes the fights are prolonged and violent. The lack of an umpire in wildlife fights makes them far more exciting to watch than TV. The fights are real and not for money.

Frederick and I tried to figure out why cocks never killed each other outright. The whole performance of sixteen or so cocks tearing around a booming ground, fighting, blowing up their huge orange air sacs, and booming lacked pattern. This behavior started each year in late February or in March ... long before any hens appeared on the booming grounds. It looked like merry mayhem without a purpose. The terms "territory," and "appeasement behavior," were not yet common in the ornithological literature of the 1930s and early 1940s.

We were baffled and nobody needed to tell us what must be done next: we must individually color-mark as many cocks as possible on at least two booming grounds. Fearing shock, or some other related "disease," we had all our materials in readiness before we started to net prairie cocks—one after another—on the booming grounds. If we could manage it, every cock was going to wear brightly colored tail feathers or neck tufts.

We saved feathers from dead bluejays and cardinals, pulled feathers from the speculums of duck wings to put in the neck tufts of living cock prairie chickens; and we dyed quantities of white feathers, red, green, blue, and yellow to imp their tails.

The word "imp" comes from the Latin word *imponere,* to place within. Falconers were not only the first ethologists, but they were also the first group of people that really understood the care of individual birds. As an example, when a flight feather broke, they mended it by imping a new one.

We adapted the falconers' technique, but with something very

168

different in mind! Instead of adding part of a matching feather we strove for conspicuous mismatches.

Each time we succeeded in catching a cock, we cut off a feather quite close to the skin, but so the hollow shaft of the feather protruded. Then we selected some brightly colored feather that would fit neatly into the hollow shaft. Having made sure that the fit was good we plunged the base of the colored feather into Duco household cement and then fitted it into the cut shaft on the bird itself. The cement dried in about two minutes and—with luck—the cock would wear the brightly colored feather for months—until the next molt. Imping the tip of a feather worked better on the pinnae—the long, earlike tufts of feathers on each side of the neck.

At last all the cocks on the booming ground didn't look alike to us. There is something very frustrating about having a whole bunch of birds rushing about in front of you day after day without knowing what they are doing or who they are. But even before we had trapped many, we came to realize that certain places were "pet spots" of certain cocks,

and that our best chance of catching a given individual was in his pet spot.

The recognition of "pet spots" would seem to have established that prairie chicken cocks are territorial on their booming grounds: not at all! The unravelling of the mystery was like a detective story.

In the first place, "pink tuft right" had two pet spots. Sometimes he boomed on one and then he flew across the booming ground and displayed on the other.

In the second place, *visiting* cocks sometimes appeared. These tended to scoot around the booming ground with their bodies held low and their pinnae lowered, but sometimes they "gained courage" and boomed, and a very few even set up a territory!

Most confusing of all was the electric change that came over a booming ground when hens appeared. One hen could drive sixteen cocks to distraction. I mean distraction in the exact sense of the word: the cocks were distracted from their territories. Even one hen walking the booming ground precipitates a type of frenzy. She doesn't have to do anything; she may just pick at a few willow buds and scratch imaginary lice from time to time, seemingly unaware of all the cocks displaying around her.

At last we saw that the influence of one or more hens pulls the territories of the cocks out of shape like a pencil drawn through an outspread hair net. The nearer the hen, the greater the distraction, and the more the cocks "forget" their territories.

We needed to fit one more piece into the puzzle before we could be certain that prairie cocks were territorial, and within two years the missing piece was found: prairie chickens can distinguish each other's sex by behavior only! This is very strange because any beginner can learn that the neck tufts of the cock are about three inches long and those of the hen are far shorter—only about one inch. Any cock that behaves like a hen and keeps his neck tufts down is "treated like a lady." Any hen that raises her long slender neck with its short pinnae has declared her true sex—female.

We published our findings on territorialism in a gallinaceous species in 1949. That same year David Lack published on territories of British black grouse, a species with a similar display. He cannot have had the fun that we had, because black cocks are big and mostly black and the hens are far smaller and brown.

They can tell each other's sex at a glance.

How to tell chickens by their faces

It has always amazed me that grade school teachers can memorize the names of twenty to thirty children in one morning, and correctly associate the right name with the right child. This is phenomenal.

I've queried quite a few teachers about this. They are pleased at my sincere admiration of their feat, and not infrequently they ask, "Why do you want to know?"

"Well, I study birds and I'd like to learn your technique."

Not one could teach me his technique, so I developed one of my own and now grade school teachers find *me* phenomenal: I can tell individual prairie chickens apart!

The trick is to give each bird a *name*. A cock who favors his left foot and hobbles about becomes "Lame left." It took Frederick to point out that only if the leg has sustained a permanent injury will he always be "Lame left." After all, he might get well!

Dark near eyes
dark quad
deep necklace

White both sides of eyes
faint quad
pearl necklace

Dark near eyes
deep smokey quad
grassy streaked necklace

White before eyes
faint line quad
necklace has right blob

171

The most reliable way of telling prairie chickens apart is by their faces. The bird-book names for the parts of a bird's head were cumbersome and didn't fit our need for quick descriptions just to name and recognize individuals. There is an area near the quadrate bone, close to the angle of the jaw, that ranges from solid black, to smoky, to freckled, to pale, to no markings at all. The areas just before and just back of the eyes may be white, mottled, or dark. The necklace at the base of the neck varies enormously; it may be deep, narrow, pale, or even asymmetrical.

I have mentioned four parts that can be described, and once we got the hang of it, it was just as easy as memorizing red hair—freckles—tall—ears stick out.

Hens tend to remain sleek, are not seen repeatedly, and are far harder to memorize than cocks.

By the time the booming season is at its peak and the hens are finally appearing on the booming grounds, most of the cocks are so battle scarred that we can recognize them by knocked out tail feathers, broken primaries, and puncture wounds on their air sacs.

Feathers are eventually replaced, wounds heal, and we know that the names we give these cocks will not carry through until next spring. It takes but a moment to sketch the puncture wounds on the left or right air sac of a cock, but again it was Frederick who sounded a warning note.

"That cock, dark quad, white back of eye, and checkered necklace, is right in front of my blind. I sketched the puncture wounds on his left air sac."

I nodded enthusiastically, having just found puncture wounds useful.

"Here are my sketches at twenty-minute intervals," he muttered angrily. "Those puncture wounds were ticks—just ticks—walking across the air sac."

Aunt Ruby's box

It always gave us delight to drive down our long driveway flanked by tall pines. Not until we reached the walnut grove could we see our beautifully proportioned house and marvel that Walter Ware, a pioneer, had fitted the low, simple lines of New England farmhouses into the Wisconsin landscape.

We never locked our doors and we never worried about having anybody steal anything. . . .

Late one afternoon we drove home through the pines, but when we got to the walnut grove, I gasped, "Somebody's stolen the windows!"

Frederick pressed his foot on the gas pedal, and as we roared nearer he sounded incredulous. "The windows are still there; they just took the glass!"

We rushed into the house so we could see how much damage had been done. No breeze blew into the rooms; the windows were still there. Somebody had *washed* the glass in all the windows of the whole house. Instead of the dead fisheye look that we'd become accustomed to, the panes were so clean that it appeared they were absent; when the light struck them just right they sparkled.

Two monogrammed bath towels from my trousseau, with dirt ground into them beyond recovery, were stuffed into an old pot. There was a small, neat note on the kitchen table. The Mannegolds—German-American aristocracy—had driven up from Milwaukee to see us. They had waited and had decided to do something useful while waiting.

I wrote Frederick's Aunt Ruby, wife of the criminal lawyer Clarence Darrow, about the day we thought the windows had been stolen, and how we could buy milk for five cents a quart if we supplied the bottle tops (which I cut out of cardboard with my manicure scissors), and various details of our rural housekeeping. It was fun to write to her: she was the only member of the family who didn't consider me "plucky"; she didn't criticize my housekeeping, and she sent extraordinary Christmas boxes.

Not long after my letter, Aunt Ruby's box arrived; we opened it eagerly. Neither of us had had enough to eat on a regular basis for several years. I had even come down with a mild case of beriberi and food was never far from our thoughts.

Each item in Aunt Ruby's box was labeled, and most labels contained a message or admonition. I wish I'd saved some of her bizarre little notes. Some were scrawled in purple ink, and others had been dashed off on one of the first "silent portable typewriters." The individually wrapped packages were packed—or shall I say "floated"—with masses of ribbon-cut waxed paper that I had normally associated with Easter eggs.

"When your Uncle Clarence and I were in Hawaii, we became very fond of these little fish. You will note that they are preserved in wine. Do NOT!!! serve them with wine. Buy some *unsalted* crackers and serve them with very fine brandy, and *do* save them for special occasions."

The same box contained a large bottle labeled "Applejack"— which turned out to be the very fine brandy.

"Have been saving milk bottle tops for Fran. Enclosed are 56. They can be washed several times."

174

"The maid tells me that the hotel is throwing away a quantity of towels and sheets. Your Uncle Clarence and I find nothing wrong with them. After sheets tear, they can be made into pillowcases, and old towels can be cut up for washrags."

It is now fifty-three years later and we still have a few items of linen labeled *St. George Hotel*.

"A newspaper man—delightful, and a great admirer of Clarence— sent us some Russian caviar. Norman Thomas and Lillian Gish thought it perfectly delicious."

The package contained *eighteen* large tins of imported caviar.

"Do eat this little tin of tongue, smoked in wine, *all by yourselves!!!!!*"

"These little packages of cheeses come from a Norwegian acquaintance. Are you aware that your Uncle Burt believes that part of the Hamerstrom family came from Norway?" We ripped open one package of cheese, a little round box—and guzzled Gruyère—perfectly aged Gruyère. Then we opened a tin of caviar and I sliced some homemade bread. The first bite was delicious, but have you ever tried eating caviar without butter or margarine? We could afford neither.

Matter-of-factly I said, "Let's save the caviar for tonight's meat." I pulled frost-bitten leaves off an old cabbage head and cooked up the whitened inside leaves. Then I sorted out the food from Aunt Ruby's box and put it on the kitchen table. That sparkling display of luxuries must have cost at least $60—more than we earned in a month—and there was no way we could convert it to cash to buy potatoes.

After supper I picked up the milk bottle tops, sheets, shirts, and miscellany to put them away. An old hat, passed down from Aunt Ruby, was remarkably heavy. It was rolled around a large tin of pickled lamb's tongues. Then I took all the crinkly green paper out of the box to make sure that nothing had been missed.

There was one more item: a package of three bars of Pear's soap with a note wrapped around it, "Remember to visit Arthur Krock. He can help you in many ways. Fran can go too. Just tell him who you are." Aunt Ruby didn't need to spell it out: Frederick was to tell Mr. Krock— or whoever else was recommended to us—that he was Clarence Darrow's nephew. We never went to see any of these people; none of them were biologists.

Pear's is still my favorite soap.

Plenty of sunlight

We knew we were good at nest finding. When we had worked under Paul Errington in Iowa, we had proven it. We had found 503 pheasant nests. Now we tried the same techniques—searching methodically in likely looking terrain—and failed to turn up a single prairie chicken nest. Farmers found them while haying, foresters found them while tree-planting, but we couldn't find a single nest. We decided to change our tactics and mark down where the hens went after a successful copulation. Maybe they went straight to the vicinity of the nest site! But we didn't give up our old pheasant approach. We still walked the Leola Marsh looking for nests. Dragging a rope between us and the occasional use of a borrowed pointing dog were no more successful. We *never* found a nest.

The farmers, however, watched these goings-on with a great deal of tolerance. Sometimes they asked what we were doing, but more often they asked why we didn't have any children. We explained that in 1935 we had decided that the world, *including* the United States, was overpopulated and that we had decided to have only two children and to have them late in life. Our primitive contraceptives worked for nine years and then we deliberately discontinued using them. (One was a mixture of cocoa butter, quinine, and something else, brewed on the kitchen stove in tin cigarette boxes.)

One evening I made a dramatic announcement. "Darling, I think we are going to have a baby. My stomach feels all funny and bloated."

Frederick didn't even look up from the book he was reading. He just said, "So does mine."

I dismissed the whole idea, but I made a mark on the calendar.

Thirty-five days later I knew. After an especially hard, hot day in the field, I lay down on the blue sofa and announced, "We *are* going to have a baby!" I lay on the sofa waiting. The deep wisdom of my man still fascinates me. He didn't say a thing and didn't look up from his book.

I waited for him to come to fan me with a magazine, or to hold my hand and to murmur, "Are you all right?"

He did nothing of the sort. As far as I could tell he kept right on reading his damned book.

After what seemed about twenty minutes he remarked, "It's your turn to get the water."

We pumped the water into big, heavy milk cans and lugged them into the house. Ladies in a delicate condition were not even supposed to hang a picture!

Quivering with outrage and indignation, I lay on the sofa and glared. At last I got up and pumped all that water and carried it into the house. It was a turning point in our lives. I stayed on the sofa a long time before I got up and did it, but it was one of the best things that ever happened to me.

Motherhood was not going to smash a research team which lasted fifty-nine years.

Frederick's concern for me was not only psychological but also practical. He got Eddie Gordon, our family doctor, to refer me to the very best obstetrician in Madison. As it happened, Dr. M. was a "society-type doctor," unaccustomed to wildlife biologists.

The doctor examined me and said, "You are three months pregnant. Why didn't you come sooner?"

I didn't like to explain that when my stomach had felt all funny and bloated, Frederick and I had both attributed these symptoms to indigestion. I just hung my head.

Then I did some quick mathematics. "That means the baby will be born about *October!*"

October was right in the hunting season! Could unkind fate incapacitate me during the time of year we both most looked forward to? It didn't, but Dr. M. and I had no idea that my hunting season was safe and that I was about to be delivered of a ten-month baby—not a nine months' pregnancy, but *ten*.

Dr. M. said, "You'd better give up tennis."

Tennis flashed across my mind. My governess had taught me lawn tennis with the graceful underhand serve; then at Milton Academy I was taught the overhand serve; and then a new tennis instructor had come, the very year the Japanese were winning matches by shifting racquets from hand to hand. His first ambidextrous pupil sent him into transports, and he gave me a lot of lessons my parents never paid for!

Tennis was part of the world I'd left behind. I said only, "All right."

"But you may continue to play golf." Golf! That dull game that I'd been forced to play to be polite and to make up a foursome to oblige my father's old cronies!

Again I just said, "All right."

Dr. M. had not forbidden me to hunt ducks and prairie chickens; he had not forbidden me to climb trees to band hawks. I left well enough alone, even when he put me on a strict diet.

He appeared somewhat puzzled that I had not put up any arguments. He needed some sort of rebuttal to size up his patient. I can see his point. I think he—quite rightly—had the uneasy feeling that I was not trustworthy. He was right; if he had ordered me not to hunt, I would have disobeyed and said nothing.

He countered with an absolute rule: "I insist that you get plenty of sunlight." To tennis and golf I had not registered in the normal manner of his usual patients. "Do you *promise* me that you will get plenty of sunlight?"

"Yes."

This promise didn't give him much grief until I came in for a late summer checkup. I had spent many hours looking for prairie chicken nests and gathering vast quantities of blueberries, blackberries, and some raspberries. The country was wilder then and far more thinly populated. It was my custom to hang my dress from the handle of my berry basket so that I could slip it on quickly if I spotted somebody in the distance.

Dr. M. started with questions.

"Morning sickness?"

"No."

"Backache?"

"No."

"Discomfort?"

"I'm hungry all the time. If I were a cow, I'd be getting all I wanted to eat."

"A *cow?*" Dr. M. laid down his pen. "What's a cow got to do with it?"

I should have explained that Frederick and I had minored in veterinary medicine. Instead I spoke with simple authority. "Pregnant animals shouldn't be starved."

"You're not starved."

"I am. Ask Dr. Gordon."

Reluctantly Dr. M. called him in for consultation, and Eddie asked, "How much walking are you doing, Fran?"

"Ten to fifteen miles a day I suppose—maybe more." I handed Eddie my diet: four ounces of meat, one slice of toast, lettuce, tomatoes, and so forth. Eddie, bless him, suggested that I be taken off the diet entirely. He winked, shook hands with Frederick, and left.

Dr. M. hadn't needed to ask me whether or not I was getting plenty of sunlight. My face and neck and arms were so deeply tanned that my eyeballs showed strangely white. A nurse steered me into a little side room, told me to undress, slip into a stiff white garment, and lie on the table. Then she covered me with a sheet and departed. In a moment or two Dr. M. started his examination. There seemed to be something wrong with his breathing. He raised the sheet and the garment higher and higher. When he came to the white semicircles under my breasts he sputtered, "How do you feel?"

"Fine."

He pulled down the garment, replaced the sheet, and departed in haste.

Frederick, having had a look at the doctor's face, pushed his way past the nurse and asked, "Are you all right?"

"Yes, I don't know what's gotten into him."

I was getting a bit scared myself, and when Dr. M. arrived with another doctor, I studied the two worried faces and my alarm grew.

Then, suddenly, I knew exactly what was wrong: neither of these dear gentlemen had ever examined a white female patient who had spent essentially all summer out in the sun without clothes!

I started quivering and choking, which must have added to their alarm, but I was only trying to suppress my laughter. Then I tried to sit up to explain and was pushed firmly back down. It was very hard on all three of us. They must have thought that I had Addison's disease, and here I was trying to explain that I hung my dress on the handle of a basket. Perhaps they thought my mind was slipping too.

Finally I had to overcome my reticence and spell it out for them. "You said I was to get plenty of sunlight. I did. I went *naked!*"

Life will never be the same again
school of thought

Mrs. Leopold and her circle of friends very kindly invited me to attend meetings of The Reading Club—known irreverently by the younger generation as The Eating Club. I liked to go to their meetings and savored both the learning and the little cakes that were served afterwards.

As soon as The Reading Club discovered that I was expecting a baby, I was bombarded with advice, admonitions, and even commands:

You will have to give up your wild ways and tend to your baby.

You can no longer live up north in that unheated house.

You and Frederick must move to Madison; he can do the field work on weekends. You will find that a baby is a big responsibility and will take just about all your time.

All these delightful ladies had children. "*Unutterably depressing*" was my reaction to their comments.

I enumerated what I had learned from The Reading Club to Frederick on our way home to our beloved prairie chicken country.

He stopped me when I repeated, "You can no longer live up north. . . ."

"How about the Eskimos?"

Suddenly we were both laughing uproariously. We gave The Reading Club still another name: we called it *The Life Will Never Be the Same Again School of Thought.* Having given them a new name, we could reexamine their values. We were free.

In spring I had teetered on Frederick's sunburned shoulders for a "leg up" to band young red-tailed hawks. In summer I had tromped the marshes and meadows to look for prairie chicken nests and to gather winter stores of wild foods. And then when the leaves of the popples turned gold and the hunting season opened, we spent much of our time hunting.

180

It was always a disappointment to me that Frederick insisted that essentially every bird we killed had to be made into a museum specimen. To retain the best flavor of the rich, dark meat, prairie chickens, shot in the Lake States, are best roasted for a short time in a hot oven and *with the skin on.*

We had no idea how to tell which chickens had hatched the preceding spring and which were older. Aldo Leopold always came up to hunt chickens with us, and our hunting pattern did not change. We started early in the morning, flushed a flock from a grainfield, and followed it. Following a flock of prairie chickens is rather like following a big game animal: one learns its habits largely by reading sign. Shotgun in hand, we learned a great deal about their autumn habits.

At noon we cooked lunch, building a small fire and often just roasting meat over oak coals with an apple or two as a side dish. Then, if the day was pleasant, we basked on a sandbank and talked over various matters. Leopold unobtrusively led the discussion. "Why do prairie chickens undergo a ten-year cycle? Why does the population *crash* about every ten years and then come up again?

"We've got to understand the pulse of this phenomenon. Do they sometimes breed at an accelerated rate? Is the rate the same at low densities? Read Charles Elton. We must learn to count those chickens and find a way to distinguish between the young birds and the older ones. . . ."

Then we stamped out the ashes of our cook fire and hunted until

Frederick imitates the professor's stance.

dusk. We came back to our house in the pines. We drank whiskey out of tin cups and I cooked supper. The fire popped and crackled and then died down. We talked. Aldo reiterated. "Count those chickens. Get counts of the winter flocks."

"But we counted and trapped a winter flock of thirty and kept trapping and caught thirty more," I interjected.

Frederick simply said, "Aldo, it appears to me that winter is the worst possible time to count chickens. If we want to learn what is happening here, we must count in spring."

"Well, they've got to be counted."

Aldo in the handsome tweed hunting garb he always wore, leaned across my kitchen table to add, "And remember production. Can you distinguish between birds for the year and old birds yet?"

With Aldo's admonition in mind I went out to get specimens to see if I could find a way to tell the young birds from the old. I was collecting, which is not as much fun as hunting—the ulterior motive subtly subverts hunting to "work." At any rate I spotted a prairie chicken sitting on top of a haystack in a farmyard. I sneaked up on it, never suspecting that I was being watched. Gun in hand I crawled on all fours through a muddy puddle not unvisited by cows, between the house and the barn.

When I got close enough I let fly with my shotgun, a Parker 20-gauge; and my prize slid slowly down the haystack and landed on its back.

The farmer roared from his doorway. At first I didn't quite catch what he was yelling. He shouted, "Nice shot!" Then he added, "Come in and have a cup of coffee."

Chicken in hand, my gun at rest in the crook of my arm, I walked toward the doorstep.

"Didn't know it was a lady!"

I felt it my duty to explain the difference between collecting and hunting and I wanted to explain that I would never shoot any bird in such an unsporting manner except for collecting, but I was "outnumbered" by the joyous enthusiasm of one farmer. ". . . belly-crawled all the way from the gate. That chicken didn't have a *chance*." Hunting was different in those days.

It was at about this time that I remembered how Harry Pry, an old Scottish gamekeeper, had taught me the way to kill upland game birds so they would pluck easily. "Bite them in the head, right back of both ears, and it relaxes their feathers so they just fall off."

We didn't want the feathers to fall off the chickens, because we

182

wanted to make museum skins of them. But it gave such a quick easy death that I bit a few heads and discovered something very interesting: birds of the year "bit easily" and older birds had tough, entirely resistant skulls. Long before other techniques were worked out, we had found a way to age prairie chickens.

We soon set up the Hamerstrom free plucking service: "for *nothing* we will pluck your prairie chickens and get them oven-ready." We drove around the marsh and wherever we found hunters who had been successful, we made our sales pitch. We didn't study the hunters carefully; we just tried to make sure that we could get our hands on their birds. The hunters, I later learned, studied us with some amazement. They watched us sort out the chickens by sex according to feather pattern; and then they watched me pluck each bird, eviscerate it, look at the gonads, and hand Frederick the crop and gizzard. Of course we were not plucking those birds for *nothing:* we wanted information on age, food habits, parasites, and such things. Frederick told the hunters what we were doing and why—in part to keep them entertained while they waited for me to finish plucking.

After the material we wanted was safely in labeled paper bags, there came a moment when I had to interrupt, "You don't mind if I bite their heads do you?"

I don't believe a single hunter answered me with a clear-cut, "Yes, go right ahead." Many gave the impression that they had not correctly heard what I had said! Nobody said, "No," so whatever sounds they made after I posed the question, I went right ahead and bit heads. The birds lay in a row on the ground and Frederick had the paper bags ready in the same order. I glanced quickly at each bird to make sure my bite would come just back of the ears and called out my results, "Bit easy . . . bit easy . . . hard . . . shot-up (can't use that one) . . . bit easy . . . bit easy, no, let me get this one again. Darling, it bit easy, but it seems harder than most of the young birds. Maybe it hatched earlier?" Frederick recorded the information on each bag. Later we found more scientific-looking ways of determining age.

Later, in fact many years later, old prairie chicken hunters still would come up to me, waggling a finger gleefully in my face, "I know you. You're the one that bit them heads!"

Dental floss

We hunted hard and checked other hunters' birds day after day. In the evenings we worked the bars in a nearby town. Frederick took those on one side of the street and I took the other. Successful hunters, as well as the unsuccessful, sat on barstools and told stories in the evenings. To get our hands on more specimens, we listened to separate the former from the latter and then offered the Hamerstrom free plucking service. It was a lot less work for a hunter to get up and open the trunk of his car and let us get his birds oven-ready than to take them home and have to do the job himself. Some hunters just handed me their car keys and said, "Go ahead."

Frederick detested working the bars. There is something about his kindly face and manner that attracts drunks like flies to a jampot. They put their arms around his shoulders, some even weep; and they tell him the sad story of their lives. Not letting go of his shoulders, they weave to and fro, and my delightful husband has never found a way of extricating himself.

Never in all my life have I encountered anyone with such a strong sense of duty as Frederick. No matter how unpleasant, distasteful, or boring an undertaking may be, his conscience forces him to finish it or do it again if the *work* requires that it be done. I'm better at visiting sick aunts and things like that. And I'm better at visiting bars.

I found the bars fun. Innumerable beery gents and some perfectly sober ones offered me drinks and sometimes, when all the birds had been bitten, robbed of their crops and gizzards, and returned neatly to the cars, I accepted a drink—not beer but a glass of port—and joined in the hunting yarns myself.

Each evening, after we had worked the bars, we looked for each other. The main street of Hancock was only a little over a block long, so this was not much of a problem. If Frederick found me first, he was apt to find me listening to some old hunter with rapt attention, "Got three in one shot; two fell into the willows, and I just wung the other. Spot," the hunter stroked the undistinguished head of a large mongrel at his feet, "this here's Spot. He's got dog sense; he went for the wung one first!"

"The wung one?"

"Yeah, just shot in the wing. I wung it."

The hunter looked around the room appreciatively and spotted Frederick.

"This must be your hubby! Come and have a drink. Your wife has been telling us the most interestin' stories."

Much as I wanted to stay, I knew it was impossible. Frederick had given me a look: it was time to go home. In fact it was time to get out right quick because a big farmer, deep in his cups, was already weaving his way directly toward my "hubby" to tell him all his teary troubles.

"Whoops!" I shouted. "We've got to get back and feed." I ran for the door, and Frederick, trying to give thanks for the proffered drink, was forced to cut them short in order to keep up with me.

We drove home in very different moods. After a while Frederick asked, "What are we going to feed?"

"Ourselves, I suppose." Frederick looked puzzled. "People will always let you go if you say, 'I gotta feed.' I was just trying to help you get out of there. You didn't want to *stay*, did you?"

"Good God no!"

The baby had been expected the last week in September, and October was already upon us. With some justice I might have pleaded my delicate condition, but such a softy approach never even entered my mind.

Frederick saw to it that the car always had plenty of gas each evening in case I should give a night alarm. After all, the doctor was 100 miles away. We continued with our normal and rather strenuous lives.

One day, just as a long string of geese passed over the marsh, I felt a little pain in my stomach and looked at my watch to note the time. Labor pains were supposed to start at twenty-minute intervals. The geese flew northwest and way out of sight. Then two mallards dropped into a ditch only about a half a mile away. When I got to the spot I'd marked down along the ditch bank, one flushed wild; I dropped the other right in the water: a fine greenhead to add to our meager larder.

My tennis shoes had come untied retrieving the duck, so I stopped at the top of the ditch bank to retie the laces. It was awkward to reach down to my foot. To my surprise Frederick, who was some distance away, drove the car right across the meadow and straight to where I was. "Are you all right?" he asked anxiously.

"Yes." I held up my dripping duck.

"You were in such an odd position. I thought the baby was coming. Let's settle on a signal," he continued. "When you think it's time to head for Madison, fire *three* equally spaced shots."

We agreed on this. Not until the rabbit season opened did he hear three equally spaced shots, and that time it was just rabbit hunters.

Frederick started carrying sterile dental floss in his pocket fearing he might have to deliver the baby and tie off its umbilical cord all by himself. After all it had been due in September. October had passed, and it was now *November!*

On November 8 we hunted ducks all day, then I helped carry in firewood for the winter and cooked supper. It was during supper that I had my first inkling that something might be about to happen. Unobtrusively, I put the kitchen clock where I could see it easily and marked down times on a piece of scratch paper. About forty minutes later I exclaimed "We go!"

We started getting into city clothes. Having waded in peat most of the day—in jeans because I had no way of fastening my hip boots to a belt—I considered taking a bath and then decided against it because it took so long to heat up the bath water. I put on a skirt and pulled on some heavy, "service-weight" stockings.

About two and a half hours later I was sitting on the edge of a hospital bed begging a nurse to let me take a bath.

"No, Mrs. Hamerstrom. I hardly think that will be necessary."

I pulled down one stocking and the nurse disappeared with dispatch. She returned a moment later with a nurse wearing a different sort of cap—who took one look at my legs and said, "Mrs. Hamerstrom, if you feel up to it you may have a shower immediately."

Alan's birth certificate states under "duration of pregnancy": ten months. It wasn't until Elva was born two years later that I realized that normal babies can look like embryo witches with red, puckered, disorganized faces, long fingernails, and unearthly black hair on their heads.

Alan looked like a cover photo on the *Ladies' Home Journal* with well-formed features and creamy, attractive skin. First, I took off his diaper to ascertain his sex for myself. Then I kissed the top of his head and started licking him. It was good. When Elva arrived, I was robbed of one of the joys of motherhood. Elva's skin tasted of some sort of medicinal soap.

It is a great pity that our research at the time our children were babies was on birds, rather than on mammals. I learned a few interesting things about mammals, but I wasn't really tuned in. I did have an opportunity to notice something about suckling rhythm, in spring when we were planting a long row of white pines to celebrate Alan's birth. One day when Frederick and I were slit-planting, I let my shovel slip from my hand and just walked back to the house without offering any explanation whatsoever. It was simply time to nurse my baby, and the signal from my body had been just as accurate and strong as if an alarm clock had gone off in my pocket.

When Elva was born, I was in the hospital exactly three days. She was wheeled into my room in some sort of a baby buggy with a squeaking wheel. I paid no attention to the squeaking wheel at the time and simply chafed because hospitals separated mother and baby except for the brief periods of nursing.

At the end of three days I returned home. Alan had a little toy cart that he liked to pull along the floor. A wheel of the cart squeaked and that squeak could set my milk to flowing—or if Elva heard it first, it set her to crying. Sometimes I think "civilization" is a bit nutty.

Fran and Elva.

Do you want to go to Africa?

Our house in the pines was not a bad place to bring up a baby. We could bank the fire in the wood stove so it would last all night. Country houses have cold floors and—as heat rises—any heated room is warmer up near the ceiling. We hung a thermometer on the edge of the baby basket, and raised or lowered the basket; so the baby, at least, would enjoy the right temperature most of the time.

There were other problems. Frederick had already put off getting his Ph.D. for a year so we could continue, with our stipend of $50 a month, to work on prairie chickens, but both of us knew that we couldn't live forever on this salary—cutting popple poles to make trap frames, making our own netting out of string, and going to burned-down houses to look for old nails to straighten, to hammer prairie chicken traps together. Now that there were three of us, it was time to get a "pay job" . . . and there were no prairie chicken jobs available.

Most especially, there was no job that could keep us working on the chicken population we had worked on so long, so in the spring of 1941 Frederick accepted a secure position as curator of the Edwin S. George Reserve, a division of the Museum of Zoology of the University of Michigan . . . with freedom to work on anything we wanted to. Frederick stipulated that he wanted to take his vacation in the hunting season, and Mr. Gaige, director of the museum—somewhat puzzled—acquiesced. We had a surprise in store: not only were there to be vacations, but *expeditions* as well. In March, Mr. Gaige proposed to Frederick that he might want to go on an expedition for a month or so.

Frederick's answer was prompt and enthusiastic. "Oh, *yes,* could we go in April? That would be just right; we need to continue our count of the prairie chickens on the Leola Marsh in Wisconsin." We went, and our baby spent much of his time in upside-down prairie chicken traps instead of a playpen, or in the back of the car, which we had fixed up for him.

Just a year later Mr. Gaige again raised the question of going on an expedition, but this time he made his intention quite clear, "Would you like to go to South America? Or perhaps Africa?"

Frederick admitted that we would love to go to Africa, but stated that it was of the utmost urgency to return to the Leola Marsh to count chickens. Mr. Gaige agreed, but it was plain that South America—or Timbuktu—would have pleased him more.

By the third spring, World War II had started. Africa was out of the question. Mr. Gaige told us where to apply for a permit to get gasoline to go on a "scientific expedition" to Wisconsin.

Alan, our inquisitive two-year-old, had outgrown playpens. Our neighbors, "Uncle Warren" and "Aunt Ethel," would keep him while we were away. That settled, we went to the courthouse to apply for the permit. The long flight of courthouse steps had me puffing and I was wearing Frederick's old plaid shirt—my "maternity smock."

The man giving out permits was neither friendly nor unfriendly.

"Scientific expedition?"

"Yes."

He wrote this down. "To Wisconsin?"

"Yes."

Again the pencil filled in a blank on the form.

"Personnel and equipment: how many of you will be going?"

Frederick and I answered simultaneously.

Frederick said, "Two," but I said, "Three." I gave Frederick a sharp kick in the shin and repeated, "*Three.*"

"Equipment?"

"Yes, traps and blinds."

He shoved the paper toward Frederick and said, "Sign this."

Frederick signed it unhappily. As soon as we were out of earshot, he demanded, "What made you say *three?* You know Alan will be staying with Aunt Ethel."

"I know, but there's a better chance of getting gas with three going."

Frederick spoke in anger, "What got into you? There'll be *two.* Just you and me."

We stood on the courthouse steps and argued. "I'm going back to change it to two. I won't sign my name to a lie."

"But, darling, it won't be a lie. Did you forget that we'll have the next baby before we leave!"

Lumbago

The war years and to a large degree the five years in southern Michigan separated us from our chickens. Try as we might, we couldn't forget that in central Wisconsin lay a wilder, more untamed country and that we wanted to work on prairie chickens more than anything else in the world.

In 1949 we pulled up stakes and left a modern rent-free house and a secure job. I have always been impressed that Frederick, with two small children to support, had the courage to quit when he felt he should.

We wanted to work together, but most administrators were afraid to hire a female biologist. After weeks of job hunting a telegram came. The Wisconsin Conservation Department wanted a prairie chicken biologist and would hire *me* too! So we found and fixed up another abandoned farmhouse—a big house with a ballroom that had never been finished because the boys had to go away to fight in the Civil War!

All this was extraordinary luck. Our next stroke of luck was, I'm sorry to say, the misfortune of a neighbor.

The lumbago of John Rozner may have altered our whole lives. John lived in the far north end of our study area some twenty miles from our house. Little did we dream that the miserable pain in his lower back in the autumn would cause us to make a record catch of prairie chickens.

Pain caused him to stay indoors as much as possible, and he just couldn't manage to harvest his corn. The shocks stood in the field ready to harvest, and then the snows came—the deep, deep snows came and prairie chickens congregated. They were hungry and consumed the corn from the outsides of the shocks until there was practically nothing left for them to eat.

The vast number of hungry prairie chickens trying to eke out an existence in the Rozner corn made us realize that we were dealing with a pack! Packing is a phenomenon that the early settlers described in various imaginative ways, and perhaps my description is imaginative

190

too. It seems to be the result of a "snowballing" effect: young chickens stay near their mothers until about September, then these family units merge and are joined by miscellaneous cocks to make flocks of thirty or so, which hang together. Sometimes, but not every winter, the flocks merge and form *packs*. Packs may consist of two or three hundred birds. When flushed from corn stubble, they zoom out of the field like bees from a hive; they circle and take off in a great body heading away over the popple woods, the marshes, and the farmlands.

The Rozner pack was plainly a most unusual opportunity. Four of us undertook to trap it: Frederick and I and Os and Mary Mattson. We moved traps by trailer—about eight at a time.

Finally, we had hauled forty-eight traps from stations miles away and made our biggest set to date. It was perfect timing—food supply almost exhausted and birds still coming in to feed. Actually, I have a hunch that the Rozner station was a turning point in our skill as trappers and in our efficiency as biologists. I shudder to think how often we had just placed a trap or two wherever we saw chicken tracks. The morning catch on March 13, 1950, was good, but the afternoon catch shortly before sundown was almost more than we could handle.

We had considered two bags of birds—five per bag—a good catch heretofore. Now we kept running back to the truck for another bag, and still another. Os and Mary and Frederick and I rushed from trap to trap in the gathering dusk, and when night fell we found ourselves shouting to each other, "Have you got all the *bags* of birds?!"

Prairie chicken is removed from trap.

No more than five chickens per bag.

The bird is weighed and banded.

The banded chicken is released.

193

We processed that big catch and then, weary and ecstatic, we drove home to light the fire in the big stove and warm up the stew. It had been a good day.

Normal operating procedure was rather different. Ordinarily we each ran a trapline about thirty miles long, twice a day. We covered as much ground as we could by car and snowshoed the rest. For some obscure reason it took us awhile to realize that big catches are often made during a thaw, rather than when the temperature is really low. However, it didn't take us long to learn that when the temperature drops right after a thaw and your clothes get wet, you get colder than you do in powdery snow.

That first year I had my own car, a used and battered telephone repairman's truck; and I made a pretty good catch alone. The rules of the project were in one respect inflexible. Never handle a chicken with gloves. Take off your mittens and use your bare hands. And there is good reason for this. The feathers of their drumsticks come off very easily; it was just common sense not to release bare-legged birds in the dead of winter. Bare fingers don't pull feathers out.

My catch was not enormous, but the thaw had just turned to a good sharp freeze and my wet hands had taken a bit more cold than I realized. I could hardly wait to get into the cab of my truck with the bags of birds, start the motor, and warm up. My teeth chattered, and my soggy clothes increased what we now call the chill factor. Thank heavens we'd never heard that demoralizing expression in those days!

I put the bags of birds on the floor of the cab and tried to turn the key to start the motor but my fingers couldn't manage to move it, so I slipped both hands inside my clothes next to the skin of my stomach and waited. I tried again, but I couldn't seem to get my thumb and index finger to meet. I almost got the wind up. How often had I been told that one small mistake in cold weather can be the end of the line? I couldn't get my mouth down to turn the key, but after several tries I managed to turn it by using the knuckles of my index and middle fingers. The motor burst into a satisfactory roar. I processed the birds and went home to tell Frederick of my adventure. He examined my hands with concern. Suddenly, with all ten fingers working again, it didn't seem such a close shave anymore.

Packs of prairie chickens tend to attract predators. When hawks and owls behold traps full of prairie chickens, they make repeated attacks, causing the chickens to thrash about and injure themselves.

194

Occasionally during the skirmish, the talons of a large raptor nail a chicken right through the netting.

We finally learned to cope. But for several winters, whenever we ran into this sort of trouble, we just gave up and moved the traps to another station. Just one hawk or owl, weighing less than four pounds, could force us to lug hundreds of pounds of equipment out of a good station. As we were generally trapping in somebody else's cornfield, we carried bags of our own corn to bait the traps with. Carrying corn into a cornfield is better than being accused of stealing. Os is an enormously powerful man, and I remember carrying four bags of corn—which is heavy—into a faraway cornfield with him, as well as twelve traps. It took several trips on snowshoes. I took one end of each load and he took the other, and I prided myself on not suggesting that we stop and rest. And then, when we had a goodsized trapping station baited and set, we found a snowy owl working that pack. The next day we moved all the traps out again. By mutual consent we didn't carry the bait back out too.

Most of the farmers soon respected us, for we worked at all sorts of odd hours. We knew that the worse the weather was, the better our catches were apt to be. And we always seemed to be hurrying. One farmer, mystified after watching Frederick and me set up a station, asked, "Is anybody *timing* you?"

We felt that the farmers really had it hard, having to milk cows every single day and night, and they thought we had it hard, working outside in all weathers. They were good to us, and we sometimes planned the end of the trapline so we could stop in and get warm in somebody else's kitchen before going home to our own cold house.

But one farmer had me really scared. Frederick dropped me off to pick up a catch, while he drove on to the next station. It was getting late in the day and we were behind schedule. I snowshoed into the cornfield where a huge farm dog was working our traps. He had already killed two chickens and was after more of the same kind of excitement. I got the birds out of the traps and put them into bags, at which point the dog decided that he wanted to bite *me*. It is very hard to do anything at all when holding two fluttering bags of chickens over one's head out of reach of a serious dog, and even harder to kick the dog away when encumbered by snowshoes on both feet. Snowshoes are considerably bigger than tennis racquets, and you can kick just once. After the kick there is no way of getting the snowshoe back onto the ground, and the only alternative is to fall down. If I kicked once and failed to intimidate that enormous dog, he had a chance at me sitting helpless in the deep snow. Furthermore, my main aim was to protect the prairie chickens in the two bags I was holding above my head. Prairie chickens weigh about two pounds apiece, and I had to snowshoe back to safety holding some twenty-two fluttering pounds above my head.

The dog was a bit off base out in the cornfield. I yelled and shouted orders at him like, "Lie down," and "Get out of here." I didn't dare shout, "Go home," because that is just where I was heading! I was heading for *his* home where Frederick was going to meet me.

Somehow I managed to get to the farmhouse, and the dog didn't really bite me until I was almost at the door. Somewhat frantically I banged on the door and was let in. I didn't like the looks of the place, and I didn't like the looks of the man who had let me in. I figured that was no place for a young woman to be: the choice was inside with the man or outdoors with the dog and my precious chickens.

"Your dog bit me," I said accusingly.

"Never bites nobody."

I laid the bags of chickens on his floor and drew up a leg of my wool pants. There was a good-sized rent in the pants and enough blood on my tender pale skin to convince anyone that his dog really had bitten me. But I hadn't helped my cause. He didn't seem to be looking at the wound. That lonely old man—I suppose now that he was about forty—looked at a graceful feminine leg suddenly exposed right in his kitchen and he leered.

The next half hour or so I was nasty. Good and frightened, but nasty. He tried to pat my hand and I yelled, "How dare you keep a dog like that! Wait till my husband comes and see what he says!"

I had visions of his chasing me round and round his kitchen table like a villain in a 1920 movie. Now that I look back on it, I still don't know how matters would have turned out if Frederick hadn't "saved me" by knocking on the door. I probably panicked too soon, but I wasn't used to visiting strange men with a three-day growth of stubble on their faces and having them call me "Dearie."

Don't you move a muscle

Ordinarily one writes a lot of letters to solicit help when something has gone *wrong*. In the spring of 1950 we were faced with a major crisis because everything had gone so well. We, with the help of Os and Mary Mattson, had put numberd colored bands on 298 prairie chickens! There was no earthly way that three project members, even with Mary's help, could possibly cover all the booming grounds on the study area to see where the winter-banded birds might turn up.

A few graduate students and friends had helped us in spring for years when we were on our first shoestring study, but this was the Big Time. We needed more eyes to read band numbers. I put ten thin pieces of paper and nine thin sheets of carbon paper into the typewriter and wrote a sort of "To whom it may concern" letter. It ran something like this: "Dear——, We have an emergency. We have banded so many prairie chickens that we need help. Come if you can. We live in an ancient, somewhat primitive farmhouse without modern conveniences, but we have lots of room and, if need be, can supply food."

I ran this communication, complete with nine carbon copies, through the typewriter several times, stuffed the letters into 3-cent envelopes and mailed them to just about everybody I could think of who might come.

Over 100 people came. One flew in from New York and stayed six weeks. People came in trucks and Cadillacs, they arrived on motorcycles, and two boys hitchhiked from Illinois.

At any rate, there was never again a need to *invite* anybody to come and help with the prairie chickens: the word was out that it was exciting, demanding, and an experience not to be missed.

I agreed. I wanted everybody to get a chance to watch the prairie chickens boom; there is nothing like it.

Frederick agreed too, but he soon said, "I don't want more than ten observers at a time, and I want the best ones at the peak of the season when the hens come in."

Another bunch of boomers.

Little by little I developed a fair knack for segregating the best observers from the others: professional wildlifers tended to be very good, veterans of World War II were better than bird-watchers, high schoolers were mostly too young; and some ancient individuals of both sexes, wearing trifocals, kept good notes and read bands accurately.

On the other hand, not all presidents of big companies had a knack for reading bands and one gentleman, Allen Slichter, was membership chairman of the Society of Tympanuchus Cupido Pinnatus, one of the foundations to save prairie chickens. He flatly stated, "I'll get you plenty of the right sort of members, but I absolutely refuse to get up early in the morning to get into one of those blinds to watch the prairie chickens." His contributions to the Society were invaluable.

In some respects the Society of Tympanuchus Cupido Pinnatus reminds me of President Truman's daughter's wedding: she invited only 600 intimate friends!

(Not everybody can get into the Society. Somewhat diffidently, but eager to buy more land for the prairie chickens, I once proposed a chap who was said to have lots of money, but gangster connections. My suggestion was turned down with a resounding "No.")

But I digress from the selection of good observers for peak seasons. They were selected in January each year. People had asked for

198

booming season dates throughout the year, so I soon let it be known that reservations would not be made earlier. In January I placed a large calendar on my work table and sorted out the letters. (I always felt rather a fraud, as the calendar was still empty.) I started with Mrs. G., whose daughter-in-law has a hummingbird feeder, and who is looking for a home for her darling kittens, and who wants to come. Her stationery is pink and strongly scented (prairie chickens can't smell) and she says she would like to bring a camera.

"Hum," I said to myself, looking at the calendar. "She is plainly old, or she wouldn't have a daughter-in-law, and I'm not at all sure that she can take cold weather well. It would be heartless to put her into late March or early April. Making observations in early May is not apt to be demanding." I write:

> Dear Mrs. G.,
>   Fortunately we have an opening on May 4 and would be delighted to have you come to watch the prairie chickens and help with our observations. Please bring a sleeping bag, warm clothes, and hip boots. We will expect you at 7:30 P.M. on May 3. Please let me know promptly if this is not satisfactory.

That accomplished, I write "Mrs. G." on the calendar. The first "boomer" of the season has been assigned.

The next letter is from the chief of the Research Section of the Wisconsin Conservation Department, our own bunch. I don't even have to think. They are the very best, and I put them down for April 19–20, the most important dates of the season.

Bill Brooks wants to bring a class from Ripon. He brought an unruly city-type boy once, but only once. I check the calendar again. April 17 and 18 are also important dates.

Then I pull out a scribbled note: "Fran, I have a bunch of Cub Scouts and I really want them to see the chickens." Harry Croy has conned me into letting children in again. He is a good Scout leader, and kids can take the cold well.

> Dear Harry,
>   You and your scouts may come on April 2. They will need plenty of warm clothes. Tell them it's going to be colder than sitting in a duck blind.

So it went. Year after year I wrote personal letters to each applicant.

Mrs. G. came and was much younger than I expected a mother-in-law to be and also far plumper than I had envisioned her. She arrived the year that we had a pet flying squirrel.

Dan Berger, the new project assistant, our daughter Elva, and I had captured a flying squirrel coming out of a hole in a popple, and I'm sure we only managed to catch her because she was a bit slow and very pregnant.

She gave birth to young in Berger's mother's garage. One of the young squirrels grew up in our house. This endearing pet was terrified of company. It had several hiding places and it was always at home on a member of the household, to whom it could glide from tops of doors or bookcases to hide beneath a warm shirt.

Mrs. G. came earlier than she was supposed to. As it happened I was cooking supper and I saw her legs cross the cracked, tilting cement of our back stoop: well-turned calves and somewhat swollen ankles in nylon stockings. She was short and wearing high heels.

She knocked on the back door and I continued frying onions with canned tomatoes to pour over the hamburgers, for the hungry crew was assembling. I just shouted, "Come in."

Mrs. G. opened the door with that falsely timid smile that most of us put on when nobody welcomes us correctly at the door of a strange house. After that everything happened quickly.

Mrs. G. took one step into the kitchen. The flying squirrel, atop the kitchen cabinet, panicked at the sound—or possibly the scent—of a stranger. Mrs. G. felt a rat-sized mammal scrabble down the front of her pink knit dress and claw its way inside her bra.

Mrs. G. yelped, then screamed. She started to beat and claw at her chest with both hands. Berger and Socha, both sturdy outdoor men with big black beards, jumped to save the squirrel. Mrs. G. felt herself seized and pinned against the door of the refrigerator. When she was satisfactorily immobilized, Berger, who was wearing a hideous pair of yellow sunglasses that made his six foot three inches

even more sinister, commanded, "Stand perfectly still. Don't you move a muscle."

Berger has a way with animals. I stopped cooking and got him half a pecan. He tightened his grip on Mrs. G.'s shoulder, roughly commanding, "Don't you dare move." Suddenly his voice was gentle. "It's OK." He made soft clucking noises by gently clicking his tongue against the roof of his mouth and simultaneously he tapped the base of Mrs. G.'s throat with the pecan. "Cluck, cluck, cluck, tap, tap, tap." In a moment the squirrel scratched its way upward and dove inside Berger's shirt with the pecan.

Leaving Mrs. G. to her own devices in the vicinity of the refrigerator, we all followed Berger into the living room and watched anxiously as he checked the squirrel over for possible injuries.

At last I went back to my cooking. Mrs. G. was still standing by the refrigerator, holding on to it with one hand.

"It's all right," I said pouring tomato and onion sauce over the hamburger. "You didn't hurt it at all."

The following January I received a nice letter from Mrs. G.—again on pink, scented paper. "Please give me a date to watch the prairie chickens and if not too inconvenient for you, I would like to bring two friends."

Harry's Cub Scouts

Essentially everything we did was connected with the prairie chickens—but not quite everything: we were never able to squelch our interest in the birds of prey. Officially, Frederick was working full time for the Conservation Department, but I supposedly worked only 60% of the time so if the children came down with measles or something of the sort I would have plenty of time to nurse them. Actually we worked almost every waking hour, but my 40% free time gave my conscience a rest when I went loping about the marsh catching and banding hawks and owls. I always figured if I wanted to spend my free time playing bridge, it was my right to do so, and if I happened to prefer trapping hawks, that too was my right. The department more than got its money's worth from me.

I did, however, have to be careful about public relations. To put it more simply: it was up to me to avoid criticism. In those days hawks and owls were considered "vermin." It would have been better public relations to catch them and wring their necks than to put bands on them and let them go. At that time Portage County still paid a bounty on marsh hawks, which had been protected by the state for some time.

My solution was to keep a low profile. I hid my traps from the public, and when I went to check them I ambled across the meadows as though going nowhere special, when I really wanted to run to see if I'd made a catch. I also took advantage of just about any quick opportunity to catch a hawk.

One day when I was driving home after moving blinds from one booming ground to another, I spotted a red-tailed hawk perched on the far side of a pasture. The gate was open, so without a moment's hesitation I swung into the meadow and reached simultaneously for a baited trap. It's not too bad to drive on a frozen pasture without permission, but to my dismay my wheels cut through the sod; a low spot lay directly in my way and I gunned the motor to ram the car through without getting stuck. Mud and sod hurtled on either side of the car. First the front wheels hit a depression and then the rear wheels fell into the hole and stopped. It would take a tractor to get me out. The redtail was long gone. Dejectedly, I walked to the nearest farm for help.

The farmer was very pleasant, until he found out *whose* field I was stuck in. The trail of destruction left by my tracks on the field was beyond belief. He hitched up a chain and pulled my car out backwards. And the huge treads of his tractor almost dwarfed the damage I had done.

"Look at that! Just look what you've done!"

I picked up a sod in my bare hands and placed it carefully back in a rut. This pitiful attempt to right matters caused him to ask me one more anguished question before he drove away. "Who's going to put all that back?"

"I am. I'll see that it's done."

Such a silly statement depressed him more than ever.

"I *promise*. I promise it will be all right by noon tomorrow."

I thought I heard a little snort before the roar of the tractor motor drowned out further conversation. He didn't believe me.

Harry Croy has an absolute flair for breaking rules at the right time. Not only did he bring those Cub Scouts, but he brought more of them than we expected—and he brought them the only time I really needed them.

Shortly before noon the following day the farmer, who was "just going by," stopped his tractor. The field must have seemed covered with small, gnome-like children busily patting down the remaining little unevennesses with their little hands. The field I had desecrated was now again a smooth, even green.

He watched for quite awhile and then he turned his tractor around and drove back home.

He had something to tell his wife.

The funnel trap and boop, boop, boop

Even present-day research projects sometimes fall flat on their faces because the investigators haven't the foggiest notion how to catch and mark the animals they are working on.

Aldo Leopold used to say trapping seems to lie in the blood. Our blood was that of seafarers. Frederick's ancestors were Vikings, and I am said to be a direct descendant of Captain Flint, the pirate. Maybe both our ancestors illegally captured lovely ladies from foreign ships, but this hardly seems the best inheritance for knowing how to trap the wily prairie hen—especially as the cocks are easier to catch.

Sometimes, when rather shy neighbors drop in and conversation becomes difficult, Frederick and I argue with some gusto which is better: his Vikings or my pirates. It tends to break the ice. We avoid the discussion of trapping. Once a trapping discussion is started we simply forget that anyone else is in the house.

We have built hundreds of traps and devised and/or modified dozens of designs. We have caught more prairie chickens in funnel traps than in any other device. At first we tried the then standard tall and narrow funnels, and the prairie chickens walked in and out of them as though they were doors made specially for entrance *and* exit. Broad, sloppy funnels made of unreinforced chicken wire were far better than the standard, tidy, rigid funnels we first devised. Once a prairie chicken is caught and has eaten its cropful of bait, it tends to walk the edge of the inside of the trap, now and again trying to get out through the soft netting with which the trap is covered. Round and round they go and, in theory, each time they come to a funnel they walk up over it. Soft, floppy, unreinforced funnels soon mash down so that they work like self-shutting doors.

Of course we had read the old books and articles in *Forest and Stream* to learn how to trap chickens. The old-timers had found trapping so easy that our industrious efforts were put to shame. They often used a tip-top trap, set in a cornfield, and they had to empty it frequently. This sounded like an easy method for getting the winter's meat supply, and surely we could adapt it for banding.

It is great fun to watch a prairie chicken land on top of the trap, prepared to eat ear corn, and watch him slide unwillingly down into the trap. He can't take off and fly as he cannot possibly regain his footing; his footing is falling away from him every time his feet, more or less running backward, add to the speed of his descent into the trap. In less than a minute he is inside and the counterweight has moved the top of the trap back up, ready for the next innocent bird.

What wasn't fun was that we couldn't tack the netting onto the trap loosely enough so that the birds wouldn't injure themselves occasionally. To solve this problem, we covered the traps with burlap, knowing that chickens would not struggle in the dark. This innovation ran afoul too. The slightest bit of wind caused the traps to drift solid full of snow. We soon learned that the real trick was not just to catch birds, but to catch them without hurting them.

What we learned from the old books about trapping was simply irritating. What we learned from them about the temperament of prairie chickens was utterly frustrating.

My envy borders on rage whenever I look at a picture of prairie chickens happily sitting about on the backs of chairs in the kitchen of an early settler, while some woman in a long skirt stirs a pot on the stove. I want to be that woman! Frederick is perfectly content observing wild animals (preferably individually marked) in their natural state. I am not.

My mind has an ethological bent and I wanted to live with prairie chickens as companions. I wanted them to come when I called, but in general I wanted them to have their being quite naturally—indoors and out—without their paying any particular attention to me. I have managed such relationships with eagles, hawks, owls, mice, squirrels, foxes, raccoons and—with some degree of success—with green herons.

When a storm is about to burst, it is not uncommon for various creatures to scratch on doors or sit on window sills waiting to be let *into* our house. No prairie chicken has even indicated that it wanted this privilege.

I realized that my best chance to tame prairie chickens was to start with newly hatched chicks, and Frederick gave me every possible opportunity to acquire some. Each time we found a nest that had been doomed by a mowing machine, I held the eggs close to the skin next to my stomach while Frederick drove me swiftly to the nearest setting domestic hen, or—more often—back to our house. Hatchability of prairie chicken eggs is excellent; those chicks are determined to come out of the shell. I have even brought off a hatch in the oven of our old kerosene stove with the burners turned way down. And later, after we put in electricity, I got a little incubator, and brought off another splendid hatch of fine, lively chicks. They followed me about on the lawn, and my happiness was so great that I could barely leave them long enough to cook for the family.

They didn't seem to want to eat much, so I put them in a nice warm container with plenty of light and offered wild strawberries, grated egg yolk, and hundreds of living insects.

Prairie chickens differ from domestic chickens in the way they rear their young. The domestic hen tends to lead her brood, and the chicks watch her pick at this and that. They appear to follow her example. The prairie hen, on the other hand, keeps her chicks from getting too far apart by calling them from time to time, but other than that it is my impression that her young are out of control in that they eat what they please and learn to do it all by themselves by trial and error.

The prairie chicks I hatched in an incubator had no sense for eating anything. They followed me after a fashion, came when I called, "Boop, boop, boop," but they almost entirely neglected to eat. Like all the other prairie chicks I tried to hand-rear, most died on the second or third day of life after their nutritious little yolk sacs had been absorbed; their sibs gradually weakened and died over a period of about two weeks.

A few people have successfully reared prairie chickens. Hurst Shoemaker in Illinois reared a substantial number, and some of the

Part of the pack at dusk.

cocks grew up and displayed to him as though he were a hen; Arnold Kruse reared an astonishing number in North Dakota in the 1970s. One chap dipped living mealworms in batter for food and even raised prairie chickens in battery brooders—those trays that domestic chickens, destined to become fryers, grow up in.

My friend, Pat Ware, once said to me, "If Fran Hamerstrom had lived 300 years ago she would have been burned as a witch, for her way with wild animals is uncanny."

She was right only in part; I have failed in the one species I most wanted to work with as a companion. Furthermore I'm glad that I'm living right now. I can very often figure out just what almost any wild animal needs or wants without really putting my mind on it, it's usually just obvious to me and I find the thought of being burned as a witch repugnant.

I never relinquished my dream of living with a tame prairie chicken. Now and again an acquaintance would send us a newspaper clipping about a prairie cock who inhabited an airport and displayed on the wings of the planes, or of a filling station attendant who could throw his hat toward a prairie cock and this bird—showing the close bond that I had hoped to establish—displayed to the hat.

These reports invariably reached us weeks, months, or years after those eccentric cocks were no longer displaying or were dead. If I could only get current reports!

One day when I was washing my hair in a bowl of hot water on the kitchen floor, the telephone rang. It was a game warden. "There's a prairie chicken down here in Marquette County that's hooked on a manure spreader. It follows it around all the time."

I pushed my long, wet hair out of my eyes and shouted into the receiver, "Can you catch it?"

"I've already caught it. I put it in a chicken coop. I think it's *lonely*."

Maybe that warden should have been burned as a witch too, because I think he was dead right. I ignored details and shouted into the receiver, "Can you catch it again and get it to us?"

People's reactions to the Hamerstrom household vary, but are almost always extreme. Some have said that the conditions are perfectly appalling; and others, in a tone of reverence, have soberly stated that they never felt nearer to God.

I figured that a prairie cock that had fallen in love with a manure spreader might find our ménage a happy home.

I moved our bed out of the north porch, where we usually sleep in summer, and installed pine boughs for cover. The cock, magnificently healthy, arrived aflutter in a burlap bag, and I released him in our summer bedroom (Frederick was very nice about it).

I have no idea how many hours I spent with that cock. I read in his presence and slept in his presence and spent every free moment in his presence. Not once did he mistake me for his manure spreader.

Then I decided to get tough. That bird was fed corn and other grains, but I withheld protein. If he wanted protein he had to come to me for it. Day after day I dropped squirming earthworms on the floor of the porch and called, "Boop, boop, boop."

He learned to rush toward me for those goodies if I stood very still, but I got to feeling more like Simon Legree than a companion. Finally, reluctantly, I gave up. I netted him, banded him, and released him in our garden.

The next day I called, "Boop, boop, boop." There was no response. I never saw him again.

Had I had sense enough to go to Marquette County myself and record the sound of the manure spreader, I could have played the sound back to him. Perhaps he would have come flying from afar to put in among my pansies and lilacs. He might even have followed me into the house and caused my cup to run over: he might have perched on one of my kitchen chairs.

Try as I might, I never succeeded in making that bird happy, but I have some small consolation: never have I made my man unhappy by playing the sound of a manure spreader right inside our house. Frederick is musical—and his hearing is far more acute than mine.

The love life of the prairie hen

The love life of the prairie hen lasts about five days each year. After most of the cocks have established territories and boomed for a month or more, the first hen is apt to appear on the booming ground. The moment she arrives the cocks near her increase the intensity of their booming. Their huge orange air sacs are blown up like distorted balloons. The cocks beat a rapid tattoo with their feet and move around the hen like mechanical toys. And there is a new sound on the booming ground—the "ladies present" call, which sounds rather like the high, clear honk of the Canada goose.

Those cocks that are unfortunate enough *not* to have the hen near them cackle in excitement and "flutter jump." The flutter jump is far different from the majestic beauty of a booming cock. Flutter-jumping cocks fly awkwardly almost straight up into the air as though crippled and come more or less tumbling down only to cackle and flutter jump again, no doubt in order to attract the hen. (Cocks do not flutter jump when a hen is near; they already have one!) The first day that a prairie hen visits a booming ground she appears *indifferent*. Her behavior is almost indistinguishable from that of a hen wandering about in a meadow all by herself! She appears to ignore all the wild excitement she has generated and seems to wander about on the booming ground at random. She picks at willow buds and such, but this is not real eating; it's substitute behavior, like a lecturer pulling at his ear when he doesn't know what to say next. When Day 1 is past, *indifference* is over.

On Day 2 the hen has undergone a subtle change: she is *aware*. She walks the booming ground, moving through the territory of each cock. She was courted yesterday but is courted even more intensively now, and it is perfectly plain—even to a person—that she is aware. She reacts without taking initiative. As many as four cocks may boom around her in what I've called the "Indian War Dance." She holds up her long slender neck, declaring her femininity: a simple statement—nothing more.

On Day 3 she is *flirtatious*. She has developed a quick little wing flick, and she tends to run away from each courting cock—but she never runs very far. After all, she has the power of flight and could easily just fly away from the booming ground. A flirtatious hen stays right close to those cocks. And by now she is staying right close to certain cocks; she may have singled one out.

On Day 4 the hen has reached the *seductive* stage. Her movements are slower and more deliberate; she spreads her wings wide in invitation, but she still runs away. Each time she runs from a cock, she runs a very short distance. Now white feathers may appear near the shoulder. These are excitement spots.

We suspect that excitement spots are an adrenalin reaction—like hair standing up on a cat's back—and we also suspect that the prairie chickens themselves are unaware of the excitement signal. We have seen these excitement spots appear under three different circumstances: just before a big fight (in cocks), just before copulation, and sometimes just before death.

As far as we have been able to detect, excitement spots are of no practical value to prairie chickens. They are of enormous practical value to a wildlife photographer: he knows precisely which bird to focus on.

On Day 5 the hen has at last reached the *receptive* stage. She may arrive on the booming ground still in the seductive stage, but each time she spreads her wings in invitation and crouches, she holds the invitation a little longer—sometimes so long that the cock actually places his foot on her back, but if she isn't ready, she scoots out from under. When she is completely ready, she holds, and the cock mounts.

A prairie hen is never forced. Rape, so to speak, is unknown. The prairie hen is mounted when she is receptive, and not until she is good and ready.

This sequence—indifferent, aware, flirtatious, seductive, and receptive—has some variations but it is typical of the many banded hens we have known in over twenty-five years of watching booming grounds essentially every morning throughout the entire spring.

We didn't find out all these things alone. We had help from about 7,000 miscellaneous observers.

In some ways the notes we expected from them were simplified. For example, we didn't expect observers to follow the path of any given hen, and certainly not to follow the kaleidoscopic paths of sixteen or so hens walking one booming ground simultaneously, some aware, some seductive, etc. And to further confuse the picture, the hens may put on a

These hens are indifferent.

A flirtatious hen.

sister act and stick together like a bunch of giggling girls downtown on a Saturday night.

We spared most observers this welter of confusion and, as far as hens were concerned, just asked them to count them, record their band numbers, whether or not copulation occurred, with which cock, and was it successful?

Every evening after the new arrivals put their duffle on their bunks, we held a briefing for the ten to fourteen observers going out into the blinds the next morning. The questions asked about hens were all straightforward and needed no explanation except the one about successful copulation. If a cock mounts a hen and makes contact before getting knocked off by another cock, and the hen "rouses"—shakes her feathers violently—and if the cock thereupon tears off to fight or intimidate another cock, and the hen leaves the booming ground within ten

212

A receptive hen.

The triumphant moment.

minutes, the copulation was successful. It is *that* hen's last visit to the booming ground and time for her to reprogram her body for egg-laying. Sometimes, a month or so after a successful copulation, we have seen a banded hen return and have assumed that her eggs had been broken.

Theoretically, the territorial system should prevent conflict and make for uninterrupted copulations, but over and over again, the immediate vicinity of a seductive hen became a jumble like the pile-up on a football field. Even professionals had trouble taking good notes.

Ordinarily, I preferred to be by myself every morning, but when Colonel Nial Rankin, husband of the Chief Lady-in-Waiting to the Queen of England, came to watch the prairie chickens, I volunteered to let him share my blind, hoping to learn about the doings in the palace. He proved to be an outstanding observer. To my amazement, he read every band number correctly with my scope whilst mumbling, "Magnificent equipment you have... magnificent." It appeared he was too shy to talk, so I told him about the love life of the prairie hen.

I learned nothing about the palace, but when it came time to wash the huge stack of dishes we had accumulated I heard a cultivated voice inquire, "Couldn't I help you?"

I tossed him a dish towel, which he caught dexterously, and soon I learned a bit about what I assume was the attitude toward dishes in the palace. He wiped the top of each dish, then he wiped its bottom, then he carried it across the kitchen and held it up to the window to make sure that both the top and the bottom of it gleamed—after which he walked back across the kitchen and placed it in the cabinet, as though it were the egg of an extinct bird.

It was plain that it would take all morning to get the dishes wiped at this rate, but just as I was about to yell for another wiper, the colonel gave a dry little British cough and said, "Maybe I shouldn't tell this one, but Her Majesty was amused. . . ."

I had no idea the British told stories like that! I listened to one after another, laughing and astounded.

The Queen was one up on me: she was amused by a story I didn't understand at all, and it *did* take all morning to get the dishes done.

The Second Breakfast

The Second Breakfast was the high social point of the day. There was no hurry. Some very fine amateur chefs have cooked the Second Breakfast, but usually I served a big tray of toasted cheese sandwiches (if you pass around just an ordinary tray somebody is sure to say "thank you," put it on his lap, and start eating, thinking they are all for him!).

After the cold hours in the blinds the warmth of the big stove—and for some of the novices, perhaps the sheer relief of having gotten back safely—made for a merry, noisy atmosphere. Frederick brought in more coffee one day, as a big black man in a cream sheep-lined coat accepted another sandwich. I noticed his accent was British. "Astounding, Mrs. Hamerstrom. Such fighting ability! Your prairie chickens are astounding. Where can I buy some?"

"You want to *buy* some prairie chickens?" Fencing for time, I stammered, "Where do you live?"

"Jamaica." He explained, "I simply must take some back with me to cross with my fighting cocks."

"I'm afraid it's not practical." Across the room a wispy little girl was trying to pull off *my* hip boots. "Would you mind helping that girl pull off those boots?"

The magnificent gentleman from Jamaica crossed the room, introduced himself to the small, startled freshman with a charming little bow. She grabbed both arms of the red chair, and leaned back. He knelt to ease the first boot off: a pool of muddy water formed on the floor. He eased the second boot off: a larger puddle ran out of that one, spreading over the boards and down into the cracks.

I gave my friend from Jamaica a broad grin—approving a job well done. Then I lent the girl my fur-lined moccasins to warm up her skinny, white feet.

I owned *two* pairs of hip boots and almost never got to wear them myself! And Frederick bought himself a brand new pair of rubber boots one year; he never got to wear them once all booming season. Our boots, our parkas, our mittens, were worn by others day after day. So few people followed instructions and brought the right clothes . . . and we were toughened to wind, icewater wet feet, and the raging spring storms of central Wisconsin.

It had been a good morning. But there were sixteen boomers and only two of us to check their notes. The dirty dishes left over from the First Breakfast were hidden under the kitchen stove. Time to get to work.

The purpose of the Second Breakfast was not purely social: it was our chance to check everyone's notes and straighten out any confusion in band numbers, etc. If people just left their notes with us we often had to hound them for weeks by mail to answer questions that they couldn't even answer anymore.

We had dawdled long enough. It was 9:30. We had already worked seven hours and wanted to get to bed by 10:00. I looked across the room at Frederick. He hadn't been dawdling; I had. I'd been telling people stories about prairie chickens, quite forgetting that we were short-handed! Frederick had been checking notes and looking up band numbers for heaven only knows how long.

I seized the nearest boomer by the wrist and asked, "Have your notes been checked?"

"Er, no."

We settled down with his notes. Sixteen cocks and eleven hens. I got up to compare with a big pile of other notes from the same boom-

ing ground. He had all the band numbers right on the cocks, but he missed the hybrid.

"Anything funny about that cock way over to the left?"

"Funny about it?"

I set his map of territories in front of him. "Here's green 23, the one that sometimes comes and fights right in front of the blind." He nodded. "And then there's the unbanded one who fights with him." He agreed again. "And off to the side and a little farther away, there's this one. Anything funny about this one?"

The boomer looked at me as though I were psychic and asked very slowly, "How did you *know?*"

"Tell me about him."

"You can see where I kept erasing. Sometimes I was sure he was a hen because his neck tufts were too short, but then he boomed!"

"Good observation. That's the hybrid cock—a cross between a prairie chicken and a sharp-tailed grouse."

I initialed his notes and reached for somebody else's.

Frederick appeared unexpectedly, "There are two cars still out, and you'd better have a look in the kitchen."

I put down the notes and rushed into the kitchen. "Oh, no!" I moaned. Somebody had found the dirty dishes, piled my grandmother's lovely silverware in with the aluminum cooking utensils, and was adding boiling soapy water. "Silver can't be washed with aluminum. It ruins the patina." I poured a bucket of cold water into the dishpan, fished the silver out quickly, and stored everything back under the stove. "Thank you for offering to help, but somebody will come to do them." It was one of my better white lies. I didn't add that the "somebody" would be the two Hamerstroms.

"Now where were we?" I asked, settling back to checking notes.

"You were just starting."

I looked at "arrival time of birds." His birds arrived nine minutes late. "What time is it?"

His watch was nine minutes behind. "Did you synchronize your watch with Dr. Hamerstrom's last night?"

"No, was I supposed to?"

"Maybe nobody told you. OK, fourteen cocks and two unbanded hens. Are you sure both hens were unbanded? Could you tell for certain?"

There was a sound in the kitchen I didn't much like, so I put the notes down to take a look. The would-be dishwasher was standing guiltily by the refrigerator. "I was just putting the butter away."

217

I took the butter dish from her gently and said, "We leave it at room temperature so it will spread."

"Now," settling down to the notes again, "could you see both legs of both hens?"

Frederick, who does not like to raise his voice and prefers to walk quietly across a room to ask a question, called, "Fran, where are yesterday's notes from Hakes booming ground?"

To his surprise I didn't shout back. I pushed my way through the throng and whispered, "They were absolutely no good. I burned them."

"I've spent at least twenty minutes looking for those notes." His voice was beginning to lose its timbre from sheer lack of sleep.

I added, "I'm sorry, I should have told you."

Suddenly a great clatter of new, happy voices moved from the back door into the living room. The lost carloads had finally arrived! What a relief. At any rate we wouldn't have to go out to the marsh to look for them. But it was harder to settle down and check the remaining notes with the newcomers telling everybody what they had just seen. I made toasted cheese sandwiches for them and heated up more coffee.

When I got back to the living room I saw Frederick with his shoulders hunched up trying to check the notes of a gray-haired man in a plaid shirt. He was deliberately ignoring a rather large woman in a beige knitted dress who kept trying to attract his attention.

"Dr. Hamerstrom," she exclaimed, "I saw the dance of the hens!"

"*Tell* him," I shouted across the room, "*tell* him about the dance of the hens!"

Encouraged by my enthusiasm, she raised her elbows and tripped in a semicircle in front of Frederick's chair on her plump feet.

Frederick's fists clenched and he threw me his worst Chief Thundercloud look. He thought I had picked this unfortunate moment to have some fun!

The moment that marvelous woman raised her "wings" and went into her dance, I knew that for the first time ever, the dance of the hens had been observed, because I had seen the same hen. "What time did you see it?" The lady and I compared times. The dancing hen—and we never saw another like her—danced in front of that lady and then she flew to my booming ground and danced in front of me.

Losing sleep over dancing hens is worthwhile.

Can you trust 7,000 observers?

In some ways Frederick and I were naive when we started working on chickens; in other ways we were not. We started right out trying to distinguish between good, accurate observers and the other kind. Later we had plenty of ways of finding out. Every observer had to turn in his field notes, so we soon knew the band numbers, colors, and positions of all the regular cocks on each booming ground. After all, we built up a whole series of maps of each booming ground, detailing even minor changes in the positions of some of the cocks. *But* it was harder to read the band numbers of the hens; they seemed to spend a lot of time hunkering in the weeds, they might visit more than one booming ground, and besides, each hen's total days on a booming ground tend to be only five in all! You can be sure that we put what we hoped were the best observers where we expected the most hens!

After each evening's briefing we brought in red wine and had a discussion period. It was during the discussion period that Frederick— or whoever gave the briefing—had to make up his mind. The best observers had to be put on the key booming grounds. The decisions were always difficult to make because *we cared so intensely.* We wanted the data.

I'd look at a group of brand new faces: There is Ed Peartree. He's blind in one eye, but I think he has what it takes. (Right: he was one of our top observers for some nineteen years.)

And that chap Brown doesn't seem very well coordinated. I'll put him in a blind with me as a recorder. (Wrong: Brown kept up with me—almost running—and made it into the Lauritzen booming ground before the chickens got there, and his observations were perfect. I didn't learn until a year or two later that he had an artificial leg!)

We tended to discount the abilities of females, but some of these proved us very wrong. Marie McCabe (Mrs. R. A.) could sit in a blind, with those dreamy Madonna eyes of hers, and could read the numbers and colors of prairie chicken hens that came onto the booming ground in the half-light of the early dawn—and again and over again she was proved right. She'd catch the bands of those hens on Day 1 of their love life and give us a chance to follow up on the whole sequence.

Eventually we set up some ground rules: professional wildlifers were top of the heap. Hunters had quick eyes and an uncanny knack for reading band numbers. Presidents of large companies were far more accustomed to giving orders than to taking them and did not really pay attention to instructions very well. I remember one: Frederick was giving the briefing that evening and I heard him say, "Your notes will be taken in pencil."

An egregiously distinguished-looking gentleman, with well-brushed silvery hair and a commanding deep golden voice, replied, "I always take notes with this gold pen. It was given me by the President of the United States."

Frederick brushed this comment off as though it were a fly buzzing about his scrambled eggs at breakfast. "You will use pencil!" Almost as an afterthought, but governed by innate courtesy, he added, "Ink freezes."

However we may have failed to sort the good observers from the rest during the briefing, we would know with certainty how we had fared when the notes came in at the end of the morning: we could trust the notes of those who had made a good map of the territories and read all the cock bands correctly. No one went home before his notes

Briefing.

had been checked, and the originals stayed with us. New boomers had no idea that we had such an efficient cross check on their observations!

Poor observers sometimes simply couldn't see well enough. Other poor observers we lumped among the prudes: they tended to behave in a silly, rather suggestive manner and, when pinned down, were forced to admit that they had observed a copulation.

Another group was the suggestible. One evening during the discussion period someone asked me if we had wolves on the study area. I told them about the only two times we had seen coyotes, members of the wolf family, on a booming ground. Here are my field notes: "*The coyotes came in from the north and worked the whole booming ground. They behaved like sheep looking for vegetation, rather than prairie wolves a-hunting. Slowly they walked around the whole booming ground and one after another, each cock was flushed. Then one coyote came right up to the blind. His eyes were within inches of mine and I suddenly realized, 'This is, after all, a wolf' and became uneasy. Then the coyotes sat to watch the show. Two coyotes and I watched the prairie chickens display. It was a grand moment. Then the coyotes loped off . . . and disappeared.*

"*I saw the coyotes once more, the very next day, but the wind was wrong. Both of them scented me; it was as though they tripped over an invisible wire. They just took off.*" I had found my experiences with the coyotes mighty fascinating, but I didn't expect my description of these two, long ago mornings to brainwash one third of the boomers at the briefing!

When the notes came in the next morning, coyotes had been seen from *three* different blinds! Frederick was aghast. So was I, but I had a good idea of what was up. I practically battled with the boomers who insisted that they had seen coyotes. One backed down right quick and honorably admitted that all he had seen was a sort of shadow that might have been a farm dog or something. However, the other two struck with their coyote stories.

Twice in twenty-five years of chicken watching have coyotes been seen. Once, during a briefing, were coyotes vividly described. Thrice were coyotes reported by boomers. Guess when? The morning after my vivid description!

So much for suggestibility.

There is a far worse problem: the outright liar who sticks to his lie. There fortunately aren't many of these people, but they cropped up from time to time. I kept waiting my chance to find out *why* people ever behave like this. We've spotted them off and on: they insist that they saw something that we know to be impossible. We have many ways of checking up on them without their knowing.

At last I had my chance! Just what I wanted. A professor of psychology arrived with his students, and the professor himself had some peculiar discrepancies in his notes: he had reported a pink and white spiral band (we have never used pink and white spiral bands) and he reported a three-digit number (we have never used three-digit numbers).

I asked one of the students to pass out the toasted cheese sandwiches so I could reread the professor's notes carefully. Some of his numbers and colors were impossible.

The professor, sitting on the bench beside me, lit his pipe and smoked quietly.

"I'd like to ask you about one of the birds. The cock with the pink and white spiral band on one leg and the number 357. How good was the light when you recorded this?"

"The light was fine." He answered easily.

"Was the sun already up?" I persisted.

"Yes, bright sunlight." The professor uncrossed his legs and appeared a little less relaxed.

"You're not color-blind are you?"

222

"I'm certainly not color-blind!"

Plainly, he was indignant at the very suggestion, so I added quickly, "I didn't think so. You got most of the colors right."

He relaxed a little.

"How far away from you was that bird?"

The professor answered, smiling and in a condescending tone. "The bird was in perfectly plain sight and so near that I could see every detail. It was right in the middle of the booming ground all morning."

He started to get up to leave, but I said, "Just a minute. You see, I want to learn something. We have never used pink spirals and we never used three-digit numbers. Besides we know the colors and numbers of every cock on that booming ground.

"You're a psychologist," I continued delightedly; "I've been longing to ask a psychologist. Perhaps you can help me? Why do people report things that are impossible and then stick to them even after they have been proven wrong? Is it compulsive like kleptomania?"

The professor knocked the ashes out of his pipe. "I was not wrong. I know what I saw."

"And you're absolutely sure?"

"Absolutely."

Somehow my golden opportunity to learn from a psychologist why people tell lies and stick to them slipped between my fingers. Perhaps it was my fault. I was too eager to learn the cause of this phenomenon to appreciate the plight of the poor professor surrounded by his students and caught in two outright lies.

He never came back.

On being helpful

Some boomers were forever helping each other or helping us. There was the time that "the Duke," a fellow graduate student and now a famous scientist, came up with Bob McCabe to watch the chickens. He brought 200 mousetraps with him and stated, "I want to set them in a creek bottom." We got to the creek bottom, baited the 200 mousetraps, and found ourselves setting all his traps for him, while he sat under a large white oak. I figured he wasn't feeling well, but as soon as we got back to the house, he regaled us with stories about all the amusing things his black bearers had done in Africa. The rest of the men peeled potatoes, and I cut up some meat and onions for the mulligan. At last McCabe interrupted, "Why don't you help? Why don't you go pump some water, and while you're at it, take the slop pail out too."

As soon as the Duke was safely out of the house, I said, "Bob, I don't think he's feeling well."

McCabe picked up a long potato peel, leaned back, and fanned himself with it. Imitating the Duke's haughty intonation, he mimicked, "And when I snapped my fingers they came running; one built the fire, one unfolded the bathtub, and one beat a drum to chase away the evil spirits."

When the Duke came back into the house, McCabe was sprawled on his stool, cowering in mock terror from the evil spirits, and managing to keep the potato peel fan moving.

We tried not to laugh, and I thanked the Duke when he set the water pail down on the floor. Then I gasped, "What's in it?"

The water was dirty and had a bilious scum. Frederick was mystified, "Where'd the dirt and oil come from?"

The Duke drew himself up rather grandly and announced, "I suppose you know that one primes a pump."

McCabe was the first to take in the full enormity of what had happened. Fists clenched, he roared, "So you put on your thinking cap and primed the pump with the slop! Go pump till the water comes clean."

We took twenty-minute turns at pumping far into the night. It was a short night: breakfast was at 3:00 A.M.

We were always short of sleep during the booming season. With luck we got to bed by eleven. Frederick tended to get up at 2:30 A.M. and let me have twenty minutes extra sleep. With luck we got back into bed by 11:00 A.M.—sometimes even by 10:00—for our nap. Up again to eat, move blinds, fix equipment, and prepare for the next group of boomers. What with loss of sleep, excitement, cold, and all the stimulating people with whom we wanted to stay up, we lost ten pounds apiece on four meals a day each spring. Sleep was our most precious commodity; you don't just go to bed when there's work to be done or when some of the most fascinating biologists in the world are right in your living room expounding theories or telling yarns.

There are so many ways one can lose a nap. Tom Gilliard, from the American Museum of Natural History, came to watch the chickens and to bring back three or four boxes of prairie vegetation for a display case. Frederick, Dan Berger, and I all volunteered to dig the plants for him; but no, he had to hire a boy! He was *not* going to trouble us with any twenty-minute job. He wanted to hire a boy. That blew another nap. The high school couldn't find a boy, the grade school couldn't find a boy, and none of the neighbor boys were interested. At last I called Larry Crawford, also on the chicken project, and said, "Larry, can you do us a favor? I know it isn't your job, but could you just go dig up some plants for Dr. Gilliard?"

"Sure."

By then it was Larry's supper time, and he'd been working crazy hours too. That little job of digging up those plants had cost the Prairie Chicken Project at least six hours by sundown! We never did find a boy, and Gilliard never found out that it was Larry Crawford of the Game Management Division who dug up his plants!

Lack of sleep may have made me somewhat uncharitable to the helpful. Two well-dressed ladies drove in from Buffalo, New York, at 11:00 one morning, just as I was going to slip into bed. "We don't want to trouble you. We came a little early," they said in their nice, well-bred, Eastern voices. "Perhaps you could recommend a farmhouse that could puts us up for the night?"

"You can stay right here. We have four guest rooms. You can take your pick of any two, or share one."

"No, my dear," the older lady pierced me with her firm blue eyes, and smiled. "We are *not* going to trouble you. Just a simple farmhouse?"

Throughout my childhood I had been trained not to argue with ladies of this very type—ladies from that other world I'd left so far behind. Even the intonation of their voices reminded me of my teachers and some of my more forceful aunts so I meekly spent my nap time telephoning our neighbors trying to find somebody who would take them in. Nobody wanted them. But Mrs. Cook, our neighbor to the north, had sounded uncertain, simply saying, "Why, Mrs. Hamerstrom, I don't think we could do anything like that!" She was worth another try.

At last—exasperated—I commanded the ladies, "You wait right here." Then I jumped into the car and roared into the Cooks' driveway. Mrs. Cook and I argued for almost an hour. Now and again Mr. Cook chipped in a word or two. Finally Mrs. Cook said, "Well maybe, . . ." and I exclaimed, "Thank you ever so much."

Finally—utterly exhausted—I tiptoed into the house hoping not to wake Frederick. The ladies were sitting quietly at our dining room table reading. There was a buzzing sound from the next room.

"What's that?" they asked anxiously.

"That," I answered bitterly, "is the alarm clock telling me it's time to get up."

I just don't know where *to spit*

My family not only dreamed about what their only daughter would do; they planned it. I was groomed to feel at home in the capitals of Europe and qualified to become the wife of an ambassador. The dream and the plan were that I would become an international hostess.

By a curious twist of fate I did become an international hostess, but instead of flitting about world capitals, I helped my husband entertain in quite a variety of abandoned farmhouses. The farmhouses—needless to say—were no longer abandoned after we moved into them, but never once did we move into a farmhouse that anyone had lived in recently, and we fixed them up the way we liked them, rather than conforming to the American standard of living.

Our house tends to be full of *"gabboons"*—a politer term would be apprentices.

The word "gabboon," I have been told, was once spelled with a "C" and referred to a wretched African tribe, forced into slavery by a more powerful tribe—to be fed on scraps and to conduct low forms of labor.

Most of the gabboons are mine, and my loyalty toward them is strong. (Many, but not all, have gone on to distinguished careers.) In recent years I hardly know how to address the new crop because they are so much quieter and more polite than the earlier ones. In the early years they were a rowdy lot, and even I was appalled at some of their ways. One Christmas they brought us two turkeys wrapped in foil, which I popped into the oven and roasted. When we sat down to feast, Frederick, who was carving, gasped, "Fran, these birds aren't drawn! You cooked them with the guts in!"

"Why," I stammered, "they were wrapped in foil." Turning to the gabboons I asked, "Where did you buy them?"

"Buy them!" they howled. "We stole them!" And one added virtuously, "We plucked them for you."

Most of that rambunctious group had arrived in a beat-up old car, but three had hitched-hiked from Illinois. It had taken them two days.

Knowing they had no money, I was mystified. I asked, "Where did you spend the night on the way?"

This simple question was greeted by beating on the chest and yelling. It appeared that some of the gabboons—determined to help us with our research—had developed the art of arranging for a free room just about any time. They explained, "It's simple. Stir up just enough trouble and a free bed is offered you—a nice warm room in a jail."

Six or eight might come for a weekend; more often there were only two or three, and these might live with us for months. As Frederick found their table manners distressing, I'd put a big bunch of flowers on the dinner table and seat the gabboon with the worst manners behind the bouquet. I used to pick a lot of flowers in those days.

As luck would have it, when our first distinguished European guest was about to arrive, we had a houseful of gabboons. I gave them a strict briefing. "Watch your table manners. Don't hunker over your food and gnaw on the bones. And don't wear undershirts at mealtime."

Tom Oar, a rodeo rider, deliberately mistaking my meaning by pretending that I was forbidding an undershirt under his shirt, asked, "What if it's cold?" He looked outdoors and managed a fake shiver.

"You know perfectly well what I mean. You don't have to wear ties," I shouted in a voice unbecoming to an international hostess. His brother Jack listened with interest, ready to take sides if need be. Blood sometimes flows when gabboons take sides.

I assembled all the gabboons, lowered my voice, and simply said, "Look, you idiots, this visit means an awful lot to me."

Then Gustav Kramer—the brilliant biologist who invented an artificial sun to study bird orientation—arrived, eager to pick up American expressions, especially slang.

Kramer asked, "How do you say *prosit* when everyone holds up his glass for drinking?"

"Here's mud in your eye!" I replied.

"People actually say *that?*"

"Yes."

Kramer tried this toast out on the gabboons that very same evening and was rewarded by a delighted respect. "And here's mud in yours!" they roared.

The next morning he asked, "How do you greet in the country? Do you say 'Hello' or 'Hi'?"

"You say, 'How are the chickens?' " I answered with a straight face.

"*That* is what is said in the United States?"

"Yes," I answered. "Look, I have some mail to get out and some shopping to do. Why don't you come with me?"

Frederick and I had worked on prairie chickens for years. The whole town knew it, and I knew the local people's stock question.

Kramer and I drove to town.

The postmaster smiled and asked, "How are the chickens?" I smiled knowingly at Kramer.

The grocer just asked me what I wanted, but a dear old man wearing an ancient red plaid jacket and a toothless smile wandered over to me and asked, "How are the chickens?"

That did it. Kramer was convinced.

It is my misfortune that I never had the chance to watch him walk up to a total stranger in the United States of America and ask with charm and confidence, "How are the chickens?"

But Kramer's troubles weren't over, nor were mine.

The gabboons—to show what dainty table manners they had— stuck out their little fingers at mealtimes. Some of them, only fairly surreptitiously, opened their flannel shirts, exposing great hairy chests, or pulled up their sweaters, exposing their stomachs, to let me know that they were *not* wearing undershirts. Jack and maybe two others tried to prevent this display.

The gabboons were taking sides! But mercifully, no fight broke out in front of Kramer.

Sometimes it was just me against the gabboons. For weeks they had used an irritating expression. Over and over again when Frederick or I had asked a difficult question the reply had been, "I just don't know *what* to say." And each and every one simpered when he said it. It was maddening.

I had taken a good deal of satisfaction by walking up to any gabboon who came out with this idiot phrase, looking him straight in the eye, and saying, "Ich weiss nicht wo ich spucken soll."

None of them knew German and none had the faintest idea that what I really said at them in disgust was, "I just don't know where to spit."

Jack had a good deal of control over the gabboons and this time he was on my side. Never once did he expose his hairy chest at mealtimes, and I don't think he once raised his little finger to advertise how dearie-delicate his table manners were supposed to be. Jack not only was

229

Senior Gabboon but he had memorized that one German phrase. He happened to be leaning against the music room door when Kramer asked him a question that he couldn't answer. He straightened up, and his answer was like a field of daisies in June—so sure, so right. Jack answered, "Ich weiss nicht wo ich spucken soll."

His accent was perfect.

Grand Central West

Once the word was out that prairie chicken watching was both adventurous and useful, we soon had to turn away up to 140 applicants each year.

Evening after evening as new groups arrived we hoped they would be on time. Some students had been coached in an almost military manner: they formed a line with their sleeping bags over their shoulders and waited, almost at attention, to be shown their sleeping quarters. Our house was built by an English gentleman named Walker, the first judge of Waushara County. It has high ceilings, transoms over the doors, and although we have lived in it since 1949, I still don't know how many rooms it has. Most of the boomers slept in the ballroom—an upstairs ballroom that runs the full length of the house. It holds five double-decker cots and sometimes three single cots as well. These take up much of the floor space; the walls are lined with dress forms, costume trunks, deer antlers, two antiquated sewing machines, books, tennis racquets, and more. . . . Cobwebs form interesting patterns on the unplastered walls, bats squeak in the rafters, and squirrels scuttle in the walls.

Our ballroom appears untidy, but it is full of items we might have use for some day. We kept the guest rooms tidy and reserved them for couples. We have four guest rooms with double beds and an extra nook with a double bed in one of the upstairs halls. All in all we could sleep twenty-three people without dislodging a member of the family. Twenty-three was far too many to help with the chickens at one time, and we tried to hold the numbers of boomers down to about half the capacity of the house.

Our children grew up with the booming season as a natural part of spring. Sometimes they mingled with the boomers, and sometimes they didn't even look up from their books or toys. (Most American adults don't notice children anyway.) Each evening they watched a dozen or so ornithologists, hunters, students, Europeans, New Zealanders, South Americans, grouse experts, etc., come through the kitchen and go upstairs lugging their duffle.

Alan, oblivious of boomers, muses.

One late afternoon our car stuck on the marsh and we finally got home about nine-thirty—two hours after the boomers had arrived. Elva—about eleven at the time—met us at the door. "I showed them their beds, and I briefed them because you didn't come."

Frederick and I were both exhausted. He said, "Good evening," to the mass of assembled men standing in our living room. He took a deep breath and started firing questions at one and then another:

"How do you distinguish between a cock and a hen?"

"The cocks have three-inch neck tufts. Hens have one-inch tufts. If it booms, it's a cock."

"When are you to map the territories?"

"When there are no hens on the booming ground."

"How do you know if a copulation is successful?"

"The hen ruffles her feathers all up, the cock chases another cock, and the hen leaves the grounds inside of five to ten minutes."

One after another the answers came back, prompt and correct.

232

Frederick got out the jug of red wine. "The briefing is over. Now I'll assign you to blinds."

I started cooking breakfast for sixteen. Whoever didn't give the briefing got breakfast started. Count out sixteen plates; put thirty-two eggs in a bowl; fry sixteen slices of bacon till almost done; make a big pot of coffee. Elva joined me in the kitchen. "Perhaps you could let Hammy know that the man with the Badger T-shirt is color-blind: he can't go alone."

I slipped Frederick the message and congratulated our small daughter for having done a fine job.

It never seemed quite polite to write total strangers and say, "Come at 7:30 P.M., *but don't come before.*" As a result a good many groups of boomers arrived before. They arrived before we had finished eating our supper, or even earlier. This was fine if they were old friends, but it was awkward to cook, eat, plan the work, and entertain new arrivals simultaneously. Frederick just moaned when carloads arrived early. we need one reasonably quiet meal. He prefers a rather hermit-like existence anyway; he likes to plan ahead, and when Alan suddenly named our ancient farmhouse *Grand Central West* at supper one evening, Frederick sputtered, "That's just what it is!" I had just ladled the stew into bowls, when car doors slammed in the driveway. "Damn it," he continued, "I haven't even read day before yesterday's mail and here come the smiling faces."

I rushed outside to intercept the group and returned in a moment or two. "They'll be back at exactly 7:30."

"Who were they?"

"I haven't any idea. They're boomers. Darling, I *did* read day before yesterday's mail: the state wants us to band woodcock, and those people are out there right now pinpointing the peenting grounds for us. I told them how to listen for male woodcock making the peenting noise. They find the peenting grounds; we trap the woodcock."

We had our supper in peace.

Soon the woodcock project became so fascinating that we began to welcome early boomers. The minute I detected their arrival, I intercepted them, handed them some pieces of paper towel, and asked them to mark each peenting ground as exactly as possible. The next evening we set our vertical, almost invisible mist nets by the markers and made our catch. This fine symbiotic relationship didn't always go smoothly. A group of wildlife students from Minnesota marked more peenting grounds than any other group. Rain kept us from setting up the nets but didn't keep me from sending the next bunch of early birds out to listen for woodcock . . . just to listen . . . that's all I asked them to do.

At 7:30 the group reappeared. The leader, a young man, radiated a noble glow and his group stood behind him beaming. "We found a lot of litter and picked it up." He and the members of his party held out pieces of paper towel as though they had just accomplished some fantastic ceremony.

"Put them back," I roared. "Those are markers. Do you know how to put them back?"

"No," he gasped.

He took the markers from each member of his party and headed for the wastepaper basket.

"Don't throw them away. They'll all go out again tomorrow night if we're lucky enough to have a good crew."

I took the towel scraps from him and put them in a paper bag. "You couldn't help it," I said kindly. Apparently not a single member of that group noticed that each piece of towelling had been fastened to the ground with a stick and that by some astounding coincidence peenting woodcock had led them unerringly to their precious "litter!"

Frederick asked me, "Would you like to give the briefing tonight?"

My answer was short. "Not at all."

I went out and netted a couple of woodcock. This put me in a better frame of mind, but we had lost our big catch that spring.

234

Look out for the English

We were pretty well tuckered out, for the home crew had been out well before daylight for seven weeks. We didn't just get up early once or twice; we did it every day, seven days a week. And the day hadn't started out just right—nothing really wrong. One lady, the last to come downstairs for breakfast, arranged a whole row of bottles, jars, skin creams and such on the wash bench in the kitchen. Quick eaters had almost finished their scrambled eggs, and the slow eaters were making good progress. Frederick left the table to see why there was still an untouched plate. He viewed the array on the wash bench in horror. The lady smiled and said, "I'm going to wash my face," and added, unscrewing the cap of a bulbous pink jar, "I do this every morning."

Frederick moved closer, almost blocking her from some of her equipment. "You will either wash your face or you will eat breakfast."

The lady raised silent pleading eyes, like a begging puppy and gave a little sob, pushed her possessions into some sort of a rubberized sponge bag, and rushed toward the only plate of bacon and eggs.

Dick Hunt announced, "Let's get going. The North End is about to leave. Line your cars up back of mine."

The lady redoubled her efforts with her fork, but found Frederick looking at her. She reached for a paper napkin and whispered, "I can just take this with me."

"No food in the blinds!" he ordered.

I slid in beside her, "Look, just eat, don't argue."

I tried to find her later to explain why we can't let people take food in the blinds. They leave waxed paper, banana peels, and all sorts of stuff that we have to clean up later.

Toward the end of the booming season we got a frost warning. A frost warning in mid-May puts us all on edge: it means that hens are apt to return to the booming grounds in substantial numbers. We need a fine group of observers to cope with reading band numbers in spite of rather tall grass, and we want excellent notes. Frederick said, "What sort of people are we having tonight?"

A boomer emerges.

I got up from the supper table and handed him the list. "That boy, Kozlovsky, was here before and did a good job, Mike Cudahay brought us a whole side of bacon last year, but I don't remember what his notes were like; I think all the others are new. Mr. and Mrs. English were highly recommended and they are bringing *two* scopes."

The boomers came piling in just as we finished supper. I showed them their beds, welcomed them, and gave them routine instructions like, "Wear your boots to breakfast. We leave immediately afterwards, and nobody has a chance to run upstairs to get anything he might have forgotten."

Frederick started making preliminary lists of who had hip boots, who had brought his own scope, who wanted to photograph, etc. "Where are Mr. and Mrs. English?"

236

"I'm putting them in Posey's room; they aren't here yet."

7:40. "Have the English come yet?"

"No."

8:17. "Fran, will you read that letter from the English and make sure they have the right date?"

I handed Frederick the letter. They had the right date.

9:04. Frederick herded everybody into the big room. We had waited long enough for the English. In fact, we had never delayed starting the briefing so long before.

At 7:15 that same evening our good neighbors, Mr. and Mrs. Crawford, watched a strange car turn into their driveway; a moment later, a young couple bounded into their house and shook hands. "We're the English."

Mrs. English stooped swiftly and exclaimed, "What a darling puppy," while Mr. English seated himself on the sofa.

They admired the lovely old farmhouse, the Wisconsin countryside, and the ladies shared an interest in home upholstery. I suppose the conversation may have flagged a little from time to time, for the English—patiently waiting for the briefing to start—failed to state their business. Country courtesy kept the Crawfords from asking the direct question: Why are you here? And unexpected visitors were such a rare treat that it was not until 10:00, almost three hours after the unexpected guests had arrived, that Mrs. Crawford brought out coffee and cake: the country signal that it's time for guests to go home.

Mr. and Mrs. English enjoyed the cake and coffee and settled themselves even more comfortably on the Crawford sofa.

After a while Mr. English inquired, "When are the Hamerstroms coming?"

"The *Hamerstroms?* Why we don't expect the Hamerstroms tonight."

Mr. English leapt to his feet. "You mean they don't *live* here?"

"Why, no," Mrs. Crawford said gently, "they live way over there. We can sometimes see their lights from here. They must have gone to bed. They have to get up terribly early every morning . . . long before daybreak."

The Hamerstroms had finally gone to bed. And after a brief, peaceful sleep, there was a scratching sound on the windowsill. Frederick turned his head slowly and saw a man trying to help a woman through our bedroom window.

I was awakened by the roar of my man: "What the Hell do you think you are doing?"

Frederick always puts on his slippers and bathrobe before emerging. Barefoot, in his pajamas, I rushed outdoors. My flashlight found them right by our window. "Who are you?"

"We're the English. We didn't want to disturb you."

"Then why didn't you walk in a door? They're unlocked."

"Unlocked?"

"Did you really bring two scopes?

"I'll show you to your room. We'll call you at two. That's in about three hours. Sleep quick."

The next morning Frederick said, "I'd have killed them if I'd had a baseball bat." It was a bad beginning, but we learned to love the English.

Halloween

When our children were small, we received a perfectly standard invitation (printed) to attend the annual meeting of the German Ornithological Society, which I had joined because they sometimes had good papers on grouse in their journal—and prairie chickens are grouse too.

I rushed to Frederick and shouted, "Look! We're invited to a meeting in Germany." Our son, age seven, and our daughter, age five, followed me into the study, noticing that something beyond the normal excitement of the household was up.

Frederick looked at the "invitation" with mild interest. "Just think!" I shouted, "we can study black cock and capercaillie. They are so closely related to prairie chickens. It is our *duty* to accept."

He looked again at the piece of paper. No expenses; just printed; nothing personal; and then he gave me his answer. "It's impossible. We can't do it. We don't have the money."

For three or four days I burned most of the meals— not on purpose—and I walked in the woods to soothe my soul—and I wrote poetry. I think I managed to get the whole darn thing out of my system in five days. Hopeless, we can't go.

Then I forgot it.

About two weeks later Frederick asked, "Where would we leave the children?"

"Leave the children? *When?*"

"Leave the children *if* we go to Europe."

"No problem. There's my mother, and Aunt Ethel. And lots of people love our children. It is very bad for children just to be brought up by their parents. They should be exposed to numerous good adults."

Before we could study grouse in the marshes, moors, and mountains of Bavaria, other arrangements had to be made. After we arrived in Germany, Adalbert Ebner, of the German Forest Service, spent a number of days telephoning, coaxing, and trying to line up the right contacts for us. At last he announced, "We are in—totally in. Oberforstmeister Karl Beringer, the chief forester, has personally invited us to afternoon coffee."

Adalbert looked at us appraisingly, "You will make a very good impression." He said it again, as though to convince himself. "A very good impression." Americans were not particularly popular right after Germany had lost a war. Plainly, Adalbert wanted to tell me not to wear the tattered jeans that I persisted in wearing in the woods.

The next day we took the train for Marquartstein where a junior forester was to meet us. Adalbert relaxed when we got on the train. He said, "Fran, you always do things perfectly—just right for the occasion—it is an art."

I was wearing a plain white peasant blouse, a handwoven Bavarian skirt, and only another woman would have detected that I was wearing any makeup at all.

Both men were wearing those little green hats with chamois beards sticking up at the sides. We got happily off the train and started to wait. I jumped up onto a luggage truck, swung my legs, and admired the scenery while the men paced up and down the railroad platform. Everybody is always a little late in Bavaria, so it took us quite a while to realize that nobody was coming to meet us. Something had gone wrong.

Adalbert asked for directions, and we trudged up steep mountainous roads to our destination. Beringer, bowing, met us at the door. He exclaimed in distress, "But you walked!" We pointed out that we were sorry to be late but no one had met us.

Beringer jumped to the telephone and ordered, "Schuster is to appear immediately." And in a very few minutes a tall blond forester arrived.

Beringer looked at him scathingly. "Didn't I tell you to meet the Americans on the three o'clock train?"

"Yes, sir."

"And why didn't you?"

"There were no Americans on the train."

Schuster got a good dressing down. He kept peeking at me. There was no way he could explain that he thought all American women wore horrid bright colors and too much makeup, and it wasn't until I spoke to Frederick in English that he really believed that the girl he'd seen sitting on the baggage truck was actually American.

The house of the chief forester was almost royal. Persian rugs lay on polished floors, brocade drapes graced tall windows, and heavy, spookily carved dark furniture looked as though it had been in the family since the Middle Ages. Frau Beringer—a magnificent brunette—poured coffee into delicate china cups and two beautiful teenage daughters passed cakes on silver platters.

Herr Beringer was the most magnificent sight of all. He stood a bit over six feet, with his curly gray hair in the first Einstein haircut I'd ever seen (the year was 1949). Dark eyes flashed dangerously under fine black brows, and his arching nostrils made him look like a proud prince out of some ancient fairy tale. Seldom—if ever—have I beheld a man with such an aristocratic and haughty bearing.

After coffee Herr Beringer invited Frederick to look at his gun collection. I followed close at their heels, but Frau Beringer pulled me gently away. "Let's let the men talk."

I couldn't tell her that I didn't want to miss a single one of her husband's hunting stories, so I followed her. She showed me the house, which struck me as a cross between a castle and a museum. Dazed by the splendor and beauty, I didn't know what to expect when she said, "Would you like to have me show you something special?"

I nodded, and was guided to the kitchen. Frau Beringer linked her arm with mine and stood perfectly still. Plainly there was something I was supposed to admire, but I hadn't the foggiest notion what it might be. Overwhelmed by the fantastic things I'd seen in the last hour, I was at a loss.

She gave my arm a little squeeze, disengaged it, and opened the refrigerator door. "Think of it. It is an electric American refrigerator!" It was touching. She and her daughters dusted and polished and cared for the treasures of the ages in that huge house. They did it with love and understanding, and now their work would be a little lighter.

Herr Beringer took us to the railroad station in his car when our research came to a close. And then he stood on the railroad platform and waved and waved again with a large white handkerchief. And we waved back. Paths sometimes cross for so short a time.

But the train didn't leave the station. We waved and he waved. Minutes seemed to turn into hours. Here was Oberforstmeister Karl Beringer waving a handkerchief at us, and we were getting to feel more and more foolish waving back. He waved with perfect aplomb, and plainly planned to keep waving until we were out of sight.

At last we left our seats and went to the open door. Just then the train gave a lurch and got under way. I shouted, "You must come to see *us* sometime."

241

We watched Beringer getting smaller and smaller in the distance till we could barely see him waving his handkerchief. Heavens only knew when we'd ever get to Europe again. He'd probably be dead.

Back in Wisconsin we returned to our rigorous routine and published a paper on our European findings as well. An airmail letter from Germany arrived in August. I struggled through the miserable handwriting and announced, "Beringer is coming."

Frederick—considerably startled—asked, "*Here?*"

"It's all right. I'll warn him."

I wrote Beringer airmail, an honest—and maybe even lurid—account of our circumstances. "We do not live the way you do. We live in an ancient farmhouse without plumbing. We pump our own water, and the house, built before the Civil War, is crumbling apart—no telling when a ceiling is going to fall down. Of course you're very welcome, but I thought we'd better let you know. We do have good hunting."

Beringer replied, "I can only stay with you a week."

A *week!* We planned that week. Forestry tours, grouse hunting, and we planned every single evening so he could savor something new in the United States.

After he arrived, we planned to introduce Oberforstmeister Karl Beringer to American Negro spirituals. Anybody with all that culture had better hear them. It happened to be Halloween night.

Our children, Alan and Elva, got dressed up and appeared in our living room. "Excuse me for a few minutes. It's Halloween. I'm taking the children to town and I'll be right back."

"Is this Halloween a National Festival?"

"I don't really think so. . . . We have some fantastic music—American spirituals—that we are sure you want to hear."

I took Alan and Elva dressed up as ghosts to Plainfield and rushed back to entertain our distinguished guest. Frederick had produced a bottle of red wine and was preparing the record player.

Beringer met me at the door. "How often does this not quite National Festival occur?"

Finally, I caught on. "Would you *rather* go to Plainfield?"

"Yess. That would be preferable to me."

Frederick stashed away the records, and we set off for town: Honor Bright, with no plan in mind.

As we moved past the Johnsons' house I asked Frederick to stop. "Stop *here.*"

Quickly, in German, I briefed Herr Oberforstmeister Karl Beringer. "Walk up to that door, ring the bell, and demand, "Trick or treat.""

Dear old Mrs. Johnson opened the door expecting small children. She found herself confronted, not by little children, but by a tall, terrifying man whose black eyes and arched nostrils loomed in the half-light. Beringer took one step toward her, bowed, and bellowed, "Trrrick or trreet!"

Mrs. Johnson gasped, held her hand to her mouth to stifle a scream, and clutched the door frame.

Frederick and I were hiding behind some spirea bushes to watch the fun. But Frederick decided the fun had gone a little too far so he leapt to the porch to reassure her. She had known him at least twenty years, but now she failed to recognize him. Two giant men confronted her at her own door: trick or treating!

Fortunately, Elisabeth Johnson appeared at that moment. "It's all right, Mother. It's just the Hamerstroms."

But even Miss Johnson, who had been a major in the United States Army and had traveled over much of the world, looked a bit startled when Beringer towered over her and bowed

Competing foundations

Very few people like tongue. My parents often served cold cuts for summer luncheons and then the children got cold tongue for supper for several days thereafter. I find cold tongue with a dab of sharp mustard absolutely delicious.

When it came time to do something for the chickens, to save them before their range disappeared, Frederick and I gave a series of luncheons on the lawn under the elms. We invited influential conservationists, to try to stir up interest in saving a species that many thought was already doomed in Wisconsin. We hoarded our money for these occasions and bought ham, cheese, tongue, sandwich bread, and, of course beer. And we expounded on the plight of the chickens.

Without exception these luncheons all ended in the same way. Everyone agreed that "something must be done for the chickens." Then they all got back into their Cadillacs and drove away. The only tangible result of these parties was that the Hamerstroms had enough leftover tongue for dinner—for supper—for breakfast.

But over 7,000 people came to watch the prairie chickens booming and the chickens themselves produced one dark horse and then another.

An old hunter spoke up at the Second Breakfast one day. "You know, I'm a member of the Wisconsin Conservation League. We're all getting old and were just planning to disband. We have some money left in the kitty."

Money!

The League was delighted to buy eighty acres of chicken land with the money in the kitty.

The next dark horse was Paul Olson of the Dane County Conservation League. He watched the prairie chickens boom on the Buena Vista Marsh and promptly launched the Prairie Chicken Foundation. I quote: "Let the boys at Canaveral hurl their rockets at the moon and at whatever swirling worlds there are. I respect their discipline and their sense of high adventure—but in the cold predawn of the Buena Vista as I listen to one of the last authentic truly wild American voices—I achieve *my* adventure."

244

Paul Olson.

The Prairie Chicken Foundation (with the help of a dark horse of its own) bought many acres of chicken land.

Then, too, there were private purchases by individuals. The Gordon Kummers made the first. Reuben and Meta Paulson, farmers from the southern part of the state, said, "I guess we can make our old car do another year." They bought eighty acres. And so did the Clarence Jungs—right where the domain of the chickens was about to be threatened by agro-industry.

Dory Kummer Vallier has a knack for running into just the right people at just the right time. She ran into Bill Sullivan and said, "Bill, you've just got to help the prairie chicken."

"Help the prairie chicken? Hell, I didn't know he was in trouble."—Bill Sullivan.

245

It was so that the Society of Tympanuchus Cupido Pinnatus was formed. Bill elected himself "Tympanuchus," Jack Pelisek became the "Quill" (Secretary), and Bill selected a "Council of Chiefs."

Frederick and I watched this amazing organization grow. He opined, "Good works do not have to be done in a sepulchral atmosphere."

Now the Society's address is: S.T.C.P., Russell C. Schallert, Tympanuchus, 735 West Wisconsin Ave., Suite 1177, Milwaukee, WI 53233. (Not everybody can get in, but it's worth a try.)

Luncheon parties under the elms and leftover tongue now seem long, long ago. Two foundations amicably competed with each other to save the chickens. Now each spring the prairie chickens boom and the mellow sound rolls over the meadows. More land set aside would make it even more likely that Wisconsin will keep its chickens forever.

Going into Society

Smokey the Bear has perhaps been the worst enemy of the prairie chicken. They thrive after a fire! John Curtis, the great ecologist, stated that in Wisconsin the white man has changed the north by fire protection even more than he has changed the south by intensive agriculture.

Frederick says, *"Smokey the Bear is the greatest ecological hoax ever perpetrated on an unsuspecting public."*

Fire is a natural and a necessary part of our landscape. John Curtis has *set* fires to save orchids. Game managers are now setting fires (known as controlled burns) to save prairie chickens. Prairie orchids and prairie chickens alike face extirpation when vegetation gets too tall.

Not all fires are good. Some do enormous damage. And controlled burns must be set not only in the right place but also at the right time of year. That day—so long ago—when I played tennis and failed to fight fire is a good case in point. A fire, catastrophic because it swept over the Great Plain during the nesting season, sealed the doom of a whole race. But fire was nevertheless essential to the survival of the heath hen. Now we know that controlled burns at the right time of year might have saved that bird from extinction.

The Great Plain was roughly the size of our study area, and our study area had one of the densest prairie chicken populations in the world.

In 1941 there were prairie chickens in every county in Wisconsin, including Milwaukee County with all its cities and subdivisions. But those nice, untidy farms in the northern part of the state were obliterated by *zoning:* people were moved out and the forest took over. And in the southern counties intensive agriculture, perhaps combined with competition from the Chinese ring-necked pheasant, obliterated flock after flock.

The decline of the heath hen and of the prairie chicken was variously blamed on disease, on overhunting, on foxes, on cats abandoned by the summer people and left to go wild, and on "them white owls."

247

Let her roar—saving a prairie.

We drew blood from prairie chickens and examined the guts of shot birds to test for disease. We were able to rule out overhunting. The decline of the prairie chicken was plainly not due to cats, foxes, or owls. It was like a jigsaw puzzle with one of the pieces missing, and at last we found the missing piece. Prairie chickens needed a *home*. The hens needed the right sort of place to lay their eggs and rear their young. This wasn't their only requirement. It was just the hardest piece to fit into the puzzle.

Somehow we had sense enough not to stop after our great discovery. (Habitat is a household world now, but it wasn't then.) Frederick was offered chances to triple his salary if he'd go to Washington. (He just laughed.) Now that we had found a key to part of the puzzle, we had a lot to find out. The foundations were buying land in forty-acre blocks. How far apart should these purchases be? Only banded birds could tell us.

We named each purchase and one of these, bought by the Society of Tympanuchus Cupido Pinnatus, soon just became "Society." It was a

248

fine piece of nest-brood cover, and a food patch on it turned out to be a good trapping station in winter. It was on my trapline.

Late winter is a particularly good time to catch prairie chickens. They are down in weight and push eagerly toward the bait. My trapline consisted of twenty-seven miles and I had a lot of ground to cover. I took a shortcut and rammed the car into a major snowdrift. It can't have taken me much more than an hour to shovel out, back up about half a mile and go around the long way; but I had a good catch, and it took me some time to process all the birds.

One more station to run! And I was about two hours behind schedule already! I'll never know what caused my next mishap, but the car slithered off the road. Now I not only had to shovel but I had to jack up the rear wheels and put boards under them to get moving again.

It was Sunday, and the road into Society was terrible. Actually I hadn't expected to get stuck until I hit that road. The Wagon Wheel Tavern was on the way to Society, and they had a telephone. The barkeep was busy. Church was over and the tavern was jammed. There were no women in the tavern, and my arrival aroused a certain amount of attention. An amiable drunk asked me what I would have, and gradually conversation practically ceased while everybody watched developments, as in desperation I explained I didn't want a drink. I wanted to telephone. A man in overalls on a nearby barstool nodded toward the telephone. It was behind the bar, well out of reach of the customers.

I jumped, threw my belly on the bar, reached across, and seized the phone. By now everybody was listening. I called home and, worried lest I not be able to reach the birds in the traps in time, I must have sounded utterly distraught. "I'm going into Society and if I'm not back in an hour rescue me."

I rushed out of the tavern, jumped into my car, and disappeared. I can almost imagine those in the tavern, "Know what that woman said? I heard her."

"Yeah, I heard her too."

And he played the electric guitar

One of the biggest landowners in the prairie chicken country was something of a mystery man. He posted his vast acreage with conspicuous signs—TRESPASSERS WILL BE PROSECUTED—and was occasionally seen to patrol the edges of his domain in a big black Cadillac. He may have spoken to me once when I was trapping a broad-winged hawk that I wanted to band. At any rate the big black car slid up beside mine, and a man with a strong Chicago accent wanted to know what I was doing. There were prairie chickens on his land; he was reputed to be rich, and if I hadn't been so startled I would have tried to persuade him to set aside portions of his land for prairie chickens to nest on— instead of plowing up almost all of his property.

His dark glasses masked his facial expression. His voice was unfriendly, so that I didn't even pull myself together enough to ask permission to go on his land to count the booming prairie cocks in spring.

We needed those counts.

I took matters into my own hands the following spring. I pulled on hip boots, and very early one morning I drove straight onto The Big D Ranch, sneaking in on an almost unused farm trail. I hoped to get the chickens counted and be gone before anybody was up and about.

The road was unused for good reason. When I had barely made it through puddles for not quite a mile, the bottom dropped out of the road and I sank my truck in mud—down to all four hubcaps. Time to face the music. I had to go to those Chicago-type farm buildings and ask somebody to get out a tractor. I brushed my hair, and when I got quite close to the buildings, I took off my jacket and hung it over my arm to hide its raggedness. Men are usually gentler with a woman, and I was glad that I, not Frederick, had to confess trespass!

I didn't enjoy walking up to the front door of that big, modernized farmhouse. And I felt even more uneasy when a handsome, swarthy man with curly black hair said, "Step right in." But the voice was mellower than the one I remembered.

250

"I've done something awful. I got my truck stuck about half a mile north of here."

"Yeah?"

"I'm stuck on your property and it's going to take a tractor to get it out."

"I'll send out the boys."

"Oh," I exclaimed quickly, "I'll go out with them and help."

"It's breakfast time. You stay and have breakfast with me." This man didn't sound unfriendly at all. "Annie," he called into the kitchen, "fix breakfast for two, and make some of them muffins."

"Ever hear an electric guitar?" Without waiting for an answer he took a guitar out of its case, seated himself on the sofa next to me, and started playing *Santa Lucia*. The delicate aroma of bacon floated into the living room. I studied my host's face. It was a strong face, but it didn't look mean.

He looked at me inquiringly after he finished, and I said, "That was lovely, Mr. . . .?"

"Just call me Sid."

"Yes, Sid."

He played another tune and started singing with a good deal of gusto and rolling out his *r*'s like an Italian opera singer. The music was awfully loud, and I was glad when Annie came in to set the table. I knew Annie! She was one of our neighbors! I said hello, but Annie just barely nodded her head and kept right on putting breakfast on the table.

My chance had come! I let Sid eat a few mouthfuls to put him in a good mood, and then I told him about the prairie chickens on his own property and how wonderful it would be if he would set some land aside and just keep it in grass.

"You want me to do that?" he asked.

"*Could* you?"

"How much land do ya want in grass?"

"Well, the best would be about forty acres in each square mile."

Sid swallowed the last mouthful of his breakfast, pushed his plate back and said, "That's only about one sixteenth of the ranch . . . not much of a problem."

I could hardly wait to get home to tell Frederick, and the boys had just returned with my truck. Annie's husband was one of "the boys."

"Got another song you might like to hear." Sid took up the guitar again, and I didn't dare offend him by telling him I was supposed to be at home cooking for a houseful of boomers and helping Frederick check their notes.

Sid knew a lot of songs, but I finally made my escape. It was almost noon by the time I got home. The boomers were gone, and Frederick was washing the dishes by himself. I grabbed a dish towel.

"What happened?" he asked. "Get stuck?"

"Yes, and it was the best thing that ever happened. Darling, the Big D Ranch people are just wonderful. I met the owner and he promised to set aside scattered forties for the chickens. He says it's no problem! No problem at all. He wants to help the prairie chickens. He's perfectly charming."

I looked at the map of the Big D before I went to bed and dreamed of flocks of chickens and the sound of their melodious booming all over the ranch in spring.

A few days later I ran into Annie in the post office. "Annie! What a wonderful man you work for!"

"Huh?"

"Sid—he's going to change the farm plan and set lots of land aside for the chickens."

Annie wrinkled her nose. "That Sid ain't the owner. He's hired help just like me—and he got fired yesterday."

Of possums and public relations

Anybody who is in danger of becoming a living myth had better proceed with caution. Some people have an absolute knack for getting talked about; it is one of my failings, and not all the talk helped the Prairie Chicken Project.

I've found the myths to be based on fact, and when you get down to the kernel of truth in the story, it is based on an innocent episode . . . for which nobody had requested an explanation.

For example, we had two tame horned owls on our front porch, Ambrose and Zuleika, and we hoped that they would breed there. Wild horned owls came to visit our tame owls and sat in the tall elms in front of the house and made music in the evenings. I wanted the wild owls nearer so I could watch them better, so I devised a "visiting owl's chair."

One Sunday morning in spring, when the frost was out of the ground, the neighbors passing our house on the way to church saw me and my son Alan digging a big hole in the front lawn. I can almost hear their comments: "Isn't it nice? Maybe Mrs. Hamerstrom is going to put in a rosebush."

Alan and I worked fast, and on their way back from church the neighbors were treated to the sight of two people planting the grayish, knobby trunk of a long-dead tree. Nobody stopped to ask why we planted a dead tree, but some of the neighbors tended to be a bit self-conscious when returning my friendly waves.

This wasn't so bad because what I was doing out by the front door was not being paid for with taxpayers' money. I tried hard to conform, and I don't think it was until August that I *perfectly innocently* gave somebody another story to spread.

There was a banded male marsh hawk that I passionately wanted to catch. He ignored all the usual traps, so I fashioned a series of small nooses and put them on his favorite fence post, hoping to catch him by his toes. I hid and watched that bird. He chose a new post. I moved the contraption to his new post and he selected another. The only thing to do was to shag him back to his old favorite perch by making all the other potential perches unattractive to him.

I got up early the next morning, armed with 100 rubber bands and a large kitchen knife. I cut vegetation and fastened each bunch to a fence post, leaving only his favorite post with nothing on it but that little circle of nooses.

At last there was no place for him to perch but on that one post. I looked around. There was a pickup parked by the road, and somebody had been watching me for heaven only knows how long. Then I looked around again. The goldenrod was in full bloom and had been by far the easiest vegetation to cut. I had decorated almost 100 fence posts with bunches of flowers!

I ran toward the truck, plunging through goldenrod, nettles, and spirea. I waved and called to the man in the truck. I *had* to catch him and explain what I was doing and why, but he drove away. This was more serious: I was out on the study area, and I felt another myth on its way to that mysterious country telegraph that passes on juicy morsels of information: "Know what us taxpayers are paying for now? Those prairie chicken people are putting *flowers* on top of fence posts! Flowers! And you and I gotta pay for it."

Rumors started sizzling, and more and more fuel was added. During the past winter when the snows had been deep, we had simply

unset one prairie chicken trapping station by tipping all the traps upside down so the birds could feed on our bait at will. That story got back to us: ". . . they left them traps out in the field and they never went back. I'd hate to tell you how many chickens froze to death. There wasn't a single snowshoe track into that field for more than two *weeks!*"

When the story got back to us, we explained that the traps had not been set and not a single prairie chicken had died in them, but how many people had heard the story and believed it? Stories have a way of shifting. More than likely this one was what got the next one going: "They are putting so many bands on the legs of those birds that they can't fly."

Frederick, with his gentle politeness, explained to everyone he had a chance to talk with that the three bands we put on each chicken weighed only two grams, and that the chickens weighed about a thousand. Most people had no conception of how heavy a gram might be, so I'd add, "Those bands don't weigh the chickens down any more than a Hershey bar in a man's overcoat pocket weighs him down." Over and over again, we were not believed. We didn't know it then, but things were warming up for what later was to be known as the Prairie Chicken War.

We always tried to do our work well and to be good neighbors too, but now we spent quite a lot of time avoiding criticism.

In late summer the American Ornithologists' Union met in Madison, and after the meeting two carloads of people who wanted to see prairie chickens came home with us. This was unexpected and I didn't have much on hand to feed everybody, so when I saw a lot of fresh ear corn lying by the roadside where a truck had taken a corner too fast, we all got out and picked up corn for supper. Next I stopped for a fresh-dead possum. I find possum too fat to be tasty, but some people like it. Konrad Lorenz, who was in the United States for the first time, eagerly took the possum from me, exclaiming something like "Bauchtier! fabelhaft!" He looked at that possum with as much delight as I would have examined a road-killed kangaroo. Then he left it on his lap and asked questions about the landscape, the animals, the vegetation, and the Indians. It didn't occur to him to ask me about local public relations.

Frederick's carload of ornithologists peppered him with questions, and his car tailed the one I was driving for most of the hundred miles north to our house. But not the very last bit of the way. I turned up the dirt road to our house, and Konrad Lorenz made one of his swift decisions. He glanced to make sure we were being followed. Then he shouted, "Stop!"

I slammed on the brakes.

His reddish beard abristle, and holding the dead possum under his overcoat, he hurled himself into the roadside ditch and pretended to catch a possum. Having "caught" it, he ran up onto the road. Keeping the creature wriggling about in a lifelike manner with his fingers, he pretended to bite it to death. This show was especially for Jean Delacour, who was traveling with Frederick.

The car behind us, however, was no longer the one that had followed us from Madison. Two of our most talkative neighbors slowed down and then drove by very slowly. They saw me sitting behind the steering wheel with a frightened expression on my face and watched a huge and ferocious man bite a possum to death in front of their very eyes. Mrs. S. sucked in her lips: she had a story to tell, and as they passed, Mr. S. nodded slowly. He wasn't nodding to me.

The Prairie Chicken War

Frederick can be mighty stubborn. He was asking permission to trap prairie chickens on the land of Mr. L., a local politician, and refused to back down in an argument about foxes and white owls. White owls, which sometimes winter on our marshes, but never in numbers, soon disappeared from the heated discussion. Mrs. L., a broad-shouldered, capable-looking woman, came in to listen and put in her bit about foxes too. "We've got to get rid of the foxes."

Frederick pointed out that there had been foxes and prairie chickens since time immemorial and what we needed was good nest-brood cover. "Look," he said, finally raising his voice. "It doesn't matter how many foxes there are if the chickens have good habitat! What the prairie chickens need is *land,* not fox trappers."

We had crossed swords with an extremely influential man, who happened to make money trapping foxes for bounty, and we had succeeded in irritating him.

Later he and his wife retaliated beyond belief. Mr. L. got "the boys" out and circulated a petition which had hundreds of signatures and was sent to the governor of Wisconsin. The gist of it was: all you need to do for the prairie chicken is to get rid of the foxes and the Hamerstroms.

We were unaware of the petition being circulated against us, and the first repercussion from the fox discussion came from an unexpected source. Our small son Alan came home from school one afternoon and said to me, "Mrs. L. wants to shoot you."

Neither Frederick nor I laughed. We froze. It was no laughing matter. Alan got himself three peanut butter sandwiches, lay down on the sofa and said, "Don't worry. You're a much better shot than she is."

That petition was the first rumble of the Prairie Chicken War. It was simply filed, but more serious trouble developed some years later. Unbeknownst to us a mass meeting was staged. Frederick walked right into it. One of the game managers appeared at our house and said, "There's going to be a meeting in the town hall tonight. Let's go; they want you to come."

Delighted at a chance to explain the prairie chicken management plan, Frederick, softly humming, rummaged in his study and brought out some maps and charts for his presentation. Then I waved them a cheery good-bye.

To Frederick's astonishment, the town hall was surrounded by cars and more were parked up and down the road. As he approached the building, he could hear the roar of voices like the "zinging" of angry bees in a hive. He walked in. Silence. Suddenly there was absolute silence. Frederick felt a prickle of fear.

Some of the men in the town hall had heard of the management plan and a few had actually seen it.

The plan was for the state to purchase about forty acres per section in a scatter pattern throughout the marsh and keep these areas in good nest-brood cover. We had watched land-use changes and saw the coming need for some land to be managed just for chickens. Frederick showed his map and pointed out that the state didn't need any particular forty, that the map was just to show the general idea. If somebody didn't want to sell his land, undoubtedly a neighbor near-by might be glad to do so. Nobody would be *forced* to sell his land.

There were farmers in that town hall who saw part of *their own land* crosshatched for purchase! Land had been condemned by the federal government in the nearby Necedah area, and farmers had been driven out—evacuated and moved elsewhere! "And now," they shouted, "it's going to happen here. Right here and to *us!*"

Frederick came home drained and exhausted. I had sense enough not to ask him how it went. After he finished eating his late supper in an absent-minded manner, he said so softly that I could hardly catch the words, "I thought they were going to tar and feather me." He tried to smile, "And run me out on a rail."

It was long, long ago, but that was the beginning of the worst year in my life. Of course some amusing things happened, but mighty few of them seemed funny at the time.

We continued to do our fieldwork on the marsh and were grateful when friends and neighbors waved to us or invited us in for a cup of coffee. Not everybody hated us. We also had sense enough to go to the local meetings and be seen.

The next time that Frederick had to go to one of those meetings in another town hall, it was PTA night and I had been invited. I telephoned ahead and said I was looking forward to coming. This was far from the truth. I was scared, but I wasn't going to let it show. A few minutes after I had put the receiver back on the hook, the telephone rang. "Mrs.

Hamerstrom, we are *so* glad you are coming to PTA. We will have a debate." I caught my breath, for in my mind only one subject seemed up for debate right now. I could hardly believe what the principal was saying: "The debate will be on whether home economics should be taught in grade school or only at the high school level."

"Yes," I gasped.

"And we want you to be on one of the teams," he continued.

"Yes."

Frederick rummaged for his maps and set off for another town hall. I watched him get into the car and drive away, wishing with all my heart that I could go with him. My presence might keep the "party" from getting too rough.

I put on my best (and only) black dress, brushed my hair, and drove to Tri-County High in the truck—so steamed up about what might happen to Frederick that my memories of the debate are vague. The adrenalin pumping through my veins apparently caused me to put on an unusual performance. I pleaded the case on home economics with such passion that teachers and parents came up afterwards to congratulate me. In those days I was sure that home economics shouldn't be taught in school at all, and I have no idea which side I argued for. At any rate, the compliments buzzed about my astonished ears.

"Mrs. Hamerstrom, we had no idea you were such an eloquent speaker. We didn't know of your skill in forensics (I'd never debated before), and we want you for our president."

"President?"

"Yes, president of PTA."

I thanked them for the great honor and mumbled that it was really out of the question—working mother and that sort of thing.

I learned something very reassuring that evening. The Tri-County school, which was off the prairie chicken study area, was not out to get my skin. They seemed to be unaware of our troubles, and our children were not apt to suffer from their schoolmates as a result of the Prairie Chicken War. The size of the furor was limited, and the school lay outside of the battleground.

Cars in the drive

Frederick came back from the second mass meeting angry and bewildered. As far as I can recall this was the last meeting of this particular sort. Henceforth, for about a year, there were meetings right in our own house.

At about this time we bought Alan a dog and I took it to Wautoma, the county seat, for inoculations. I started home and decided to take the back roads for variety. The roads looked more and more unfamiliar, and soon I discovered that I was lost. The sun was still up and there was no possible excuse for getting lost. I stopped the car, studied the map and then—for the first time in many days—I took time to think. How could I, a professional biologist, lose my way within eighteen miles of home? I looked again at the setting sun. It gave me a clue, and I suddenly faced why I had gotten lost. It was psychological: I was *afraid* to go home.

Day after day the setting sun brought carloads of people into our driveway and into our house. For the most part they were loyal friends telling the new and often fabricated stories of what Mr. L. or somebody else had said or done toward running us out of the country. And they told us what our friends were saying: how Cecil Bender had stood right up to the town chairman, and that John Kraemer knew we were all right—he watched us at work in all weathers. Harry Chamberlain drove all over the marsh singing our praises and telling people what to think. He didn't stress competence or fairness. With deep rural wisdom he stressed two main points: these people wouldn't tell a lie—I know them—and they just love the prairie chickens.

We rarely had anything to contribute, but one evening Frederick electrified our friends by telling the story of the day. A farmer had stood right on his front steps in Coddington—a tiny town within our study area—and stated: "The government's going to flood the marsh and drive us all out. The south end is already under water and they are moving people out. Watch it: we come next."

The south end of the marsh was only ten miles from his house, but he had not bothered to look for himself. If he had, he would have found no water, no exodus, no change of any kind.

I tried to keep things reasonably normal for the children. When Alan and Elva came home on the school bus, I fed them and sometimes took them out to explore. But that left Frederick to cope with the excited babble of voices in our living room. We told both children exactly what was happening, so if they heard rumors or someone was nasty to them in school they would be armed with the same, pitiful morsels of information that we ourselves had. I'm convinced this was the right thing to do, although both children seemed to find our explanations rather boring. Elva occupied herself with a variety of pets and Alan asked me for a sheet.

"A sheet? What for?"

"I want a sheet. It doesn't have to very good, but the top of the house is my pirate ship and I want to put up a flag."

Alan cut a skull and crossbones out of an old black dress and Mary Mattson sewed them on one of my old sheets. And in due time another story floated back to us: the Hamerstroms are spies. They are flying the flag of a foreign nation on top of their house. This was announced with much gusto, and then the teller of this particular tale lowered his voice and hissed in a sibilant whisper: "Must be *communists!*"

He passed this information on to the bluegrass crews. One of the major industries on the marsh was the harvesting of bluegrass seed. Machines known as "strippers" were pulled with tractors, and men rode the strippers. A rotating cylinder, covered with what appeared to

be extruding nails, whirled the tops of ripe bluegrass into boxes or "hoppers." From time to time the tractor stopped, and the seed was unloaded into burlap bags. Now and again a young prairie chicken was whirled into the hopper along with the seed, but in general the bluegrass acreages were the heart of the prairie chicken area: vast expanses of land, managed to produce grass by periodic burning.

Needless to say, the bluegrass harvesters, who were known as strippers too, took sides in the Prairie Chicken War. Bluegrass seed is ripe for harvest about the first two weeks of July, when most of the young prairie chickens have hatched but can't fly very well yet. Frederick and Os and I went from crew to crew and asked each stripper to tell us how many broods he had seen and how big the chicks were. The three of us could have walked the marsh from dawn to dusk, day after day, and not gleaned as much information as we could get by simply asking the strippers.

I loved interviewing them, and whenever a stripper stopped, I used to unload his hopper so he could rest his aching muscles. At the end of the day the heavy bags had to be loaded onto trucks, and my muscles were easily up to hurling bags of seed up to the top of the load.

Most of the strippers had milked cows early in the morning, finished their chores, and then put in some fourteen hours or so on the bouncing, clattering machines before going home to milk and finish up the evening chores.

The Prairie Chicken War altered our happy approach to the stripping crews. Some were so hostile that none of us liked to ask them about broods, and stories started flying: "Those prairie chicken people want to get rid of *us*. They saw a dead chick in my hopper."

We kept pointing out that a few dead chicks didn't matter a bit—that the seed industry was just wonderful for prairie chickens.

Not only did we have assembled cars in our driveway every evening but there were cars assembled around the taverns, and we well knew that we were among the chief subjects of conversation. As far as we knew, Frederick and Os were bearing the brunt of the talk and nobody had focused his attention on me. My time was to come.

Knitting on the street

And then, unexpectedly, we got a call from a professor at the university. I answered the telephone, but Professor V. said, "I'd rather speak with your husband." Odd way of putting it.

"Telephone!" I shouted, "and it's just for you!"

We hadn't had any trouble with the university, so I went back to mending equipment without feeling particularly uneasy. Frederick was at the telephone a long time, mostly listening, and when he finished I could see that he had bad news.

"What is it?" I asked.

For a moment I didn't think he was going to tell me. He just kept looking at me. Finally the words came. "They are talking about *you*."

"What are they saying?"

"He didn't want to tell me over the telephone. I told him we'd come right up."

I nodded slowly, and then getting on with the practical aspects, I said, "Let's dress up as though we were giving a lecture. It can't hurt to make a good impression."

Frederick changed into a suit and polished his shoes before putting them on. I put on my new beige stockings, a black dress, and high-heeled shoes. Then I fixed a quick cold supper for the children and left them a note:

> *We'll be back tonight.*
> *Here is your supper.*
> *Alan, please undo the buttons on the back of Elva's dress so she*
> *can get into her night clothes.*

Frederick drove to Stevens Point with one hand so he could hold my hand with the other. They were talking about *me,* and I had given them so much to talk about: the flowers on the fence posts, planting the dead tree, or the sunny day I wore a raincoat. There were so many things that I felt steeped in guilt and didn't have sense enough to remind myself that I hadn't done anything really wrong—not as far as I knew.

264

When we got to the professor's house, Frederick brushed aside his greetings and said, "Well, what is it?"

Professor V. answered in a low voice, "The children aren't in bed. Won't you sit down?"

We seated ourselves uncomfortably on his big, soft sofa. He suggested that we should learn good public relations and help our neighbors with haying and barn-raising, but for the most part we discussed inconsequential matters while romping children managed to delay bedtime. At last Mrs. V. brought us some drinks and quietly left the room.

Frederick's voice was unsteady. He set his drink down untouched and, leaning toward the professor, he demanded, "What are they saying?"

The professor leaned forward and gave us the news. "They are saying," he paused, "that Mrs. Hamerstrom has been seen knitting on the street!"

"*Knitting?*" I asked.

"Yes," he nodded soberly. "*Knitting . . . on the street.*"

I looked up at him as though I were a little girl who had been caught doing something wrong and asked, "Is that so bad?"

Professor V. was surprised at the question.

At last he mumbled, "Why no, I suppose it isn't."

Mass hysteria plays queer tricks. Said in a certain deep tone, *seen knitting on the street* has an ominous ring, reminiscent of the sinister Madame Defarge and the French Revolution. Countless people, even a sensible professor who had tried to help us, were upset at this knitting business and failed to seek out the facts.

On the way home I laughed uncontrollably—without merriment—and then cowered against Frederick's arm and cried very softly. He probably preferred my little sobs to the wild laughter he had just been treated to.

Just about anyone in public service must have periods of great strain, but we weren't used to gossip and malice and we cared so much about saving the prairie chickens.

I still knit on the street. It's as good a place as any. And we won the Prairie Chicken War.

Years later I asked a neighbor, "Mary, remember when things were so bad and they had the mass meetings?"

She nodded.

"Why did people mind my knitting on the street?"

"Knitting on the *street?* You mean knitting on the road."

"On the road?"

"Ya. You'd go up on the marsh in the afternoon and park your car and knit—and taxpayers paying your salary!"

Mary patted my hand. "As for me, I figured it was nobody's business. You worked so hard and got up so awful early."

It was my turn to pat her hand. "I was working, Mary. I can knit without watching, and I had to wait to see what time the chickens came in to boom in the afternoon."

Mary gave a little snort of pleasure. "Now I've learned one thing and it's good.

"You learned the German way. It's the only way to knit—without watching your stitches."

The Hamerstrom rule of thirds

When we took our first pay job at the University of Michigan, Leopold chuckled and said, "You can satisfy the requirements in one third of your time." It was not at all plain to us what he meant, but perfectly plain that we were expected to do some thinking. We pondered this cryptic message and devised the Hamerstrom Rule of Thirds.

We never told our employers about the Rule of Thirds. It goes this way:

> *Spend one-third of your time on the mostly worthless red tape required by the administration.*
> *Spend one-third of your time doing what is wanted of you, and what you want too.*
> *Spend one-third of your time doing exactly what you please.*

I am convinced that this formula is unbeatable. It is not for the lazy, but for those who are willing to put in the extra time—far beyond a forty-hour week—and the effort to earn that extra "free" third to do a first-rate job.

I really hadn't figured on entertaining 7,000 house guests, but this turned out to be the most electric part of the free third. It just happened that way so we could get the job done; it was never subsidized by the state.

Furthermore, if some nimble gentleman wanted to chase me all over the front yard trying to stuff a five-dollar bill down the front of my shirt for the wonderful breakfast, I got his name and he got a receipt from the Prairie Chicken Foundation. We refused to take money. And a good thing too. If we had accepted money, our "guests" would have had a perfect right to complain that the mattresses were lumpy and the accommodations distinctly substandard.

I learned to be perfectly shameless about asking boomers to chip in food. Bill Pugh, one of the most outstanding friends of prairie chickens, who has done so much to save them, lives in Racine. Racine, Wisconsin, is the home of the kringle. The kringle is almost a coffee cake but so light and so alive with fruit and spices that it surpasses any Viennese pastry. Shamelessly, the Hamsterstroms accepted kringles from Bill Pugh and his fabulously beautiful wife . . . and if Betty Pugh whispered, "These are just for you," we slipped the kringles out of sight very quickly so we could eat them alone.

We found that the aristocrats didn't grumble, and neither did the very rich, nor the very poor. Our rather few troubles came from some sort of stuffy in-between layer. That layer would come out with remarks like, "I can't imagine how the State of Wisconsin subsidizes *this!*"

This—the house, the breakfasts, the briefings, and the good fellowship—was not what we were paid for. They were part of the third of our time that we had allotted to ourselves. I realize now that it was that extra "free" third that made it possible to save the prairie chickens.

The financial drain was not too bad because so many boomers brought coffee, eggs, bacon, and bread. But we never knew what might come in and had to keep the larder well stocked. The first time the Wisconsin Society for Ornithology scheduled a prairie chicken field trip, we failed to let Ed Peartree know that we couldn't guide an unlimited number of observers out to the blinds. Fourteen boomers stayed at our house, and nineteen more showed up unexpectedly for the First Breakfast at 2:30 A.M.! We knew they were coming, but not for breakfast! Each time one more walked in the back door I said, "Good morning," and broke two more eggs into a frying pan. I still remember a delightfully cultured voice asking, "Where do we warm the plates?"

I'm told I answered, "Oh, it's rather a warm morning." We served sixty-two eggs well before daybreak, and I was just hoping we had enough plates to put the eggs on.

After the booming season was over—seven days a week for eight to ten weeks—we sometimes just took off and went fishing with the children. Sometimes we took two or three days off without the slightest sense of guilt.

When we first started working for the Conservation Department about 1950, we were told, "A biologist's time is his own. He's expected to get the job done." Fair enough. Of course, we had to draw up work plans, keep track of official expenses, and write quarterly reports.

By the early 1970s great changes had come to pass. For one thing we were ordered to work *no more* than five days a week! To the best of my knowledge prairie chickens haven't the slightest idea what day of the week it is, and they boomed and fed energetically or not, depending on the weather. We solved that one by working in secret. We kept right on working seven days a week, but we had to cheat when reporting how many hours we worked each week.

This bothered us and was a far cry from "a biologist's time is his own." That was the union's doing.

In August of 1970 I got up early in the morning to work out some figures on population dynamics. Math is not my strong point, and I needed the cool early morning for concentration. By seven the household was moving, but I shut the door of my study and let everybody get his own breakfast.

At about 10:30 I finished running the calculator and had checked all my figures. I went over to the pond to take a break and swam slowly across the pond and back. Some of the men had left mist nets and poles on the beach. I picked up half of them to take them back and store them; then exhilarated by having finished complicated math and a nice swim, I picked up the rest and carried them toward the barn.

A strange little man in a business suit was more or less prancing around on our front lawn. I suspected he was a salesman of some sort.

"Are you Mrs. *Frances* Hamerstrom?"

I didn't like the way he said it. I was barefoot and wearing a shirt and shorts, but I pulled myself up to my full height and said, "I'm *Doctor* Frances Hamerstrom."

I liked his next question even less. "Are you working?" He didn't say it nicely, like, "I wouldn't want to trouble you if you are working." The tone of the question was wrong.

I eased the poles off my shoulder—more poles than *he* could carry, I'm sure—and asked him, "Does it look it?"

"What are the poles for?" he persisted.

"These are mist net poles. The Department of Natural Resources in cooperation with the federal government is banding mourning doves. I'm storing equipment."

The little man wasn't going to let go. He said, "This is just a spot check."

I failed to grasp what he was saying; he sounded repulsively official.

"Would you like to see my supervisor?"

"Yes."

I showed him the way to Frederick's study. Frederick has enormous dignity. He told me afterwards, "That man was sent up from Madison to see if you were working. He was pretty sheepish."

It took me about five hours to absorb what had happened. The little man was long gone, but I wanted to shake him until his teeth rattled.

Of course it wasn't *his* fault. It was the fault of the system that sent out a snooper.

Drop nets and whipping cream

It has been said that essentially all the principles used by biologists for catching wild animals were known to Stone Age man, and it would not surprise me at all to learn that the drop net we used for catching prairie chickens had its prototype in the deepest of dark Africa where Pygmies netted elephants in eons past. But we learned of the drop net from Caleb Glazener, who used it for turkeys. It revolutionized our trapping. Bait piles of ear corn were pulled out onto the marsh by toboggan. Whenever a substantial flock of chickens took to feeding on a pile, we drove six steel fence posts into the frozen ground to support a forty- by forty-foot horizontal net. Few modern houses are forty-foot by forty. It was a big net. We did not use Stone Age materials. We bought fish netting, stretched it with steel fence posts and fastened it for quick release. Our pull wires, which sometimes were a quarter-mile long, came from the hardware store.

One man (or I) was hidden in a pit in the snow with nothing to do except give the pull wire a mighty heave when the signal came. Another (seldom me) had the task of deciding when the maximum number of chickens were under the net—decisions, decisions! I learned to avoid this.

Five chickens walking toward the net and three running out. Twenty-six under at 3:15 and twenty under at 3:20, but seven rushing toward the net. I managed to get myself into that pit as often as possible. All the pit man had to do was pull the wire for all he was worth. Then six cotter pins slid through holes near the top of the fence posts, and the net dropped. The net bounded upwards once when the netted chickens tried to take off and then settled over the struggling chickens. We rushed in on snowshoes and hand-grabbed any birds that were likely to escape from the edges of the net.

Prairie chickens can entangle themselves in a net like Billy-be-damned in a matter of moments—after all, they are the wildest creatures I know. And I'd never known what to do with our children's outgrown socks; now I found a use. Each sock became a hood to slip

271

over a bouncing chicken's head: a rubber band made it stay put. Once hooded, the cocks and hens behaved like ladies and gentlemen and ceased to struggle; then we could extricate them from the net without dislocated wings and other unmentionable horrors.

There was one hitch. Sometimes only five of the six cotter pins pulled loose. Part of the net remained tilted upwards, and most of the flock escaped.

The solution came from a most unlikely source. Dan Berger and Helmut Mueller, who were helping us then, tried various lubricants manufactured by the automotive industry, but even so and all too often, one corner of the net failed to fall.

One day I forgot to bring along any lubricant, and Mueller looked at me accusingly and said, "Fran, what have you got?"

I handed him my Tangee lipstick. It was the best lubricant of all.

The press was attracted to our operations. Berger and Mueller had big black beards. I still remember a reporter from a Milwaukee paper, shivering in elegant field clothes. His pencil stopped moving when Berger ran over the bait pile and accosted Mueller. "Give me your lipstick!" Mueller reached in his pocket matter-of-factly and handed it over as the howling wind spat snow into our faces.

Helmut Mueller and Fran.

Not all our bait piles were near roads. Berger and I made one memorable set. We gunned the VW bus into the north end of the Buena Vista Marsh plunging through deep drifts. We both knew that if we could get the vehicle near the bait pile we could make a catch. The equipment for handling a big catch was more than we could carry, and there was no way that we could carry bags of chickens a mile or so to the bus without jeopardizing their lives.

How we were ever going to get the bus back onto a plowed road *after* the catch was a matter of secondary importance—simply a problem to be solved later. We shoveled through the drifts to get in, and our trail closed behind us in a smooth sweep of unbroken snow, masked by new falling snow and snow blown by the howling wind. At last we "parked" in sight of the net. We exposed the heap of corn under the net with a shovel and ran the long pull wire directly to the bus.

We waited snug in the bus with the set ready. Berger had a scope trained on the bait pile, and all I needed to do was to get out of the bus and give a mighty heave when he gave the signal. In the meantime I cooked dinner on the camp stove. It was Sunday: steak and potatoes; and strawberry shortcake for dessert.

The bus was like a little cave on an island—snug, resisting the wind, and isolated from the whole wide world. We ate our main course slowly, by which time the strawberries had thawed. Biscuits, left over from breakfast, were ready, and I sat on the floor in back of the bus to whip the rich, country cream we still could buy. Suddenly, without warning, I heard voices of strange men!

They were jackrabbit hunters and couldn't imagine why Berger was so happily relaxed inside a bus that was hopelessly stuck and far from any help.

We needed to get rid of those men. At any moment our chicken flock might swing by and be spooked by people in sight of the bait pile. I moved the eggbeater slowly, trying to think of what to say; I knew full well that if they ever realized we were doing something as fascinating as netting chickens they'd never go away.

Berger, who was sitting in the driver's seat, rolled down his window. The leader of the jackrabbit hunters said, "Young feller, you're stuck."

Berger answered easily, "We are not stuck. We're *parked.*"

The hunter absorbed this amazing information slowly. Then it dawned on him that Berger had said *we.* He peered into the back of the bus and asked, "What's *she* doing?"

Berger answered a little impatiently. "You can see perfectly well what she's doing. She's whipping cream."

One by one the old men snowshoed to peer in the window nearest to me. I spun the eggbeater with enthusiasm as each wiped the window with his mitten and peered. Without another word they snowshoed away—off into the storm.

We made our catch within forty minutes and shoveled innumerable drifts getting the bus out to where Bill Peterson, the district ranger, could pull us onto a plowed road.

I never saw the three old men again. They missed watching the big drop net fall. They missed watching us band the chickens, and they missed sampling my strawberry shortcake topped with slightly overbeaten whipped cream.

The photographers

Photographers were always a special problem. Almost nobody (there were two exceptions) could take good notes and use a camera at the same time.

The old western saloons had a barrel by the door in which, on especially formal occasions, the customers were requested to leave their shooting irons. Frederick sometimes threatened to put a barrel by our back door, but for cameras.

Photographers tended to feel free to interrupt the briefing by asking at what speed they should shoot. Each detail of prairie chicken behavior described generated new enthusiasm for the equipment they had brought with them: long lenses, wide angle lenses, special film, polarizing filters, etc.

Furthermore, with few exceptions, photographers are poor observers. So during the briefing we always asked, "Who brought a camera?"—just so we could put a good observer in the blind with him to take the notes. I know nothing about photography, nor do I intend to learn. What they say to each other is perfect gibberish to me, but there is no mistaking the tone of voice in which they speak to each other.

"I have a Ciné Special," one chap says eagerly.

"Oh!" the other replies, "that's a nice little camera. I had one years ago."

And then at the Second Breakfast they have a go at it again.

"How many feet did you shoot?"

"Four rolls."

"Did you *really?* The light was so bad today that I didn't even take my camera out of its case, but maybe you got something. . . ."

Photographers have taken knives and cut huge camera ports in the sides of our carefully constructed blinds.

It is the photographers who often have so much to carry that they want a biologist to tote some of their gear for them! And some of them have simply moved our blinds to suit mysterious purposes of their

own: backlighting, for example. But their chief complaint was usually about the inappropriate height of the windows in the blinds.

Many photographers, of course, are wonderful people and we are grateful for the pictures and films they have given us, but a certain wariness creeps over me every time I see a camera.

One morning at the Second Breakfast, Henry, a portly, somewhat elderly duck hunter, and his wife Mabel bubbled with enthusiasm for the prairie chickens, but asked me, "Why are the windows in the blind so low?"

"Low? Are you photographers?"

"No, we were just watching." Mabel added, "We took turns watching."

"You took *turns?* Why?" This whole business of the low windows was becoming more and more mystifying.

"There wasn't room for both of us to look out of the windows at once."

"We've never heard of a complaint like this before. Those windows are at eye level and every blind has six windows."

"Yes," she answered, "but our eyes were so low down. We had to take turns on our hands and knees." These dear old people smiled at each other understandingly. She explained, "We are both so very plump."

I got to liking them more and more, but I couldn't imagine what

276

on earth they were talking about. "Why didn't you just get in the blind and sit on the bench?"

"The bench?" she asked and added, "Why Henry, there *was* a bench. A nice little bench right out among the birds!"

In a dizzying moment their predicament became clear to me. Yesterday's wind had capsized their blind and blown it away from the bench as well. They had spent the morning in an upside-down blind!

Tail end of spring

Morning! The pale glint of pre-dawn outside our bedroom window outlines the barn and I get up running. It must be that the alarm clock has failed because Frederick, who usually gets up first, is still asleep. I stand baffled in the kitchen. No eggs counted out ... no plates ready ... no clutter of gear on the floor.

No boomers. The season is over and the perpetual houseparty is past until another year.

The old house is very quiet.

Pavlov conditioned dogs to salivate when they heard the dinner bell. I have been conditioned too. My internal clock is set for predawn in spring.

After booming season, the briefing room became my study again.

Boomers were sometimes discouraged from entering Frederick's study by leaving the lights off . . . and the curtains of fishnetting were often drawn to exclude owls.

The same oval mirror hangs on another wall over the same blue sofa as it did forty-five years ago when I was so uncertain and young.

We cleaned up after the booming season.

(It's ten years since our last boomers have come and gone, and I still wake up from time to time ready to run, to cook, to guide to the blinds.)

Every spring I was conditioned anew to the heady excitement of laughter, of strangers in the house—the fascinating mishmash of volunteers from all walks of life; then—not unmixed with relief that another season had gone well—there was always a sense of loss when it was all over.

It would be exhilarating to hear, just once more, the cars of the boomers pull into the drive, give a briefing, and get everybody out to the blinds before the cold gray dawn. . . .

But at the end of each booming season we had more time for the children. Time to field tough questions like, "Why is the sky?" or, "If an owl saw me pushing a baby buggy would it be surprised?"

I cannot imagine what it must have been like to be brought up a Hamerstrom child. We brought them up under rules—or better still, policies. The first, established the day Alan was born, was:

> *We do not own our children*
> *Our children own themselves*

This meant that even as toddlers they were treated with the same courtesy as grownups. Mind you, one does lose one's temper from time to time—and then apologizes.

Our second policy was: always say *yes* when you possibly can; only say *no* when you have to. When Alan asked, "Can I go barefoot in the snow?" I absent-mindedly corrected his English and answered, "You *may*."

In 1954 we were invited to go to Finland—a chance to study grouse in the far North. We held a family council. "You Alan, will go to a horseback riding camp in Arizona."

Alan's answer was a shout. "Hi . . . yo . . . Silver!"

"And Elva will go to visit her grandmother."

"I don't want to. I want to stay here and look after my pets."

Frederick shook his head, and I added, "You are only eleven; we can't let you spend the night alone in this house."

Dreary rain beat against the windows as Elva slowly left the room—I supposed to take comfort from one of her many pets. I knew no way to console her so I left her alone.

About forty minutes later she burst into the house, drenched by the downpour which was getting heavier. "I fixed it! Mrs. Jorgenson says that Nancy and I can spend the nights in their old chicken coop. We're going to fix it up for a clubhouse."

Frederick and I looked at each other. "You mean," he asked, "you plan to spend the *days* here and the *nights* at the Jorgensons?"

"Sure. I have my bicycle and it's only half a mile."

(Always say *yes* when you possibly can.)

We said yes.

Perhaps because we were a mite worried about this unconventional arrangement, we told the sheriff that the house would be empty for a couple of months and asked him to stop in now and again.

True to his word, he stopped, and when we came back his story ran something like this:

"The driveway hadn't been used for a long time. The door was wide open. I knocked; nobody came so I walked in. A white chicken squawked and jumped off a sofa, and a rabbit hopped out of another room like he was waiting for me.

"Then I opened a door and a big owl, sitting on the back of a chair, bobbed its head like it was going to come for me. I shut that door quick and went upstairs.

"None of the beds had been slept in; some kid had left crayon drawings of animals on one of them. Back in the kitchen I could smell somebody had been cooking, and there was fresh food in the refrigerator.

"I went outside to think. There were bicycle tracks in the drive. I'd missed them before. Then I heard sounds I couldn't figure out at all . . . way out back of a big plum thicket.

"I moseyed over and there was a pretty little girl, sitting in a patch of daisies, playing a clarinet.

"I didn't want to scare her, so I waited till she saw me. I asked her, 'Where are your parents?'

"That little kid smiled at me. Guess what she said?

'I don't know. I think they're in Lapland.' "

Time to trade children

Some might feel that the upbringing of our children was highly permissive. We never worried about that. We worried about the lack of cultural advantages: no governesses, no tutors, no languages, no art taught in school, no dancing school. We arranged to exchange children with European biologists.

Alan was the first to go to Europe. He went alone, on an ocean liner, at the age of twelve. We gave him a note to take with him:

> *Alan Hamerstrom is allowed to stay up as late as he pleases.*
> *(Signed by his parents, Frederick and Frances Hamerstrom.)*

Alan stayed up late the first night on board ship. Thereafter he got sleepy soon after supper. He and another boy played detective and followed an old Irishman for much of the journey. Just before they docked at Le Havre, they told the Irishman what they'd been doing and all he said was, "Is that so."

The Cunard Line was willing to accept a twelve-year-old traveling alone but insisted that the child must be met upon arrival. We arranged with a French courier service to have Alan met. One small twelve-year-old American boy, wearing scuffed shoes and carrying a battered suitcase, went down the tourist class gangplank and was met by *six* bowing Frenchmen. He was accompanied on the boat train to Paris and conducted to the Hotel Louvre. The tall windows of his room had two kinds of fancy curtains and he had a huge private bath. A courier asked anxiously if he would be afraid to go down to dinner alone.

"Not at all."

Alan dined alone in the elegant dining room, confusing the waiters not by speaking English, but by wanting hamburgers or hot dogs. After dinner he went out and hired a taxi to take him to an American movie. After the movie was over, he hired another taxi to take him to another American movie. Then he hired a third taxi to take him back to his hotel.

The next day he set forth for the north of Germany and just what we hoped wouldn't happen—did. Alan's train missed connections and he was stranded at eleven o'clock at night in a strange city not knowing a word of any foreign language. He was picked up by a Woman's Army

Corps (WAC) major who took him out to dinner and talked with him until he could catch the next train for Wilhelmshaven. One of the first things he told us about when he came back home was that he'd done something wrong.

"Something wrong?" Our small son was looking very concerned.

"I didn't pay for the WAC major's dinner. She paid and I should have."

Alan spent a year with Gustav Kramer, the man who invented an artificial sun to study bird migration, and Frau Dr. Kramer let him go on long bicycle trips with their children.

Elva, at age twelve, also spent a year abroad in Germany and Austria visiting the Konrad Lorenz family and the Gustav Kramer family. Perhaps not having dancing lessons wasn't too bad. The first dance she ever went to was in a castle.

Elva sent this photograph from Europe. "Look, I'm reading German!"

Alan and friends at the starting point of a 200-mile five-day bike trip to Oldenburg, Zwischenahn, Bremerhaven, and back to Wilhelmshaven in 1954.

284

When we started the children exchange program we just thought how wonderful for our children to go to visit in Europe. Having the European children come to visit us was wondrously rewarding. So much so that five came to stay with us: Peter, Lorenz, and Elisabeth Kramer, Dagmar Lorenz, and Silvia Ebner, daughter of a forester. Four

Dagmar Lorenz.

Silvia Ebner.

Elisabeth Kramer.

Peter Kramer.

Lorenz Kramer.

of these had a wonderful time living in an old American farmhouse, pumping water out of a creaky pump, and exploring what seemed incredibly wild country to them. Silvia was too old. She was seventeen and homesick. Twelve seems the perfect age for children to live in a foreign country. Our arrangement was simple: one year we'd have one child at home and the next year we might have three or even four (one or two of our own and the others European). Our school took in the Europeans, who picked up English as they went along, and the German schools took our children on a similar basis.

There is much discussion nowadays about the difficulty of forcing children to learn a new language. It is my impression that most children are taught new languages so late in life—in their teens—and are exposed to the new language so few hours a day—often only five hours a week—that learning the new language becomes prolonged agony, rather than a simple and natural accomplishment easily mastered in a year.

Our children knew no German when they went abroad. Alan came back with a clipped north German accent and our daughter's German is tinged with the blurred accents of the south.

A redhead is serenaded

Travel gave our children poise but dating must have been something of a problem in our house, especially during the prairie chicken booming season. Whoever took Elva to a dance or roller skating had to wend his way through all the birdwatchers to pick up his date. But there were compensations. The first time that Alan brought a girl to visit happened to be a night when a college band had come to watch the chickens.

Of course Alan and his date came in late and she was still sound asleep in the corner guest room when the band came back for a Second Breakfast. The band got all dressed up in their uniforms and practiced a bit out on the lawn. Alan emerged and asked, "What's that?"

"Alan," I said, "run up to the corner guest room. Wake Karen up. Tell her she's being serenaded. I'll dash out and get the band to look up at her window."

When a red-headed high-school girl appeared at the window, the band, in full uniform, launched into *Let Me Call You Sweetheart*. Alan took her hand and said, "I wouldn't do this for everybody."

When Alan was a Harvard freshman he shared a suite with four roommates, and he liked only one of them. They talked a lot about home: their houses, cars, and summer places. Alan said little. Finally one asked, "Alan, what sort of a house do *you* live in?"

"An old tumble-down farmhouse that hasn't been painted since before the Civil War. We all have to pump our own water and carry in wood to keep the fires burning."

"What does your father do?"

"He's a professional birdwatcher."

The roommates dropped the matter for a few days and then came out with another question. "What kind of a car do you usually drive when you're at home?"

"My mother's used telephone repairman's truck."

One day a car with a Harvard College sticker drove in the drive-way. A conservative young man got out and looked upon our weath-ered farmhouse. He examined my used telephone repairman's truck with interest.

When he walked toward the door, Frederick, with binoculars hung around his neck, greeted him.

One roommate, the one Alan liked, had come all the way to see if it really was true. The evidence was overwhelming.

We brought up our two children far from the advice of relatives and well-meaning friends. This was possible for us as wildlife research parents living out in the country—simply and naturally. We know now that the most enormous advantage we offered our children was to grow up with wild pets and native flora, and to let them grow by exploration.

Let me sew her up

Frederick pulled another prairie chicken out of one of the bouncing, wailing bags in the tiny blind. "She's gangrenous," he said. "What a mess. I'll kill her."

"Give her to me." I grabbed the hen by both legs, immobilized her wings between my knees, and examined the wound. Torn skin exposing the flesh beneath ran along her slim pulsing neck, across her barred breast, down across her belly, and just missed her hip joint.

It was February. The northwest wind tore at the small window slots of our four-foot-square blind; now and again puffs of snow seeped in to dust us and the wounded prairie hen. Instinctively, I shifted her position to protect the exposed wound from wind and snow.

"Must have hit a fence." Frederick reached for the bird. "Give her to me."

I shook my head. "Let me sew her up. It will take just a minute."

Side by side we sat on a wooden bench three feet long and nine inches wide. We argued. Seed pearls of sparkling frost clung to Frederick's black mustache, and my fingers—tight around the chicken's legs—pulled pain deep into my mittenless hand.

Behind us, in gunnysacks, the chickens we had already caught wailed and mewed their complaint. Suddenly one fluttered. One wing beat was enough to set off the chain reaction. Two bags of birds leapt as though possessed by seventeen devils of hell, and every chicken in those bags lost precious energy before release time.

Frederick gave me *the look*.

Just then a little bit of gray knitted wool—the spare sock—beckoned to me. It was wedged under his end of our bench. It's hard enough for somebody six foot one and in full winter regalia to get up from a tippy bench just nine inches high—and even harder when the roof is only four inches above his head.

"Could you lift your end of the bench just a little?"

Silence.

Frederick is not only my husband but also my boss; I am his

assistant and get a lesser salary. He has a perfect right to order me about. He doesn't: he just tells me what to do in a reasonable tone of voice.

No houses in sight. We two alone out on the marsh. White-out of snow. *One* gray sock was all that I wanted.

Taking a leaf from Frederick's book, I inquired in an offhand, reasonable tone of voice, "Why don't you lift up your end of the bench so we can start processing?"

My eyes were on the sock, so I didn't see his face. Perhaps, if I had glanced at it, I would not have pursued the matter. Slowly he eased one boot around the end of the bench, shifted his weight carefully, and pulled upwards. My muscles were primed to get my weight off that bench and reach for the sock in perfect timing with his effort. But, handicapped by the chicken between my knees, my foot slipped and I sat down with a thump.

The wailing of the prairie chickens was punctuated by a low grunt from the throat of my man.

"Sorry," I mumbled.

With a degree of instant nimbleness that I managed to muster against almost impossible odds in that cramped space, I half slid, half bounced off my end of the bench and knelt in the snow.

Frederick moved his heavy boot once more, shifted his weight carefully, and eased his end of the bench up an inch or two, and I wrenched the sock out with a mighty jerk.

Then I pushed the hen down into the sock where she would rest in her gentle straitjacket.

Meekly, I asked, "Would you like me to help you set up the scales?" Silly question: of course we were going to set up the scales and weigh and band and process and release those bags full of chickens. But I couldn't think of anything else to say at the moment. "Thank you" would have been a mite inadequate, and for once "thank you" lacked tact.

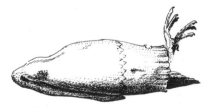

Frederick set up the scales. I untied one bag and felt carefully deep down into the warm feathery interior. I felt for both legs of *one* chicken and managed to pull a bird out of the bag without setting the rest aflutter. It took a steady hand and a good deal of practice; I was going to see to it that the model wife and perfect assistant was doing her work without blunders.

We love working together and it isn't often that the little clash of wills interrupts our teamwork. For the next half-hour or so we weighed and processed one bird after another. It became a smooth routine. Weigh, process, band, and peek out of the window to check the traps; then push the bird out of the little window for release.

Suddenly, Frederick whispered, "Chickens." A flock of about thirty came swinging in from the west, flutter-braked, and landed at the edge of the cornfield. They started walking toward our well-baited traps.

"Do we have some empty bags?"

Frederick nodded. From now on we would put processed chickens into empty bags for we had no intention of frightening the flock away by letting even one clattering chicken emerge from the window—our usual method of release.

From time to time I peeked at my patient. Her feathered feet with their delicate snowshoes—those little combs on each toe—remained upright and motionless. Would she ever run again? Would she ever fly?

At last our catch was processed and ready for release. Some of the traps seemed blackened with birds. Frederick peered out of his window. "We've got all we can handle. Let's go."

We tipped the blind, which had no door, over on its side. The late afternoon light dazzled our eyes, and fresh outdoor cold stung our cheeks and our noses. We released the processed birds, put on our snowshoes, and mushed out to the traps to bring in our second catch.

I said, "Darling, this is crazy. What made you think of working out of a blind here instead of running the trapline?"

Frederick was balancing the scales again ... "Just had a hunch today." His hunch had been good. We two were sitting in a blind chalking up a record catch.

Again we processed and released, and I produced two almond Hershey bars out of my inside shirt pocket when it was really time for us to be on our way home.

We munched. It was a good moment. Our bones ached and the

cold had taken its toll on us. A mackerel sky, laced with orange and purple, promised another big catch for the morrow.

Frederick said, "It was a good day." And I could follow his thinking: a record catch, and nothing to do but snowshoe to the car with the scales and equipment, *start* the car, push home through the drifts, and enter a stone-cold house where he would get the fire going and I would cook a good supper.

Instead I said, "Darling, please pass me the needle and thread."
Frederick said, "What?"
"The light is getting very bad and I need to sew her up now."
"Her?"
"You remember—that hen that I socked."

My man can mesmerize a prairie chicken. He held that bird while I sewed her up. Even in the bitter cold we both could detect the stench of putrifying flesh and, in the less than half light, the green of gangrene loomed ominously. His long, clever fingers manipulated the bird. I loosened the skin along the whole length of the wound, and then I pulled gently to find the *middle* of the tear in the skin . . . not the middle by math, the middle by feel. Having found my intangible middle, my fingers found new "middles"—not true middles, because my fingers had to allow for the unseemly stretchable skin of the neck and belly. I used cotton thread and an ordinary sewing needle, tying the square knots quickly and then holding up the threads for Frederick to clip my sutures.

We processed her. She weighed 726.2 grams and the bands she wore were green 23 over red. When we released her, she flew—away into the deep, dark dusk. She *flew.*

We headed home, and after we got the stove going in the kitchen, we had mulligan for supper. Then we crawled into bed. I whispered, "I'm sorry. I was pretty silly about that hen."

"What?"

"I was pretty silly about that hen today."

Frederick's only answer was, "I was *asleep!*"

That dratted hen had whizzed off into the night from the south end of the Buena Vista Marsh and I wished her well. Would she had wished me the same!

On April 28, the following spring, I came back from watching displaying prairie chickens from a blind and announced with much excitement, "I saw a hen with a brood patch!"

293

"Brood patch!" Frederick exclaimed with interest. "We've never seen a hen with a brood patch on a booming ground. We've been quite certain that one copulation is enough to fertilize a whole clutch of eggs." A brood patch—a big bare patch on the belly—implied that a prairie hen had started incubation and was coming back for another insemination.

"I saw it. Her belly feathers were every which way. And right where the brood patch has got to be!"

Frederick is a patient man. "Did you get her bands?"

"Yes, green 23 over red."

We walked over to the files and looked up the number. Then he looked at me with astonishment. "That was the gangrenous hen at Skrznecki's. She lived, but I don't think what you saw was a brood patch. It looks as though you didn't sew her belly up just right."

Ought to be the end of that hen's story, but no. I told it more than once—amusing story—and became quite a heroine for saving that bird's life. But year after year I watched the range of our prairie chickens disappear under the plow and drainage. And I began to grow up. I came to realize that the saving of one individual for sentimental reasons is nothing compared to preservation of habitat for a species.

Frederick knew this all the time.

Raincoat

From time to time all Pittman-Robertson projects are subject to federal inspection. Inspectors traveled in pairs and always announced when they were coming. On August 15, 1959, they were coming to review our project.

We never dreaded these visitations; the inspectors were biologists, and we looked forward to the chance to discuss our project. I straightened the house up a bit, made sure that I had plenty of good food on hand and, as the inspectors were not due until nine o'clock, I went kestrel trapping. It seemed a pity to waste a day, as these little hawks were passing through on migration in goodly numbers.

I just thought I'd run up and down the road to see if I couldn't catch one or two before the inspectors arrived.

Trapping was fabulous. I set two small balchatris—little cages baited with mice—by the roadside and caught two birds before I could get the car turned around. Then I noticed that while I had been cleaning up the house, Frederick had been cleaning up the car: my bands, tubes, and scales were all back at the house.

I put one kestrel in my purse, leaving the top slightly open, and looked around for something to put the next one into. (Frederick had been thorough.) All I could find was my raincoat and I feared the kestrel might smother in that, so I took off my shoes and socks and put the bird in a sock. By then I had caught *three* more birds! I slipped one of these into the other sock and then—holding two kestrels in one

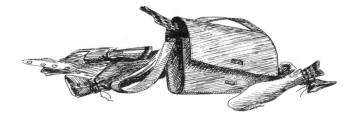

hand—I put on the raincoat, took off my slacks, and fastened the remaining two birds into the pants legs.

The sun was getting fairly high and the heat was beginning to beat down. Common sense should have suggested that it was time to quit and go home, but I never gave it a thought. Another kestrel was working one of the traps, and there were two more sitting on a wire just down the road. I baited and set out another balchatri and caught three more. I muttered "Damn female clothes." *My* slacks had no pockets—but my shirt did.

Looking carefully up and down the road to make sure no one was in sight, I took off the raincoat, took off my shirt, and hastily donned the raincoat again. It was all I had on.

A kestrel apiece went into each pocket of my shirt, and I tied one into a sleeve.

So far there had been no traffic. A farm truck went by and brought me to my senses. It was so hot that the birds in their unusual containers might suffer heat stroke. Thank heavens I hadn't put any bird in a raincoat sleeve; the broiling sun made this long, impermeable garment almost unbearable. I drove home quickly.

There was a strange car in the driveway—a long, low car bearing the unmistakable insignia of the United States on its well-polished door. I had forgotten the inspection.

I considered climbing in the window of our bedroom to change clothes, but the window was closed against the heat and our old-fashioned windows couldn't be pried open. Frederick and the inspectors were sitting at the living room table, and there was only one way to get to my clothes; I rushed past them in my long, floppy raincoat and slammed the bedroom door.

A few minutes later I emerged smiling and bombarded the inspectors with questions about prairie chickens to keep them from asking me what I'd been up to. I wasn't paid to work on hawks and, although in those far-gone days a "biologist's time was his own," I didn't want to explain why I was rushing about in the sunlight in a raincoat.

It took me a little longer than usual to prepare lunch that day because I was banding and processing kestrels in the kitchen at the same time.

After the inspectors left, Frederick asked, "What on earth were you doing in that raincoat?"

He was not prepared for my rejoinder. "Oh, darling, do you think they noticed?"

296

Our semi-secret work on hawks

Movie theaters used to be a fine place to get mice. They were open to the public. Every theater had a popcorn stand. Spilled popcorn kept the mice concentrated and breeding. We used the pounce system for catching them, but sometimes we took off our boots and laid them along the wall. Each mouse that chose to hide in a boot was very easy to catch—in fact it was essentially caught.

This esoteric information we kept to ourselves. Throughout my childhood my double life kept the powerful grownups from interfering with my passion for animals and the natural world. Throughout our twenty-three years with the state of Wisconsin Frederick and I studied prairie chickens with delight and in semi-secret we trapped, banded, and studied birds of prey. We sometimes published our findings in obscure journals, for example, *Falconry News and Notes, Hawk Chalk,* the *Purple Martin Capital News.* It seemed unlikely that our inspectors would ever delve into this literature.

All during the Prairie Chicken Project another deep-seated interest permeated parts of our being—it was our perennial passion for birds of prey.

Sometimes I feared that the big chiefs in the Wisconsin Department of Natural Resources (who paid us to work on prairie chickens) would ask, "Just how much time are you spending on hawks?" I

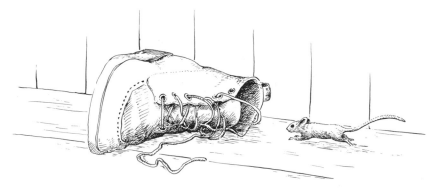

could almost hear one of the chiefs clear his throat and continue, "and on owls."

The question never came but I was ready with my answer.

"Do you mind if I play bridge in my free time?"

We published seventy papers on birds of prey.

My introduction to the falconry community was simple: I took quarry with my first falcon in 1919, quite sure that there were no other falconers in the world. But my academic introduction to birds of prey was a bit rougher. In 1935 I gathered pellets of two Great Horned owls that inhabited an island in Lost Island Lake near Ruthven, Iowa. I was just an undergraduate, but I was married and the "Mrs." in front of my name—of all things—gave me a certain prestige.

Well knowing that I was just a female made me realize that I had better get out some scientific publications and show that I could do good scientific work—Motherhood and just being sweet was not my only possible career.

It certainly never entered our heads that when we finished our prairie chicken work and the state published *The Prairie Chicken— Highlights of a 22-year study of counts, behavior, movements, turnover, and habitat,* we were on our way to an international reputation for our work on birds of prey. This I find particularly amazing because of my sex. As far as I know only four women "made it" as wildlife field biologists before Women's Lib. They were Elizabeth Schwartz, the mathematical and well-organized half of the famous Charles and Elizabeth Schwartz team; Elizabeth (Baird) Locey, of whom the Seney Refuge's manager said, "The best man I ever had!"; Margaret Altman, who worked on moose; and Fran Hamerstrom. Please do note that I am making a distinction between *field* biologists who ran the traplines, snowshoed, and battled it out in the swamps and the heat, and indoor biologists.

I paved my way toward this glorious profession by striving to get out a publication. Very carefully, I wrote up the year-round food habits of a pair of Great Horned Owls who lived on an island in northwest Iowa. I took the manuscript to Professor Paul L. Errington.

"Very nice," he said, "that should make a nice little paper." My first scientific paper! And how well I knew that as a female I desperately needed a publication.

Some months passed and one day Errington said, "Fran, where is that material you wrote up about the island owls?"

I brought it to him beaming: in my imagination I could already see my carefully prepared words under my name in print:

"This will do nicely in the horned owl bulletin."

"In the *bulletin?*"

"Yes. It just fits under case histories."

So it was that my precious first scientific publication was co-authored with Paul L. Errington and Frederick Hamerstrom. It was small consolation that "The Great Horned Owl and Its Prey in North-Central United States" won the Wildlife Society Award for the best publication of the year.

Eagle in a peach tree

Frederick and I had made ourselves egregiously unpopular in 1959. We were standing up for a principle: namely that trees should *not* grow wherever a tree can be made to grow, but that Wisconsin's public lands should have the rich diversity of various stages of the plant succession, supporting many species of wildlife—including the sharp-tailed grouse.

Anyone who has been in public service knows what these trying periods are like. Friends take you aside and admonish you in low tones, the uninformed know there is something up and don't know whether or not to be seen speaking to you, and the opposition plainly desires to pelt you with rotten tomatoes—or worse.

Just at this time the state of Ohio borrowed us from our own conservation department, to make a survey of potential sharp-tailed grouse range in Ashtabula County. Ohio rolled out the red velvet carpet. Frederick was given a plane and a pilot; I was given a plane and a pilot to make it easy for us to map likely looking sharptail habitat from the air. We were housed in a plush motel. And, furthermore, Ohio biologists and some federal personnel were sent to our headquarters so they could have the valuable experience of meeting us. It was heady, especially in contrast to the rotten-tomato climate at home.

After I had completed my survey (which went smoothly because my pilot had not gotten lost), one of the biologists mentioned that there was an eagle's nest nearby.

"Eagle! We ought to band the young."

"Waal, who's gonna climb that tree?" he drawled in what I assume was Ashtabula County dialect.

"What kind of a tree is it?"

"It's a *peach* tree."

Knowing full well that there isn't a peach tree in the world that can't be mastered with a fourteen-foot stepladder, I spoke without hesitation. "I will."

The chap looked me over with considerable interest.

"I have bands. Frederick has to go up with his pilot again tomorrow, so I'm free. Shall we start about eight?"

He shook his head slowly, walked a few yards, and then turned around to look at me again. "Eight o'clock," I shouted after him.

He nodded.

He was ready the next morning. Just in case there was more than one eagle's nest, I stowed my climbing gear in his station wagon, which was so full of biologists that I had to ask one of them to help me find room.

We drove through pleasant Ohio woods, crossed the line into Pennsylvania and parked near a dock, where I recognized quite a few of the federal personnel on hand. Everybody piled into a large motor launch. It did not occur to me to wonder where they were going or why. . . .

I watched the shoreline for peach trees. Pymatuning Wildlife Refuge abounded in tall hardwoods and conifers. Finally I asked my guide, "Where is this peach tree?"

"On an island. We'll be there pretty soon."

So I started watching the islands. When the launch was beached on an island everyone disembarked. Before I had time to ask, my guide pointed. "There it is."

High in a sky-busting *beech* tree was an obviously active bald eagle nest.

I have good professional climbing equipment: climbing irons with long spurs, a tree surgeon's belt, and a long sling to go around the tree.

My sling was obviously far too short to go around that tree trunk; besides, the giant beech was split about two-thirds of the way up, and I had no way of roping in to get past the split!

A tall nearby hemlock was my only chance of getting anywhere near the eagle's nest. I fastened my banding kit to my belt and scurried up the hemlock to reconnoiter. There was a possible route to the crown of the beech. I didn't like it, but it was possible.

One beech branch could be reached by crawling out on a hemlock limb. I hitched myself out until my weight brought the hemlock branch down so I could reach the beech branch, which was bigger than my wrist. I knew it was strong enough. The question was: could I get back? Reassuring hemlock branches below me suggested that, with reasonable luck, the beech branch would bend so I could reach some hemlock branch to take me back to earth after the eagles were banded.

I would never have tried it if I had been alone, but it was plain that all those delightful men had come to watch me. The honor of the

Hamerstroms was at stake. Besides it was long before the days of Women's Lib and not a time to chicken out.

The beech limb swooshed down with my weight, and I slithered over to the main part of the trunk like some kind of fairly awkward mechanical toy. It was no problem, and it was no problem to get to the eagle's nest. I grabbed for the bigger eaglet, but she backed off to the far side of the nest, so I banded the easy one. I had to take the nest apart a bit to find a stick with a hook at the end, with which to horse that big eaglet to where I could grab her. For a moment I looked down to see how far she would fall if something went wrong.

Far, far below me, the motor launch looked small. And on the beach there were faces—little faces of all those men watching me. I giggled.

Then I heaved myself onto the edge of the nest and pulled with my stick until that big baby eagle lost her balance. For a split second, her left wing tip was almost within teach. I lunged, grabbed it, and pulled her unceremoniously across the nest toward me. I rested for a moment or two after I finished banding her. Then I climbed slowly down to a certain slender beech limb—my lifeline. When I reached it, I rested again with arms and legs hanging down to bring a good blood supply into my muscles. I leaned against that beech limb and I didn't like it.

It does no good to reflect too long. I hitched my way back across my natural bridge with butterflies in my stomach until the slender

beech limb bent. I moved farther, and it made contact with a perfect hemlock branch. I was home!

Then I rested again, not because my muscles were tired, but because I had to put distance between myself and recent terror.

When I got down, my guide said, "You'll tackle anything, won't you?"

My answer must have puzzled him. "You have unusual accents around here."

Some peach tree!

The moviemakers

I have read of conference telephone calls and I can visualize one. I picture three or more beardless but otherwise important-looking gentlemen sitting by polished, almost empty desks discussing such things as mergers, mortgages, and moratoriums. When I heard our ring on the party line I pushed aside some hip boots left over from the hunting season, moved a basket of apples to reach the telephone on our kitchen wall, and found myself in a conference call with Dean Tvedt and Staber Reese. One of them asked, "You have a bird?"

There were two pet horned owls on the porch, many pigeons and starlings in the barn, and Joey, a convalescent horned owl, flying free. Looking through the window I could watch Nancy playing with the tail of the last calf I had cut up for her. I simplified my answer, "Yes, an eagle."

"We would like to make a film. What can she take?"

I admitted most of her quarry had been bagged hares, released for her to get the hang of hunting, but said fox would be a suitable quarry.

"Fox! You think she'd take a fox?"

The conference call lost its fearsome formality. I rested my foot on the edge of the apple basket and suspect that the gentlemen in Madison leaned forward a little in their chairs.

"I think she will. You bring the fox. It might take weeks to get a slip at a fox in the wild, with cameras in position and good light."

"And you'll have her ready? We'll set a date."

"Yes. I'll have her ready."

I was not sure how Nancy would react to a fox, especially since I had deterred her from trying for dogs by jerking her jesses each time she looked too interested; but I was sure I'd have her ready.

I planned her feeding schedule with care: full gorge that day; thereafter, till the moviemakers came, two-thirds gorge each day (the equivalent of a good meal but not a Christmas dinner); exercise every day; and then the day before Movie Day, no dinner.

It seemed so easy to say I'd have her ready. Her muscles were firm

and strong. She was bouncing, in yarak, and lovely to behold. She always did her best with good appetite on an empty stomach.

Movie Day—everything was in readiness, but anticipation got me up early. The stars were shining, auguring well for a clear day, with a light breeze from the west. I poked the fire, added a couple of chunks of seasoned oak, started the coffee, and looked out of the window. Something was very wrong. The morning half-light was deceiving, but it was plain that Nancy was not on her perch. She was on the ground, and large, dark feathers lay strewn on the snow nearby.

Still barefoot, I ran out to her, snatching up a glove on my way. Joey, the owl, had been careless once too often. Nancy had caught him from her perch and with both feet on his breast, was taking her pleasure on him. She had finished eating his neck and part of his head and was breaking into the tender, dark breast meat. I made in quickly, seeing to it that she did not swallow another morsel, but I knew that the edge was off her appetite. Nancy was not ready in the way I meant to have her ready, but she was rather sharp-set just the same.

There is an especial aura to movie people. They dress with elegance, tell lively stories, and they appear to have all the time in the world for seemingly idle chatter until the right moment approaches and the light is good. It is then that one realizes that the chatter was not wholly idle. They have been sizing up the circumstances and watching the clock, watching the sun, and just like a flock of birds that wheels simultaneously in flight without a detectable signal, the movie people decide the time has come to take pictures.

Six people were in on this, and it is unlikely that any of us will ever forget what some might deem a fiasco and what others might consider an opportunity to study reactions of released foxes and, for that matter, of people.

Staber set down his coffee cup and said, "Let's go." I took Nancy from her perch and put her in my car. The other vehicles, painstakingly laden with expensive equipment and a fox in a box, followed.

The caravan set out for one of the great open fields of the Buena Vista Marsh. I had already flown Nancy there a few days before at bagged quarry to instill in her the notion that good things emerge mysteriously from this particular meadow. Bob Davis set the box with fox where Nancy had made her last kill. The plan was for me to cast Nancy off and when she reached sufficient altitude and got into good position, I'd give the signal for the fox to be released. It was breathtaking. Nancy, cast off into the wind, circled, and quickly gaining pitch, came into perfect position. Three cameramen, two from car tops, crouched over their cameras, and exultantly I gave the signal. Davis opened the release door. Nothing happened. No fox appeared.

Nancy made her second swing over the countryside, and at my repeated and rather frenzied signals, Davis started kicking the box. Again no fox.

By now, Nancy was flying great circles in the wind and then took a perch a half-mile away. I ran toward the box shouting, cursing, and imploring, "Get that fox out of there. Get it *out.*" Davis picked up the heavy box and shook it till the fox fell out. It trotted to the south end of a long snowbank near us and seated itself comfortably, facing the cars and people.

Perhaps it cannot be said that eagles amble on the wing, but after due consideration, Nancy came slowly back and perched on the north end of the selfsame snowbank, waiting to see what I wanted her to do next. It seemed that things had come to a standstill. But eventually the fox took the initiative by wandering over in an offhand manner to sniff Nancy. Nancy watched it come, at first with curiosity. When it got uncomfortably close and was almost upon her, she panicked and opened up her six-and-a-half-foot wingspread to take off.

It is unlikely that the fox had ever before seen a stately and almost inanimate object open up like an umbrella. It ran as only foxes can.

Thus it was that the fox, not I, gave the signal for action. Nancy had a perfectly clear notion of what she was supposed to do: if something was running away and I too was running and shouting encouragement, she was supposed to catch it and bind to it, and I would reward her

306

suitably. The story almost ended in that way, but after a short and spirited chase the fox took refuge among the people.

We had picked a bare snowfield. To be sure there was a small abandoned shed near the road, but the fox sensibly selected the nearest refuge—a conglomeration of men, cameras, and tripods. There it appeared quite at home and behaved rather like a dog whose owner did not happen to be nearby.

Repeatedly we tried to get the fox out of the crowd. (I know there were only six of us, but with a fox taking refuge among us, we were a *crowd*.) Occasionally we succeeded in evicting the fox or moved away from it. Several times the fox left this hostile group of shouting people, and Nancy took wing and stopped, only to be frustrated by losing the fox among us again.

There were periods of relative calm. Good moviemen are practical; if they can't get what they are after, they tend to return with what I believe they call "footage." At one point in the proceedings the fox sat down on an untrampled patch of snow. "Hold it," called a photographer. We were glad to hold it; we were winded. Even Nancy was panting, and only the fox showed no sign of exertion. He sat as though taking pleasure in the afternoon sunlight. Tripods and cameras took position and the soft whirr of incipient footage could be heard if one turned his head enough to cut out the snarl of the west wind.

A cameraman called, "Get it to move." We had nothing to throw at it—one cannot make snowballs of deep powdery snow. I ran to my car and handed Rodd Friday an almost empty bottle of instant coffee. What a charming scene: fox in sunlight, sitting at rest; coffee bottle flying past his nose missing it by inches; fox getting up slowly and going over to sniff the bottle. It is sad to realize that editorial scissors probably cut this footage.

At any rate the coffee bottle precipitated the next scene.

The fox was moving again and outside the crowd. With one intent we all took off in full pursuit, so the fox took to the second best cover in the vicinity, namely the abandoned shed by the road. Davis by now had come to the conclusion that this was not a wild fox but somebody's pet. He wanted it, and with presence of mind he grabbed a big net out of his car.

It was at this moment that Frederick drove up to see the great fox hunt. Having seen Nancy make some magnificent flights, he undoubtedly scanned the sky as he approached the appointed place and let his eyes rove over the marsh hoping to spot my eagle stooping at a running fox. Instead he was astonished to see a fox shoot around the corner of

307

the shed. It was followed a moment later not by a golden eagle but by a man in hot pursuit. A man with a net who lunged and barely missed the fox, who fell headlong in the snow, gathered himself up and took up the chase again. Round and round the shed they went, and each time the man took a swipe with the net, he missed and fell, and the fox waited at a discreet distance. At length man and fox paused with the shed between them.

Not only in the Keystone Cops is an idea born. Moving slowly and clutching his net carefully, the man started around the shed in the *opposite* direction. It's impossible to tiptoe in the snow, but he moved carefully, stealthily, ever so slowly. The fox, too, moved slowly—also in the opposite direction. Picking his footing carefully, the man moved a little faster. So did the fox. He increased his speed. So did the fox. He ran. So did the fox. Again the spectators were treated to the sight of man pursuing fox around shed—this time counterclockwise.

Nancy sat majestically on a snowbank watching. From time to time some of us helped with the chase, while all the movie cameras stood unmanned, failing to record this episode.

Frederick had the bad grace to stand by his car laughing. But I had learned something about hunting.

An introduction

Once when we were lecturing in Europe, we were introduced by Karl von Frisch (who later won the Nobel Prize for his work on bees).

After cake and coffee served in an arbor in his garden, where it seemed to me the conversation was pleasant but idle, we soon found ourselves in one of the biggest lecture halls we'd ever been in. And we soon learned that conversation in the arbor had not been idle. Von Frisch smiled at us in a kindly way and addressed the audience.

"Sometimes it comes to pass that a young man shows a marked interest in natural history, pursues his interest assiduously, and has a distinguished career."

I wanted to squeeze Frederick's hand, but we were sitting in the front row and the atmosphere was formal.

Von Frisch continued, "Sometimes it comes to pass that a young woman shows a marked interest in natural history, pursues her interest assiduously, and has a distinguished career." I was beginning to feel uncomfortable. It seemed the professor was laying it on a bit thick. He raised both hands palms upward. "And sometimes, but far more rarely, it comes to pass that two such young people meet as a result of their common interest in natural history, and pursue their interest with diligence together and—as a result—having distinguished careers.

"I take great pleasure in introducing Doctors Frederick and Frances Hamerstrom." Von Frisch paused dramatically. "With them it was not the case. She fell in love with him because he dances so beautifully."

310

And now with the Pygmies and Indians

My childhood dream, as I have said, was to live with wild animals all my life and to marry a tall, dark man. I did both. I was married to Frederick for fifty-nine years. After he died I realized that he had skillfully avoided hot, wet places. He took me *north* on expeditions to places like Siberia and Lapland. I had always wanted to hunt with the Pygmies. My age was 83. I said to myself, "You'd better hop to it before you get old."

At the time I was a Visiting Scientist at Welder Wildlife Foundation in Texas, but I took time off every day for a month to walk, to run, to do push-ups, and to climb trees. Then I went to Mombasa on the Indian Ocean and went through the same routine in the heat—except I climbed no trees, they all had spines.

My good friends in Africa ran a biological station. For a month I stayed at the station and collected plants in the rain forest with Kenge, a Pygmy. After that I was ready to go hunting. The next time I weighed myself I had lost twenty-seven pounds.

For me it is of the utmost importance to travel alone (rather than with a white companion). I am with the native people and I don't want to keep in mind what my companion may be thinking of my behavior. For example: I had been very strictly brought up and knew that no lady brushes her hair in public. She brushes it in her bedroom, in her boudoir, or in the bathroom.

My little pup tent, pitched between two leaf-thatched Pygmy houses, was very low. Crouched on my knees and one elbow I struggled to brush my hair—living up to the standards I had been so carefully taught.

Finally I said, the Hell with it, crawled out of my tent with my hairbrush, and sat on a sort of chair that Atoka, a Pygmy, had made for me. The village seemed empty, so I gave my hair a good brushing. Then I put my head down and brushed my hair toward the ground, as I had been taught to do.

When I lifted my head, my hair was every which way, and at eye level was a sea of faces—those little men, some bearded, were watching me at close range.

Now, Fran Hamerstrom, is the time for poise. I pulled myself together and slowly finished brushing my hair, gave it a little pat, and laid down the brush.

Everybody clapped.

Nobody said, "Fran, why do you keep showing off?"

"Primitive" people test whites, just as we test them, and just as we test each other. My next test came before daybreak on my second day in the village. We went on a massive net hunt. The drivers drove the game into a 300-yard-long net, and the pouncers sat ready to pounce on whatever animal ran into the net before it had a chance to get away.

I sat on a little mound of earth (it is not nice to sit on the ground), I knew how far away a Pygmy sat to my right, but I still needed to know how far away the Pygmy to my left was: how much net did I need to be prepared to pounce on?

Moving my head so slowly that the motion was essentially imperceptible—a trick that all hunters and many birdwatchers know—I peered slowly to the left. Then I saw a flash of white. It was the teeth of a Pygmy smiling. He was doing just what I was and in the same way: neither of us would frighten game.

Next I moved my head back to its normal position and sat still; ants bit me and insects buzzed, but I sat without moving for about an hour and forty minutes.

That Pygmy must have told everybody about it because thereafter I was treated differently—accepted as a hunter!

People keep asking me, "What were you hunting?"

Sport hunters are shocked at my answer: *anything we can get!*

Subsistence hunting and sport hunting have both been important parts of my life. Sport hunters limit the size of their weapons and virtuously set obstacles in the path of success. The families of subsistance hunters may die if the hunter is not successful.

Sometimes I am sorry that I'm not a cartoonist. I want a cartoon of a Pygmy, saying to his friend, "Sure is great that the monkey season opens next month!"

Never travel with two guides. All they do is talk with each other in some foreign language or a Spanish I do not understand, while I sit in the middle of a dugout canoe and watch birds along the Amazon.

At least that's all my two guides did last year until Secundo, a famous spear fisherman, said something I understood perfectly:

"Have you noticed her long white legs?"

(I continued to watch the birds.)

Alfredo answered, "Yes, and have you noticed that the flies prefer her long white legs to our long brown legs?"

I didn't move a muscle—just kept my binoculars handy. Secundo spoke once more, "Those flies have a lot of sense."

I know they stopped talking about me, because I couldn't understand a single word after that. Secundo traveled with us for two days and then I had Alfredo to myself. He showed me how to forage in the riverbottom woods of the rain forest, and how much easier it was to find food on the nearby uplands, and he took me to blowgun hunters. We traveled for a month in a dugout canoe. Sometimes we camped and sometimes we stayed at Paul Beaver's lodge. Of course Alfredo was testing me and I was testing him. I learned how brave he was when he killed a baby aquatic boa constrictor—seven feet long. It was dangerous.

Alfredo learned how indifferent to pain I was when a piranha bit my index finger. Fortunately it bit me while we were in camp, and fortunately it bit me in a place that bled a lot.

I watched birds, feeling the warm blood run down my hand. Finally Alfredo couldn't stand it any longer and called, "Fran! you are bleeding."

I looked at my hand. The piranha had taken out a nice little chunk of meat. "Yes." And then I watched the birds again.

Sometimes Alfredo told me stories about his life. He told me about the time that he and another Indian guide had tall, muscular young

Germans as clients. These massive mighty-muscled men watched the two slender Indians struggle with the the great loads of heavy luggage that had to be carried up an embankment.

Alfredo muttered, "I do not like Germans."

"But not all Germans are the same. I like Germans. I've lived in Germany. Not all Germans are nice, but most of them are."

This, I thought, closed the subject forever.

On our last day Alfredo said, "You paddle too. We are going up-stream." I grabbed a paddle and put my muscles to work.

Alfredo kept changing the rhythm—with sudden rests. I think he was testing to make sure that I was really paddling.

Finally he said, "You *look* German."

I suddenly remembered what he said about those strong young Germans watching their guides struggle.

Alfredo shook his head in bewilderment. "You look German, but you aren't."

It is one of the strangest compliments I ever got.

I treasure my next compliment too, but it has a different ring to it. Alfredo loaded our gear into the dugout and took me to visit Ramón—a member of the Head-shrinkers' Tribe, and a famous blowgun hunter. Ramón had a rapidly growing family that was almost a village. My count was fifty-four people. They showed me utensils and artifacts, fed me, took me fishing. We laughed and we talked.

At last I said, "Ramón, when are we going hunting?"

Ramón's answer sounded as though he had a fishbone stuck in his throat. "Ungh."

I didn't add, "You have been *paid* to take me hunting." We both knew this.

Suddenly I felt white, female, and one of those pestiferous tourists.

Silence is a strong weapon.

At last Ramón loaded the dugout, and we paddled upriver. We tried one place after another. I asked Ramón, "Are birds always so scarce?"

"Ungh."

He beached the dugout by some river-bottoms. Sunlight poured into the rain forest, and the tall vegetation was thick, dry, and noisy. Ramón stepped out of the dugout and almost immediately brought down a small bird. "Bueno! Splendid!" I cheered. But we couldn't find the bird.

Next he started through the noisy vegetatation. "Alfredo, let's stay here."

314

We heard Ramón trying to make his silent way through the vegetation. Three people would have scared *all* the game out of the country. Crash, crash. After what seemed a long time, we heard him crashing back.

Ramón had two birds about the size of robins impaled on darts. The darts looked rather like long knitting needles with a wad from the silktree at one end and a sharp point at the other. They ran through the birds from up near the neck, down through the chest and the belly, and came out near the tail.

Both birds were alive and fluttering.

I wasn't brought up that way.

"¿Los mataré? Shall I kill them?"

"Ungh."

I thought of what Frederick and I had learned from the old Scottish gamekeeper long ago. "If you down a grouse and it is not dead— bite it just back of the ears. It will die *very* quickly, and will be *very* easy to pluck."

Biting heads soon became my time-honored way of dispatching small birds quickly. Absent-mindedly I bit one bird and then the other. Their heads hung limp.

Alfredo exclaimed, "Fran, you are a tiger!"

Ramón laughed nervously—and then roared with laughter. I had taught him—on his own home ground—something about hunting that he did not know. In one quick instant he had learned that I really was a hunter.

That evening we sat on a log in his camp. Paulilla, his granddaughter, brought him a plate of soup. He slid the plate over so it rested on my thigh too. We ate with our fingers, pulling out bits of fish, vegetable, and monkey meat—just like an old married couple.

I am going back to the rain forests. Pygmies and Indians, among the oldest races of mankind, have lived in forests and jungles since time immemorial and have not destroyed their habitat. No white people can say the same.

Also, wherever I have gone in my far, wide travels in "civilized" countries, in each I have encountered overpopulation with its twin horrors: human misery and despoilation of the environment.

If we are to preserve this beautiful world of ours, with its creatures great and small and their wondrous homes, we must have fewer people on earth, we must have fewer children, or the beauty of the wild will be gone—and our security as well.